THE COMPLETE GUIDE TO
FUNCTIONAL TRAINING

Allan Collins

Note

While every effort has been made to ensure that the content of this book is as technically accurate and as sound as possible, neither the author nor the publishers can accept responsibility for any injury or loss sustained as a result of the use of this material.

Published by Bloomsbury Publishing Plc
50 Bedford Square
London WC1B 3DP
www.bloomsbury.com

ISBN (print) 978 1 4081 5214 0
ISBN (EPDF) 978 1 4081 8018 1
ISBN (EPUB) 978 1 4081 8020 4

A CIP catalogue record for this book is available from the British Library.

Acknowledgements
Cover photograph © Shutterstock
Inside photographs © Mike Harrington with the exception of the following:
p 4 © Getty Images; p 43 (x2), 111, 139, 141, 142, 180 and 195 © Istock image bank;
p.238, 243, 245 (RHS) © Cybex International; p 245 (LHS) © Jordan Fitness;
p 86, 129, 140, 208, 265 taken from *Instructions re Advanced Exercises: Inch's System*, The Mendip Press Ltd
Designed by James Watson
Commissioned by Charlotte Croft
Edited by Sarah Cole

This book is produced using paper that is made from wood grown in managed, sustainable forests. It is natural, renewable and recyclable. The logging and manufacturing processes conform to the environmental regulations of the country of origin.

Typeset in 10.75pt on 14pt Adobe Caslon by seagulls.net

Printed and bound in China by C&C Offset Printing Co., LTD.

THE COMPLETE GUIDE TO
FUNCTIONAL TRAINING

CONTENTS

Acknowledgements   vi

Introduction   1

Chapter 1   The basics of functional training   2

Chapter 2   Squat pattern   43

Chapter 3   Lift pattern   84

Chapter 4   Press pattern   111

Chapter 5   Pull pattern   141

Chapter 6   Rotation pattern   178

Chapter 7   Smash pattern   195

Chapter 8   Moving and carrying load pattern   202

Chapter 9   Gait and locomotion pattern   222

Chapter 10   Supplementary exercises   233

Chapter 11   Applied programmes   277

References   307

Index   310

ACKNOWLEDGEMENTS

I would like to thank all of those who have directly and also indirectly helped in the development of this book. For all of the clients, athletes and students I have worked with and taught over the many years in this industry, thank you, I have learnt a lot from you – I'm sure I have learnt as much from you as I have passed on to others. I would also like to pay appreciation for all of the hard work by Sarah Cole and the rest of the team at A&C Black and for Charlotte Croft for her foresight in commissioning this book.

Thank you to my work colleagues and friends, Leon, Marc and Alex who have provided me with valuable inspiration, both on the technical and the business side. It is still my pleasure to read, listen and watch other coaches like the late Mel Siff, Charles Poliquin and Anthony DiLuglio, who continue to inspire me. I would like to thank my friends and family for all of their continued support, both through the highs and lows – I would not be the person I am or have reached the successes I have without your influence.

And lastly I would like to thank Jenny, my long term partner, for all of her hard work with this book – reading, rereading, and editing where needed and for encouraging me during the long days and late nights of writing, you are both a muse and a rock.

I hope you enjoy this book, and to help you implement the principles and exercises, equipment is available from Jordan Fitness, www.jordanfitness.co.uk and additional resources are available from my site, www.allancollins.me.

INTRODUCTION

The concept of functional training has been floating around the fitness industry and among those involved in the strength and conditioning of athletes for many years. It is one of the most dominant fitness concepts of the last 20 years, and shows little sign of diminishing. Every manufacturer and retailer wants to describe their products as 'functional', every instructor wants their personal training sessions to be 'functional', and every training provider wants to teach their concept of 'functional training'. The definition of 'functional' refers to something being able to fulfill its purpose or function, and so in relation to exercise prescription or fitness, functional training could then be described as training that means you are able to fulfill your purpose or function. A more complete definition of functional training is:

> The execution of specific exercises that have a positive carryover or benefit to health or the performance of the person's daily tasks, their occupation or their sport, or for improved resilience to injury.

Having studied the training methodologies popular today, it soon becomes clear that there are still questions regarding functional training and there are many conflicting opinions among the various training gurus including:

- Are bicep curls functional?
- Should seated leg extension and leg curl exercises be included within a functional training programme?
- Do stability balls improve functional ability or not?
- Is the barbell bent over row one of the best pulling exercises?
- Should I squat all the way down, only to 90 degrees or with thighs parallel to the floor?

These questions and many more will be addressed throughout this book to allow the reader to truly understand what functional training means and how it is effectively applied.

> 'It is not the acquisition of knowledge that is important, it is more the application of knowledge.'

1

THE BASICS OF FUNCTIONAL TRAINING

1

There are many forms or methodologies of training that all claim to be functional, yet they vary tremendously in exercise selection and programming. These will all be discussed in greater detail further in this section but here are the main types:

- Unstable surface training (using stability balls, BOSU®, discs, foam pads, etc.)
- Multi-planar training (such as the Gray Institute method of training, and the various duplicates of this method)
- Olympic weightlifting (exercises such as the barbell snatch, clean and jerk, modified Olympic lifts, Olympic pulls and assistance exercises)
- Unconventional training (using sandbags, conditioning ropes, hammers, Indian clubs)
- Traditional resistance training (including free-weights and fixed path machines)
- Modified strongman training (using sleds, log bars, super yokes, Atlas stones and tyre flipping)
- Many other methodologies including kettlebell, medicine ball and bodyweight suspension training.

In order to gain an understanding of how we should train, we need to understand why we train the way that we currently do. There is a phrase that encapsulates this notion: 'to understand where you are going, you need to know where you have been.'

A HISTORY OF TRAINING

'Those who don't learn from history are doomed to repeat it.'

George Santayana, 1905. The Life of Reason, Volume 1

GREEKS AND ROMANS

Functional training is not a new concept, in fact it has existed for thousands of years. Fitness training originated from the need to improve the athletic performance of soldiers. Ancient warriors and soldiers needed to combine both strength and skill if they were to survive. They had to have the ability to fight in hand-to-hand combat, to throw deadly weapons, to run towards battle or to ride into battle. An unfit soldier who could not perform these skills in battle due to lack of strength, power or endurance was not likely to survive for long out on the battlefield. Therefore, fitness and strength endurance events were created to provide the training necessary to survive long battles. This, in turn, led to the creation of the ancient Olympics.

The ancient Olympians, such as Milo of Kroton, were not just professional athletes, but were successful warriors foremost, whose notoriety in battle earned them the right to compete at the Olympics. The ancient Olympics consisted of very few events in comparison with the modern Olympics that we are all familiar with. If a method of training did not improve a soldier's ability to run fast, jump high, fight or throw weapons, there was no reason for its inclusion. The following list highlights the link between the events included in the ancient Olympics and the skills needed for combat:

- Boxing
- Equestrian events (chariot racing, riding)
- Pankration (a type of ancient mixed martial arts)
- Pentathlon (a combined event of discus, javelin, jumping, running, wrestling)

Many of the fitness methodologies invented by the ancient Greeks and Romans are still in use today.

VINTAGE TRAINING AND PHYSICAL CULTURE

Fitness did not change for many centuries, until the concept of physical culture emerged in the late 1800s and early 1900s (what we now commonly refer to as Vintage Training). Physical culture is a term applied to health and strength training regimens, particularly those that originated during the 19th century, and schools were founded in many countries including Russia, Germany, Czechoslovakia, Sweden, England, America and Australia to name a few. The schools developed as a result of the growing issues stemming from the Industrial Revolution and the subsequent inactivity of proportions of the population (particularly the middle classes), which was leading to an increase in sedentary conditions and diseases.

Each school utilised a slightly different system of training, with influences from dance, gymnastics, sports, military training and medical calisthenics (bodyweight exercises for health improvements). The influence of Greek and Roman models of strength and conditioning was still apparent.

The many physical culture systems also influenced today's health and fitness industry outside of the training methodologies, as practitioners began to promote their methods through the sale of books, journals, equipment and nutrition products. This helped to promote the benefits of physical culture to a mass market. People were suddenly able to see physical culture as a means to improving health, vitality and physical appearance and preventing disease.

Schools of physical culture became the template for today's gyms and fitness centres, and the common tools used by many of these systems were the key ingredients in today's concept of

Figure 1.1 Example of Vintage Dumbbell and Kettlebell Designs

functional training, including dumbbells, barbells, ropes, kettlebells, medicine balls and Indian clubs.

Combat training using boxing and wrestling still formed part of the fitness systems practised. Probably the most famous of these methodologies was invented by strongman Eugen Sandow and at the turn of the 20th century his system enjoyed considerable international popularity. Sandow was an accomplished gymnast and wrestler and under tutelage of Professor Attila he became the father of modern bodybuilding. A pioneer in his

Figure 1.2 Eugen Sandow, the father of modern bodybuilding.

field, he was probably the first athlete to make a comfortable living through displaying his muscular physique and considerable strength – he could perform a one arm bent press of 269lbs and a one arm snatch of 180lbs. (Most athletic people today cannot lift 180lbs (83kg) with two hands above their head in a snatch, while he could lift and hold it with just one!)

Sandow created the Institute of Physical Culture, a gymnasium for bodybuilders, in London in 1897; he trained King George V; he wrote a monthly magazine and a number of books; he invented patented exercise machines and had his own range of dumbbells, barbells and kettlebells; and he even produced his own fitness drink called Sandow's Health & Strength Cocoa! His physique was considered the epitome of masculinity and strength, and he was photographed many times and replicated in statues, mimicking the 'ideal' male proportions of statues created by such classical artists as Michaelangelo. Since 1977, the International Federation of Bodybuilding & Fitness (IFBB) has celebrated Eugen Sandow's contribution to the sport by presenting his trophy, the Sandow (a foot-high statue in his image), to the winner of the largest international bodybuilding competition, the Mr. Olympia.

Over the years the concept of improving health through lifting weights, demonstrating integrated strength and power with 'feats of strength' and a principle of lifting weights through specific movement has come to underpin the basics of functional training. Rather than training by muscles (arm, hamstring exercises, etc.) all of these muscles would be trained if all the movement patterns were worked, therefore allowing the muscles to take care of themselves. The principles, equipment and methods that worked so well in improving the health, physique and performance of clients a hundred years ago can still achieve results in athletes today.

Over this period the exercises used in lifting competitions (bent press, side press, one arm snatch) have been replaced by what we see today in modern Olympic Weightlifting competitions – the two hand clean and jerk and two hand snatch.

BODYBUILDING AND POWERLIFTING

Two of the main influences on how we exercise today are modern bodybuilding and powerlifting. Massive progressions in scientific understanding and applied knowledge have arisen from these disciplines and without them our ability to train clients for improved strength, size and power would be diminished. However, these disciplines can be considered in part to have also had a negative impact on modern functional fitness. Although modern bodybuilding and powerlifting may have brought us techniques like progressive resistance training (chains and bands), the development of fixed path machines for isolation of muscles for development, and a wealth of scientific research, some of these (like an over-reliance on fixed path machines) have brought us away from some effective, basic ideas that were used for hundreds if not thousands of years since the evolution of strength and conditioning.

Bodybuilding has evolved a great deal since the first strongmen and bodybuilders such as Sandow, Charles Atlas and Arthur Saxon trained primal movements with basic freeweights, bodyweight and wrestling. The sport again gained in popularity during the seventies when Arnold Schwarzenegger, Lou Ferrigno and Franco Columbu reigned supreme, and it has continued to attract attention in recent decades with stars such as Dorian Yates and Ronnie Coleman. Over these years though the physiques have changed from what is possible with diet and freeweights to today's exaggerated development with fixed path machines and the proliferation of steroids in professional bodybuilding.

During the 1960s and 1970s, bodybuilders' training regimes consisted of a staple of those foundation exercises known to improve physical development: squats, deadlifts, presses and pull-ups. However, the development of Nautilus resistance machines changed the face of bodybuilding. These fixed path machines allowed for a greater neural drive to a particular area, meaning bodybuilders were able to isolate a muscle for increased hypertrophy. Neural drive relates to the number of motor units activated by the nervous system – on a fixed path machine less neural energy is required by stabilisers or balance muscles (because you are seated) and therefore more energy can be focused on the agonist muscles (the prime movers) for greater motor unit activation and to allow more weight to be lifted. This is commonly seen with the barbell bench press and Smith Machine – although the exercises seem identical, more weight is lifted using the Smith Machine because there is less shoulder stabilisation required and no balancing of the bar. This is great to overload the agonist muscles, but not so great for function, which usually requires the agonists to work with these other muscles for functional movements. Unfortunately many trainers and gym users over-rely on these types of machines, and cannot understand why this type of training does not improve the body's (integrated) functional ability.

In photographs for many fitness and bodybuilding magazines, certain isolation and fixed path exercises were found to show bodybuilders' muscles at their best, meaning these particular exercises gradually became known as being the best for hypertrophy, whether they were actually used in training by that bodybuilder or not. This skewed the opinions of the average exercise to believe that these exercises were superior to others for the development of strength or size, such as the leg extension being preferable to a barbell squat.

The concept of isolation, split routines and selecting certain exercises to work individual muscles have become fundamental principles in fitness training today. Gym instructors and personal trainers are trained to write a resistance programme that works the muscles of the chest, back, shoulders, arms, core, legs, hips and calves, with exercises selected to specifically target these muscles. This method, although common practice, contradicts many of the early fitness concepts. Arthur Saxon wrote *The Development of Physical Power* in 1905, noting in the introduction: 'I shall teach you to judge a man by his capabilities as an athlete, whether a weight-lifter, wrestler or not, and not by the measurements of his biceps and chest… My idea will be, and always has been, to leave the muscles to look after themselves.'

In addition, many male gym-goers place an emphasis on the development of chest, shoulder and arm muscles, usually via an overreliance on bench pressing, and not on a well-rounded development of muscle mass (the symmetry that is usually sought in bodybuilding). Excessive overreliance of the Barbell Bench Press to develop the pushing muscles seems to have a correlation with anterior shoulder problems, and will affect the normal biomechanics of gleno-humeral movement while pressing. Standing Overhead Pressing

requires leg strength, hip stability, core stability, thoracic mobility and shoulder stability, all of which are either not required or required in very small amounts for supine Barbell Bench Pressing. A hundred years ago, Saxon (1905) summed up his response to this nicely: 'Neither do I consider a man really strong if he is in certain parts developed out of proportion to others. If a man has tremendous arms and chest and weak legs then he is only half a strong man.'

The early athletes and strongmen considered the bench press to be a lesser test of strength than any of the standing lifts above the head – the clean, jerk, press and snatch which has evolved into the modern sport of weightlifting. So why has the barbell bench press achieved such proliferation within the average gym, when in early training it was a rarely performed exercise? The answer lies in the development of the sport of powerlifting in America in the 1950s and 1960s, which increased in popularity (like bodybuilding) as Olympic weightlifting decreased in popularity. The multitude of lifts that form the core of Olympic weightlifting were whittled down into three key lifts – the deadlift, back squat and bench press – in powerlifting. These three exercises are considered supplementary or assistant exercises to the clean, jerk and snatch by Olympic weightlifting practitioners, but form the basis of powerlifting. As powerlifting increased in popularity and notoriety, so did the use of the bench press. Without the influence of powerlifting, it is highly unlikely that the bench press would be utilised by the masses to the level it is today.

The Bench Press, powerlifting styles of the deadlift and squat, fixed path machines, and knowledge of how to isolate muscles, all have a place in modern functional training, but (unlike many people's training programmes), they should not form a dominant proportion.

CORE AND UNSTABLE TRAINING

As many trainers became aware of the limitations and potential issues associated with excessive or sole use of fixed path and isolation exercises in the development of strength and fitness, so the concept of functional training began to emerge. However, the pendulum swung too far as it veered from stable, machine-based training to unstable, core-emphasised functional training.

Many fitness professionals mistakenly refer to core and unstable training as functional training. They believe that if training emphasises working the core muscles or if the surface is unstable, such as when using a stability ball or disc, there must be positive carryover to a person's performance of functional tasks. This assumption has been shown to be incorrect.

Core stability

Core Stability can be described as the ability of the core muscles to work in an efficient and coordinated fashion to maintain correct alignment of the spine and pelvis while the limbs are moving. Improving core stability can have a beneficial impact on strength in different movement patterns if the individual's core stability or strength is lacking, and if this is the weak link in the kinetic chain (the different muscles involved in a movement or task). Building up this weak link should allow the individual to demonstrate strength in conjunction with the rest of the kinetic chain of muscles.

For example, think of a functional task like lifting a heavy object from the floor – a weak back or core stabiliser muscles (such as the muscles

Figure 1.3 Unstable Surface Training

that extend the back) will limit the ability of the hip extensor muscles (the hamstrings and glutes) to produce force against a load in the lifting pattern. In order for the hamstrings and glutes to produce force efficiently to lift the upper torso and extend the hips, the body needs to stabilise and lock the core. This stable base allows the force to be efficiently transferred from the agonists (the prime movers or main muscles responsible for the movement), through the stabilisers to the load. The adage 'you can't fire a cannon from a canoe' represents the necessity of having a stable base in the production of force. Building up the stabilising core or back muscles would have the potential to improve performance in functional tasks like lifting.

However, what happens when the core muscles have reached an optimal level of strength or stability? Would undertaking additional core strength or stability training make your agonists stronger? No, it would not, and the subsequent training once the core muscles have reached their optimal level of strength would be a waste of time. Additional core training should only be prescribed when the core stability or strength is deficient in relation to the rest of the kinetic chain. In fact, correcting this deficit doesn't actually make your agonists stronger; it only allows the body to correctly apply this strength. Having strength without the ability to apply it in a functional movement pattern is a waste of strength. If you have strong hamstrings that can deadlift 200kg, but a lower back that can only stabilise 150kg, you will be limited by your weakest link and your body will only allow you to lift 150kg.

The idea of training is to develop strength through functional movement patterns and supplementary exercises, which you can then apply to a range of daily functional patterns. This is achieved through a balance of strength between agonists (the primary muscles responsible for the movement), antagonists (the opposing muscles) and assistant muscles (those that assist the primary muscles or those that stabilise nearby joints). Taking the example just given, if you have assessed that your lower back is weak in comparison to your hamstrings, you can add supplementary exercises to work the lower body, thereby improving the agonist-synergist strength balance and eventually allowing you to deadlift 200kg. What then? If you build up your lower back with more supplementary exercises, can you deadlift more? No, because now the limiting factor is the strength of the agonists (the hamstrings) and their ability to lift only 200kg. Simply performing more core training is not always the answer to improved functional strength and performance.

Unstable surface training (UST)

Unstable Surface Training involves performing exercises on a surface or object that challenges the balance of the user. For many years now the popularity of unstable training has increased, with products like the stability ball, BOSU®, stability discs, wobble boards and foam pads a common sight in everyday training facilities, and not just in the rehabilitation studios where they originated to improve balance, proprioception and stability for older clients or for those in rehabilitation from injuries or neurological conditions, like strokes.

Vera-Garcia, Grenier & McGill (2000) evaluated muscle activity in the upper and lower regions of the rectus abdominis during curl-ups performed on a Swiss ball versus a stable bench, with results demonstrating that performing the curl-up on a Swiss ball led to significantly greater abdominal muscle activity (50 per cent versus 21 per cent of maximal activity). These results were taken to mean that performing exercises, such as the overhead press, squat or biceps curl when kneeling or stood on a stability ball would improve activation much more than when stood on the ground, because this additional core emphasis would have a greater carryover to functional strength and performance. For some time, therefore, unstable training was seen to represent more of a challenge to the body, leading to the method being adopted by many fitness professionals to improve sports performance in their clients.

However, in recent years there has been a somewhat of a backlash, with many experts and researchers highlighting the limitations of using UST to develop strength. Researchers have found that muscular force output is significantly diminished when exercises like the squat and the bench press are performed on an unstable surface (Anderson & Behm, 2004; Behm, Anderson & Curnew, 2002; Koshida et al, 2008). Anderson & Behm (2004) found a 59.6 per cent decline in the maximum isometric force output (the amount of weight that could be lifted) when the bench press was performed on an unstable surface versus a stable surface. What this research shows is that although UST has its place within the functional continuum, it is important to realise that the force generated and the subsequent load lifted by the agonists during these exercises may be too little to stimulate any improvements in strength (or other improvements or adaptations like hypertrophy or power).

POSTURAL CORRECTION AND MULTI-PLANAR TRAINING
Postural correction
Linked with the popularity of UST is the focus on postural correction. Improving posture should be a crucial factor in every programme, since this will decrease stress on the associated joints and can improve the body's biomechanics (which as a result can allow the agonists to demonstrate their true strength – i.e. making you functionally stronger). Rather than only focusing on low load unstable training to improve posture, the emphasis should be on improving the agonist-antagonist

strength balance and releasing any myofascial restrictions, discussed later in this chapter (see page 34) using tennis balls, foam rollers or manual treatments (from practitioners like sports massage therapists, rolfers or active release therapists).

Multi-planar training
Another approach to training that has increased in popularity over the last five to ten years has been what I refer to as the multi-planar approach. This system was promoted predominantly by Gary Gray, an American sports therapist, and has since been repackaged by many other companies and fitness professionals. His methodology of training the body in all three planes of motion and the subsequent techniques and drills to improve joint mobility and muscle activation are very effective and as a prehabilitation and rehabilitation tool are excellent. However, the technique does have some similarities to unstable training, in that the dumbbells and medicine balls commonly used to initiate the muscle spindle activation (the stretch reflex for muscle contraction) are kept low in load (weight) in order to reach the required tempo or number of repetitions. This means its carryover to improved strength is likely to be very low, since strength adaptations require loads heavier than 70% of 1RM (approximately 12 repetitions max or heavier). It is therefore best combined with heavier strength training, as a means of increasing the ability of the body to activate specific muscles, rather than just as a comprehensive stand-alone method of training.

The following chapters will provide an overview of modern concepts of functional training, particularly the functional triangle, which should help to better explain the optimal use of multi-planar training.

UNCONVENTIONAL TRAINING

Over recent years, there has been a considerable increase in the interest in unconventional, or caveman-style, training. This includes such methods as hammer slams, tyre flipping, sled pulling or undulating training with ropes (see page 270). One reason for the increased popularity in these methods is their use in mixed martial arts (MMA) strength and conditioning and its own huge increase in popularity over the last five years. MMA as a sport will inherently embrace any method if effective, and will dismiss any method that is not. Such sports provide an excellent testing ground for the effectiveness of these unusual

Figure 1.5 Unconventional Undulating Training with ropes

Figure 1.4 Unconventional Progressive Resistance training with chains

(or unconventional) training methods, even before research can back them up.

Many of the unconventional tools used to improve strength or conditioning have developed from powerlifting methods (such as progressive resistance with chains and bands and sled training) or strongman training (such as using log bars, keg lifts, Atlas stones, etc.). Rope training particularly has become very popular in the last couple of years for improving upper body anaerobic conditioning with undulating drills (consistent, rhythmical waves in different patterns), as well as grip and forearm training.

Crossfit is a fitness franchise with gyms across the world that delivers high density circuit sessions using Olympic lifting, gymnastic, kettlebell and suspension system exercises. Franchises such as this are heavily dependant on these unconventional styles of training, and many more standard fitness clubs are beginning to consider which of these unconventional exercises or tools can be implemented into the mainstream market.

FOUNDATION TRAINING PRINCIPLES

' "Think simple" as my old master used to say meaning reduce the whole of its parts into the simplest terms, getting back to first principles.'

Frank Lloyd Wright, architect and writer

'Every science has for its basis a system of principles as fixed and unalterable as those by which the universe is regulated and governed. Man cannot make principles; he can only discover them.'

Thomas Paine, author and inventor

Exercise science is no different to any other science, in that it has certain principles at its core:

- Adaptation
- Overload
- Specificity
- Reversibility
- Acclimatisation
- Generalisation
- Individuality

All training programmes should adhere to these principles in order to successfully reach the goals of the individual.

ADAPTATION

Adaptation is any anatomical or physiological change in the body that is caused by a stimulus or stressor. Changes such as improvements in VO_2 max (maximal oxygen uptake), decreased body fat percentage, increased absolute strength on the back squat, increased bone density and improved insulin sensitivity are all examples of how the body may change and alter to the particular stresses it is exposed to in order to

survive and flourish in this new and changing environment.

OVERLOAD

Overload is the principle that the stimulus or stressor must be above a minimum threshold in order to cause an adaptation or change. Whatever the adaptation sought, the overload must be above a certain threshold in order to elicit this change (to stimulate the body to adapt), while not being an excessive overload.

Insufficient overload will not cause an adaptation, because the body is already accustomed to the stimulus (or programme), and so it is already within the body's comfortable ability. Excessive overload may also not cause an adaptation or change because the stimulus will be too stressful to the body, and the risk of injury will increase. The idea is to pitch the overload between these two levels (in relation to intensity, density or volume). Periods of short-term overreaching will help to stimulate the body to adapt, but should be carefully applied so as not to cause the body to go into an overtraining state. These short-term overreaching sessions or periods of training are commonly called plateau busters because they 'shock' the body to adapt and get past a plateau. They may seem like excessive overload in the short term, but in the long term can cause improved adaptations. Progressive overload means that gradually increasingly overloads are incrementally applied to the body over a period of time in a systematic approach in order to achieve adaptations.

SPECIFICITY

Specificity means that the adaptation will be specialised and exact, in response to the particular overload. There will always be a specificity buffer when applying overload – it doesn't have to be exactly the same as the activity you are looking to improve, but should be similar in relation to muscles activated, motor units recruited, tempo, time under tension (length of time the weight is being held or rep performed), energy systems worked, type of muscle contraction, joints used, force vector, movement pattern, load, intensity and recovery period between bouts of activity. Analysing the activity and then choosing the correct training variables will help accomplish this, but supplementary drills and cross-training can also have a beneficial outcome in relation to performance, despite the activity not being similar. For example, isolated seated leg curls on a fixed path machine can help to improve hamstring strength, correct medial to lateral head imbalances (differences between the biceps femoris and semimembranosus and semitendinosus), improve quad to hamstring strength ratios and knee stability, which when applied with appropriate squat patterns can help to improve the functional capabilities of sprinting, jumping and throwing.

Reversibility

Reversibility states that no adaptation or change is permanent; the overload must be maintained, varied or increased or the changes will eventually diminish to pre-training levels. Training variables must be manipulated and stress continued to be applied to continue adaptations and prevent adaptations being lost. Periodisation will help to maintain adaptations from previous phases of training while new adaptations are being sought.

Acclimitisation

The definition of insanity is said to be doing the same thing over and over again and expecting a different result. Acclimatisation means that the body will gradually adapt to a particular stimulus or stressor, diminishing its effects and benefits. Some individuals will acclimatise very quickly, while other individuals will continue to benefit and adapt to similar stresses (the same session) applied over longer periods of time. Clients gifted with high proportions of fast twitch fibres will usually adapt quicker to a stimulus, and thus will need to vary the session more frequently, while most clients will usually be able to follow the same session (with small micro-changes) for five to seven sessions before needing significant variation. Manipulating the training variables at an appropriate time, alongside correct recovery periods between sessions and phases of training, and the input of 'shock training' will all help to prevent or limit plateauing of improvements or adaptations.

Generalisation

Generalisation states that there are certain guidelines for training variables (volume, intensity, rest periods etc.) that will elicit the desired response if adhered to. Response to training will follow a normal distribution curve with the majority of individuals grouped in the middle and adapting in a certain way. It is generally accepted that a rep range of 6–12RM will illicit a hypertrophy effect, or an increase in muscle size, (as long as the other training variables are within optimal parameters), and we can assume that for most of the population this will be the most appropriate range to follow for an individual looking to achieve this goal.

However, there will also be individuals that do not respond to these general guidelines and will actually hypertrophy more with rep ranges of 3–5

Table 1.1	General recommendations of training parameters to achieve different goals				
	Reps	Intensity (% of 1RM)	Time under tension (seconds)	Rest period (seconds)	Sets/ exercise
Relative strength	1–6	85–100	1–20	180–300	5–12
Functional strength	6–8	79–84	20–40	120–180	4–8
Hypertrophy	8–12	70–78	40–70	90–120	4–8
Strength endurance	12+	69 or less	50–120	10–90	2–4

or 12–15RM. No one programme will always suit everyone, but if a programme works for 70 per cent of the individuals that it is prescribed to, then it is generally accepted as being successful.

Individuality

Individuality links with generalisation, in that the trainer should always consider how the individual responds to overload alongside the individual's specific requirements to achieve their goal. If a client has specific issues in relation to agonist-antagonist or agonist-synergist/fixator muscle balances, biomechanical restrictions or considerations, myofascial restrictions or hormonal imbalances, then it will be critical to consider these factors when developing their training programme. Two athletes performing at the same level, with the same experience and the same goals, may have significant differences in their programmes because of factors ascertained during the testing and evaluation process. Therefore, after testing if it is ascertained that the client requires a 3–5RM to achieve better hypertrophy, then this predominantly is the range that should be applied, despite the general recommendations of a 6–12RM.

Periodisation

Periodisation is not a principle in itself, but it is commonly explained in relation to the other principles of fitness training. In order to prevent acclimatisation, the training overload should be progressively manipulated and integrated with recovery periods to more effectively elicit the adaptations of training. Work cycles of 12 weeks, broken down into smaller phases and then into individual sessions, work very well for most individuals, with one to two weeks of recovery between cycles. Frequency of sessions, multiple sessions per day and tolerance to intensity and volume will greatly depend on the individual and their training experience.

'Obey the principles without being bound by them.'

Bruce Lee

Most of the common errors in exercise programmes result from a failure to adhere to one or more of these training principles. Although there may be some experimentation with different programmes, the principles of training should always remain at the forefront of the mind. An example of not adhering to these principles can be seen below:

Poor Programming Example:

A trainer may want to achieve greater hamstring strength in a client. They look to improve the muscles' activation by stimulating the muscle spindles of the client's hamstrings, and do this by performing a fast eccentric loading phase (where the muscle is lengthening under load). This is done by adding a pair of light dumbbells to the performance of a step and reach exercise (see page 100). This exercise will help to improve the function of the hamstrings by eliciting this stretch reflex, but will this exercise improve overall functional ability of the hamstrings? Will this exercise stimulate hypertrophy or strength by increasing the number of myosin cross-bridges or size of the muscle fibres of the hamstrings? The answer is no, and the reason is that the load (or intensity) is too low. To improve strength or hypertrophy the minimum load is 70 per cent of 1RM (12 reps or less), which is heavier than the light dumbbells used in the step and reach. Since the hamstrings have a high proportion of fast twitch fibres they respond best to 10RM or heavier. To achieve these adaptations, exercises that utilise low reps and heavier loads, such as Romanian deadlifts or leg curls, should be programmed. Although the step and reach and Romanian deadlift will both work the hamstrings, they elicit different improvements within these muscles. They should be viewed as different 'tools', used when appropriate within the periodised programme to achieve the appropriate (different) goal.

MODERN CONCEPTS OF FUNCTIONAL TRAINING

Functional training is a term that is commonly applied to equipment and training methodologies, when really those applying it don't have a clear understanding of what the term truly means.

Functional training is synonymous with the training principle of specificity – you are fit for what you do. Train using the deadlift and your ability to lift objects will be improved, but it will probably have little carryover to swimming backstroke.

So how does this apply when selecting exercises, equipment or training methodologies for 'the average person'? Every gym user, client or sportsperson should find certain similarities in their training programme because, above all, we are all human. Including movement patterns that mimic the actions that humans have been performing for thousands of years in fitness training helps us to better undertake these human movement patterns in everyday life.

There are seven key human movement patterns, popularised by Paul Chek of the C.H.E.K. Institute in the 1990s. These are:

1. Squat
2. Lunge
3. Lift
4. Push
5. Pull
6. Rotate
7. Gait*

*This was not part of the original list, but was added later (2004).

For many years I used this list without question, but a number of years ago I sat down to really assess whether it was comprehensive enough. I concluded that it was not and so developed a more complete categorisation of human movement patterns. I take no credit for devising the idea, but only for its refinement and expansion. In my defense I like to quote a famous phrase, used recently by Stephen Hawking as the title of his 2003 book, *Standing on the Shoulders of Giants.* Isaac Newton made this concept famous in a letter to his rival Robert Hooke in 1676:

'What Descartes did was a good step. You have added much several ways, and especially in taking the colours of thin plates into philosophical consideration. If I have seen a little further it is by standing on the shoulders of Giants.'

Using the theories proposed by Chek allowed me to progress the list of human movement patterns to nine major areas. We have presented this list to other experts and within our Continuing Professional Development (CPD) courses in the UK, Europe, South Africa and America, and it is becoming the standard list for movement pattern training used by master trainers in these countries.

1. Squat
2. Lift
3. Press
4. Pull
5. Rotation
6. Smash
7. Moving and carrying load
8. Gait and locomotion
9. Fighting

So what do these movement patterns mean, why the changes from the previous list and why the additional patterns?

The **squat** pattern is a quad-dominant sitting pattern, which includes parallel stance, single leg and split stance squats, lunges, jumping, landing and hopping. So why is the lunge not a separate movement pattern? When you actually break it down, the lunge is merely a dynamic split stance squat − it is still a quad-dominant sitting position, and therefore should be classified under the squat pattern. The **lift** pattern is a hip-dominant movement, engaging the posterior chain muscles and used to pick objects up or to throw them upwards or behind you. The **press** and **pull** patterns involve moving an object towards the shoulder or away from the shoulder respectively. The **rotation** pattern is a transverse plane motion, which involves the torso and hips twisting. The **smash** pattern is a flexion-type pattern as if slamming your hands or an object to the floor, such as throwing a sandbag straight downwards or slamming a hammer onto a tyre. **Moving and carrying load** is effectively moving the body again from one place to the next, but while taking a load or object with you − dragging, pushing and carrying (on the shoulders, across the chest, in the arms or in the hands). **Gait and locomotion** involves moving the body from one place to another and includes walking, running, crawling and swimming. **Fighting** is the only movement pattern that doesn't easily fit into any of the other categories and involves kicking, punching, elbowing, wrestling and grappling. This final movement pattern is commonly excluded from clients' programmes because of sociological restrictions (i.e. it is not professional to put sixty-year-old female clients in a grappling move like a rear naked choke).

THE FUNCTIONAL TRIANGLE

The functional triangle is used to represent the functional capacity of an individual within a particular movement pattern. To illustrate how this works, we will use the lift pattern as an example.

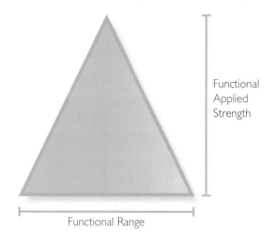

Figure 1.6 The functional triangle

Height = functional applied strength

The height of the triangle is representative of the maximum force that the individual can produce in this pattern. For the lift pattern this would be what the individual can deadlift. A deadlift of 200kg would produce a taller triangle than one that could only deadlift 150kg. We will call this functional applied strength (not to be confused with the functional strength rep range of 6–8RM, see page 22).

Width = functional range

The breadth or width of the triangle is representative of the range that the individual can demonstrate this movement pattern, whether this is measured at different speeds, grips and stances and in multiple planes of motion. For the lift pattern, this may be their ability to throw an object overhead and behind, to lift an object stood on one leg, to lift and rotate – picking an object up from the side. This is referred to as the individual's functional range.

Functional capacity

The functional capacity for the movement pattern is therefore a product of both the functional applied strength and the functional range. Too little training to develop one or the other will limit the overall capacity. This can be again represented by variations in the shape of the triangle seen in figure 1.7.

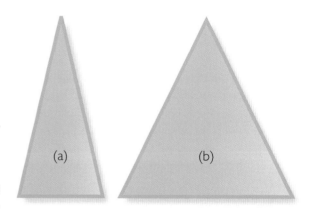

Figure 1.7 Variations in functional capacity because of functional range

Triangle (a) represents the functional capacity of an individual who may have the same functional applied strength as the individual represented in triangle (b), but they can only demonstrate this strength in a very narrow range. They can deadlift the same weight, but ask them to lift a weight from the side (lift and rotate) and they will not be able to demonstrate this strength. They should look to maintain their functional applied strength and to improve their functional range.

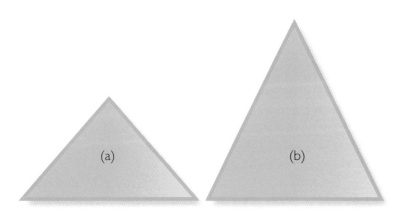

(a)

(b)

Figure 1.8 Functional capacity because of variations in functional applied strength

Figure 1.8, the second example shows that the person has spent a lot of time improving their functional range by lifting on one leg, on unstable surfaces, with rotation or repeatedly swinging a kettlebell. However, they have done this to the detriment of improving their functional applied strength – they are essentially weak.

So what about performance and injury prevention? Ask a person to perform a task that falls within their functional capacity and the risk of them getting injured is low, while the chance of them being able to perform the task is quite good (see yellow star in figure 1.9). However ask the first example to lift an object from the side

(lift and rotate) or for the second example to lift a heavier weight and the task will fall outside of their functional capacity (or outside of the individual's functional triangle – see red star in figure 1.9). They will be unable to perform that task and the chance of them getting injured goes up significantly.

Improving both functional applied strength and functional range will increase an individual's functional capacity, leading to increased performance (ability to perform a variety of tasks easily and efficiently) and to improved injury resilience. In addition to this we should consider the foundation to every individual movement

Figure 1.9 Using the functional triangle to avoid injury and increase success

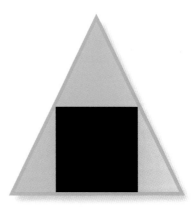

Figure 1.10 Building a strong foundation for each movement pattern

pattern (represented by the black foundation box in the functional triangle in figure 1.10). This would include posture, biomechanics, proprioception (an awareness of the body and limbs in space) and mobility to perform that movement. Without these key ingredients for each movement pattern, any training to improve strength, power or strength endurance within any of the movement patterns will be severely limited. Although they are not the only things that should be trained for optimal performance, they are what high levels of functional strength, range and capacity are built upon.

ASSESSING CLIENTS' HUMAN MOVEMENT PATTERNS

An individual should be assessed across each of the human movement patterns to determine which of them they need to perform at an average level and which they need to perform at an above average level – depending on their job or sport. A rower, for example, needs to be able to squat, lift and pull at an elite level, but does not need to be able to swim or run at an elite level (unless the boat sinks and they have to swim back to the boathouse of course!). The goal of functional applied strength for the remaining movement patterns does not need to be as high for the movement patterns used in that particular sport.

This theory also translates into everday life – the average client should look to improve their functional applied strength and functional range to cope with any task encountered in their daily life and activities, but they would not need to achieve the high levels of an elite athlete. We therefore train this client the same as and differently to an elite athlete. The same by assessing goals and starting points, evaluating areas of weakness, training each of the functional movements patterns to improve performance and increase resilience to injury; differently in that the levels of functional applied strength and functional range usually do not need to be as high or as wide for non-athletes.

THE PRINCIPLES OF FUNCTIONAL TRAINING

We have developed 20 key principles of functional training that summarise and apply the key concepts discussed above.

1. ADAPTATION IS THE GOAL AND CORRECT APPLICATION OF THE OVERLOAD IS THE KEY TO THIS

All training programmes and the exercises within them should seek to elicit changes in the body in a progressive, planned and logical pattern. In order to achieve these changes (or adaptations) the training must be above a threshold that would stimulate the body. Lifting a light weight for 8–12RM is not the same as lifting a heavier weight for 8–12RM; the weight should be appropriate for the repetition range and research has shown this should be at least 70 per cent of 1RM to cause increases in strength. Undertaking exercises or training sessions that are below the threshold for overload will not cause any strength adaptations.

The only sets performed at low intensities are warm-up and cool-down sets or 'teaching sets'. Some sessions will be deliberately planned to provide periods of recovery with active rest, low volume or low intensity. These sessions will improve the effectiveness of higher intensity or higher volumes sessions or phases only when correctly implemented.

2. TRAIN MOVEMENTS NOT MUSCLES

This is one of the most important principles in functional training, and is advocated by many of the functional training experts, including Arthur Saxon as early as the 1900s. Rather than adapting a modern bodybuilding approach to programming based on muscles (chest workout, shoulder workout, etc.), we need to design programmes based upon the human movement patterns. Although a dumbbell lateral raise and a military press will both work the deltoid muscles, the press will logically have a greater carryover to everyday activities than the raise, because it is a press pattern, while the raise is not a movement performed anywhere but in a fitness environment.

3. ASSESS AND TRAIN THE LIMITING FACTORS OF ALL THE MOVEMENT PATTERNS

Each movement pattern will be limited by a number of factors. Simply adding variations of the lift pattern exercises within your training programme will not guarantee amazing deadlift scores. Muscles in spasm, nerve dysfunction, tight antagonists and many other factors may be limiting your performance in each and every movement pattern. An assessment should be made to identify whether these limiting factors are decreasing the potential gains and, if they are, they should be corrected.

4. ENSURE OPTIMAL BALANCE OF THE AGONIST-ANTAGONIST STRENGTH BALANCE

An antagonistic pair of muscles is made up of the agonist (or the muscle that contracts and is responsible for the movement of the limb) and the antagonist (or the opposing muscle that relaxes during a contraction and is responsible for the opposite movement of the limb). Since muscles can only pull a limb when they contract and cannot push, opposing or antagonistic muscles will produce the opposite joint action when they contract or pull a limb.

At every joint there should be an optimal strength balance between these antagonistic muscles. For example, the quadriceps:hamstrings ratio, the biceps:triceps ratio or the chest:posterior shoulder ratio. There are optimal strength ratios for each of these, using certain gym-based exercises, which when achieved will help with posture, joint function, injury prevention and strength at that joint and with associated movement patterns. As an example, if your bench press is not improving it could be that the strength of the antagonists (shoulder external rotators or retractors) is limiting you; the body will not allow a heavier load to be lifted if that joint is not stable enough to withstand that load. Using the same example, the pectorals may be strong enough to bench 130kg, and the triceps may be strong enough to bench 130kg, but if the shoulder joint is only stable enough to take 100kg, then the brain will inhibit the potential weight lifted to 100kg so that no injury occurs.

In addition to the strength balance of the antagonistic muscles, a related restriction will be a hypertonic antagonist. If your hip flexors are tight, this will limit the potential activation ability of the opposing muscles – the hamstrings and glutes. When training a movement pattern, say the lift pattern, statically stretch the antagonistic muscles (the hip flexors) between sets to ensure that the hip extensors are not being inhibited.

5. ENSURE OPTIMAL BALANCE OF THE AGONIST-SYNERGIST STRENGTH BALANCE.

A synergist is a muscle which assists the agonist, or prime mover, in performing the desired joint motion. It may neutralise extra motion from the agonists to make sure that the force generated works within the desired plane of motion, or it may fix a nearby joint to provide a stable platform for the agonists to generate force. For example, during a deadlift the spinal erectors must hold the spine in a neutral position while the glutes and hamstrings produce the force to extend the hips and lift up the torso. Without this stable and rigid torso position, the force produced from the hip extensors is not efficiently transferred through the core and arms to the bar. A weak core will allow energy to be leaked out, decreasing the potential load that could be lifted. The same is true for the squat pattern; stabilisers at the knee and hip will be a limiting factor for the agonists (quadriceps, hamstrings and glutes). Strengthening the hip abductors and VMO (vastus medialis obliquus – fibres of the teardrop muscle on the inside of the quadriceps), to be able to control the forces being generated by the agonists, will ensure optimal performance in the squat pattern. The overhead press pattern is another good example, and can show how using freeweights is preferable to fixed path machines. Many individuals can generate high levels of strength performing the seated shoulder press machine exercise. But how does this transfer when performing the standing one hand dumbbell press? The lateral core and lateral hips must stabilise to provide a solid base for the agonists (deltoids and triceps) to press the load overhead. Performing the seated press variation will not develop the required strength in the synergist or fixator muscles, so when the standing variation is attempted less weight can be lifted. The strength developed on the machine is non-transferable to an applied, standing test of the same movement pattern.

6. ENSURE OPTIMAL ACTIVE MOBILITY REQUIRED TO PERFORM ALL THE HUMAN MOVEMENT PATTERNS THROUGH A FULL RANGE OF MOTION.

'Always work through a full range of motion' is a phrase commonly used within the fitness industry. But then there are also other recommendations that many trainers give to their clients such as only squat down to 90 degrees, or only lower the elbows down to the ears when pressing dumbbells overhead, or stop the bar about a fist distance above the sternum when bench pressing. Many of these recommendations go against the 'full range of motion' statement, but trainers for some reason do not question them because that's what they were previously taught. Unless the technique falters when a full range of motion is attempted, or pain is felt, then a full range should always be sought. The only exception to this 'rule' is with plyometrics, when a full range of motion would actually decrease the elastic energy generated and the subsequent force produced.

7. DEVELOP A RANGE OF MOTION (ROM) BEYOND NORMAL ONLY FOR WHAT IS REQUIRED FOR SPORT/JOB/DAILY TASKS AND ONLY IF IMPROVED ROM HAS A POSITIVE INFLUENCE ON PERFORMANCE.

Many people believe that developing greater range of motion will help to improve performance for daily tasks and sports, and will help to reduce the risk of injury. More is not always better, and persuing levels of flexibility that are beyond normal are only required for certain vocations and sports. Just as a decreased range of motion, or limited flexibility, may decrease performance and increase risk of injury, so can hypermobile joints. Certain martial arts, gymnastics, hurdling, ballet, swimming may well require greater than normal mobility at certain joints, and these should be sought if this mobility cannot be achieved by practising the sport or activity itself. A long distance runner requires a certain level of mobility to perform the gait pattern, but it will not improve running speed if the runner increases lower body flexibility so that they can perform the splits. For the martial artist that has to perform a roundhouse kick to the opponent's head, they probably would need this level of flexibility.

8. WHERE POSSIBLE DEVELOP REQUIRED MOTOR ABILITIES, SKILLS OR FACETS OF FITNESS BY PERFORMING THE TASK, ACTIVITY OR SPORT ITSELF.

This is such a common problem with many trainers that write sports-specific programmes. They believe that training time spent in the gym is preferable to time spent mastering a sport. This is not the case. Strength training should be used to complement athletic practice, not replace it. Can improving strength in the weights room translate to improved swimming speed? Yes, it can (if programmed correctly), as increased strength can translate to increased force applied to the water and subsequent increased velocity. However, the strongest individuals do not necessarily make the fastest swimmers. That is because swimming requires efficient movement through the water in addition to strength. Take a swimmer, apply an appropriate programme that makes them stronger, and this should be seen as improved performance. But without the practice to apply that strength in the water, the time spent in the gym can be fruitless. Use the strength training (or land training as swimmers call it) to improve strength and use the time in the pool to apply that strength and improve sports-specific skills. Using the principle of specificity, the land training does not need to be identical to the swimmers' stroke, it just needs to be close enough to have a beneficial carryover.

9. DON'T ASSUME THAT IMPROVING A LOW FACET OF FITNESS WILL IMPROVE PERFORMANCE.

There are certain human movement patterns, just like there are certain facets of fitness, that will translate to improved performance for an occupation or sport, and there are those that will have little carryover. If you test the VO2max (maximal oxygen uptake) for a sprinter and found that their score is low, would you spend time improving their aerobic capacity with long steady runs? Would this have any impact on the sprinter's performance? Actually, yes, it would – a detrimental one. These long, slow steady runs would likely decrease speed and power, having the exact opposite effect of what is being sought.

10. NOT ALL MOVEMENT PATTERNS ARE CREATED EQUAL.

Is one movement pattern more important than another, or should they each be trained equally within a programme? Each movement pattern is very important in its own right, or to balance out some of the other movement patterns, but it is essential that they are *not* treated equally. For example, the lift and smash patterns work opposing muscle groups, and are antagonistic in the movements actually involved – hip extension and isometric spinal extension versus hip flexion and spinal flexion. However, if an equal amount of training is dedicated to these motions – 12 sets per week for the lift pattern and 12 sets for the smash pattern, then too much volume would be applied to the flexors. If we consider these from an evolutionary standpoint, a caveman would perform significantly more lifts over the average day than smashes. This can also be seen by the size of the muscles involved – the posterior chain hamstrings and glutes are markedly larger than the spinal flexors. As a rough estimate I would advise an optimal volume ratio of approximately 3:1 up to 6:1 for the lift:smash patterns.

If there was a single movement pattern that is undertrained in today's modern gym, it would be the moving-carrying load pattern. How many times do you see someone performing a barbell Turkish get up, a dumbbell farmer's walk, a sled push or a tyre drag? We still perform these movements, such as carrying the shopping to the car, or carrying your child in your arms when they get tired, but rarely train them in the gym. Many of the unconventional tools and exercises in this book will help to train this movement pattern and fill in the gaps in many peoples' training programmes.

11. THE FUNCTIONAL CAPACITY OF A MOVEMENT PATTERN IS A PRODUCT OF BOTH THE FUNCTIONAL APPLIED STRENGTH AND THE FUNCTIONAL RANGE.

Functional capacity is a representation of your ability to perform a functional movement pattern. It is essentially the size of your functional triangle.

The height of your triangle represents the functional applied strength, your ability to produce force, and is best trained with heavier loads between 1–6RM or 6–8RM. The width of the triangle represents the functional range, your ability to successfully demonstrate that movement pattern on an unstable surface, at different speeds, in multiple planes, and many other abilities such as single leg, single hand grip, etc. This is best trained using a variety of lower load, higher repetition exercises that will challenge the body and force adaptations.

12. INCREASING THE FUNCTIONAL CAPACITY WILL IMPROVE BOTH PERFORMANCE AND RESILIENCE TO INJURY.

Performance is based on the ability to successfully complete any task that the person is exposed to, whether it is in everyday life, work or sport. When that task is within your ability level it can be performed, and when it is easily within your ability level it can be performed easily. Imagine only having the strength to do 100kg 1RM deadlifts and your job/sport requires you to perform a number of 100kg lifts within that hour or day. You should be able to do it, but the risk of you failing starts to increase and as you reach the edge of your strength range your risk of injury also increases. If you have to perform 20kg lifts repeatedly during the day, then that should be easy, and the risks of you injuring yourself should be pretty low. Improving your strength will make your triangle higher, and improving your range will make your triangle wider, and with a higher, wider triangle any task encountered should fall easily within this triangle (or ability), therefore maximising performance and decreasing the risk of injury.

13. ANY SPORT OR PROFESSION MAY REQUIRE HIGH FUNCTIONAL CAPACITY IN CERTAIN MOVEMENT PATTERNS BUT NOT NECESSARILY ALL.

The movement patterns that have been highlighted already are the foundation patterns that humans have been performing for thousands of years, since primal, caveman times. They are still performed today (or should be) by tasks that every human performs as part of their daily life. Some sports may require a mixture of these multiple movement patterns, such as MMA or rugby, while other sports rely on only a few. Time spent developing excessive strength in movement patterns not essential in that sport's performance will be a waste of time. Focus should be on the exercises that have the most carryover.

14. NON-FUNCTIONAL EXERCISES CAN HAVE A FUNCTIONAL CARRYOVER.

Is a biceps curl or seated leg curl a functional exercise? I would say they are not, since they do not fall into one of the human movement patterns. The elbow flexion that occurs in the biceps curl may make up part of the pull action, but it is not a pull. The exercises that mimic the movement patterns as close to real life as possible will have the greatest carryover – the tyre flip, the pull-up, the sled push etc. So why would the biceps curl or the leg curl still be included within a functional training programme? If you can perform a pull-up, then that is functional, but if you do not have the strength to perform this exercise, then remedial and supplementary exercises will be required to build up your strength to accomplish this task. This may be the lat pull down exercise (to work the lats and elbow flexors), dumbbell hammer curls (to work the elbow flexors) and hanging leg raises (to develop grip strength and endurance). If the reason why you can't perform a pull-up is weak elbow flexors, then this strength must be developed with supplementary drills, like the biceps curl. Once this strength has been developed, it can then be applied into a functional pattern, like a pull-up. There must be a period of application, since there are a lot of people that can lift the entire stack on the lat pull down, but cannot perform a single pull-up. But if this increased elbow flexor strength can be applied, then the non-functional biceps curl has had a functional carryover to the pull-up.

Many strength coaches therefore use non-functional exercises, like the leg extension, leg curl, seated dumbbell shoulder external rotation, supine triceps extension and many other drills, because they can supplement the big functional exercises (front squat, Romanian deadlift, standing overhead press) not just to balance out the agonist-antagonist strength balance, but also to expose certain muscles to a greater overload. If I perform three sets of leg extension as my lower body strength training, then it is non-functional. But if I perform six sets of front squats, four sets of Bulgarian split squats and then three sets of leg extension, then its inclusion is not non-functional. Performing three sets of leg extension won't undo the functional benefit of squats and split squats. But if I need more volume than the previous 10 sets can provide, but don't feel that I can perform another proprioceptively challenging freeweights exercise, then the leg extension is an excellent post-exhaustive exercise selection. These non-functional exercises are therefore best used to supplement the functional compound movements, or to prepare the individual to be able to perform these movements if they are not currently able.

15. INCLUDE EXERCISES THAT WORK THE RANGE OF THE MOVEMENT PATTERN.

Many trainers believe that a pull-up is sufficient to work the pull pattern, or the bench press the press pattern, or the cable woodchop the rotation pattern. These movement patterns, and the others, are made of different vectors (or directions) that should all be worked as part of a comprehensive training programme. A bench press, for example, will work the body in the horizontal press pattern, but there should also be a vertical press upwards, a vertical press downwards and pressing diagonally upwards and diagonally downwards. This can be accomplished using the exercises shown in table 1.2 as an example.

The different vectors will target different muscles, or different motor units within certain muscles, so it is important to work the body through the full spectrum of motion. This is the same for the rotation pattern, which is made up of horizontal rotation, diagonal rotation upwards and diagonal rotation downwards. Many trainers believe that the woodchop (diagonal rotation downwards) and the reverse woodchop (diagonal rotation upwards) are interchangeable exercises,

but they should not be used as such. The muscles used for the downward rotation at the core would be the internal and external obliques, while for the upward rotation also works the latissumus dorsi and contralateral glute. Saying the exercises are interchangeable would be like saying the pull-up and high pull work the same muscles.

The other reason to use a variety of exercises and machines or equipment so that the full vector spectrum is worked is the concept of functional differentiation. Paton & Brown (1994) describe this as when exercising a muscle with one end that attaches to a wide surface such as the pectoral muscle, the central nervous system will fine tune the activation pattern to maximally contract only a segment of the muscle (or selected motor units). If the same exercise or machine is used continuously, then this can create a strength disparity within that same muscle group, since certain muscles fibres will be trained, while others are not.

> Contralateral means the opposite side
> Ipsilateral means the same side

Table 1.2 Exercises to work a range of vectors within a single movement pattern

Movement	Exercise
Press horizontal	Barbell bench press
Press vertically upwards	Overhead dumbbell press
Press vertically downwards	Weighted dips
Press diagonally upwards	Inclined dumbbell chest press
Press diagonally downwards	Declined barbell bench press

16. SUPPLEMENTARY EXERCISES SHOULD PREPARE AN INDIVIDUAL TO PERFORM HUMAN MOVEMENT PATTERNS OR SHOULD COMPLEMENT HUMAN MOVEMENT PATTERN EXERCISES.

The group of exercises that make up the classification pattern of 'supplementary exercises' is vast.

Almost every isolation exercise is inherently going to be a supplementary exercise, since the majority of movement patterns are multi-joint, compound exercises. It is the over-utilisation of these supplementary, isolation exercises where many individuals go wrong with their programmes. Have a look at the following example of two different programmes to work the chest, shoulders and triceps:

Example 1

Order	Exercise	Sets	Reps	Tempo	Rest
A1	Machine inc. press	6	12	4.1.X.1	60s
B1	Dumbbell (DB) flys	4	12	3.1.1.0	60s
C1	DB lateral raises	6 (3 each side)	10	3.0.1.0	30s
D1	Cable triceps pushdown	4	10	3.1.1.1	60s

Example 2

Order	Exercise	Sets	Reps	Tempo	Rest
A1	Barbell bench press	6	12	4.1.X.1	60s
B1	DB overhead press (1 arm)	6 (3 each side)	10	4.1.X.0	60s
C1	Weighted dips	4	10	4.0.X.1	60s
C2	EZ Bar declined triceps extension	4	10	3.1.X.1	60s

Note – please refer to page 281 for explanations on tempo

Although both programmes would take a similar duration it should be clear that the stimulus of the second example would provide not only a greater carryover to functional performance, but also greater hypertophy, as is sought by the split session, and rep range selected. There is still an isolation exercise in the second programme, but this is to allow a complete overload of the triceps, without having to use a proprioceptively demanding exercise, which would be difficult after the first three exercises selected.

Wherever possible, freeweight exercises should be selected over more stable, isolation, fixed-path machines. If the individual is unable to perform these exercises because of poor stability, mobility or proprioception, then supplementary exercises can be used to build them up to that level. For example, strongmen would perform exercises like the windmill (shown later in chapter 10) to build up the required lateral core and hip stability, as well as shoulder stability and mobility, to optimally perform a single arm press overhead with heavy loads.

For the person that needs to develop strength or size in the calves, squats or deadlifts would be insufficient on their own to overload the plantarflexors. In this case, standing and seated calf raises would allow for specific overload of these muscles in addition to squats and deadlifts. Some may ask if these functional, compound exercises are required for the development of greater calf size, but what good strength coaches know is that isolation exercises to develop the size of the calves, or biceps, or forearms, are best combined with large exercises that will produce a stimulus on the body as a whole (causing hormonal changes), rather than just on their own.

Figure 1.11 Fat grip dumbbells can help develop a weak grip

17. GRIP STRENGTH IS A KEY LIMITING-FACTOR FOR MANY OF THE HUMAN MOVEMENT PATTERNS.

Vintage strongmen realised that a man is only as strong as his weakest link. Today most trainers talk about the core being the weak link in our kinetic chain. Making this link stronger will make an individual functionally better. This is true for any weak link in the kinetic chain, and the grip is slowly becoming just as important as other weak links.

The grip is essential for the body to hold on to an object for pulling exercises, lifting and for moving and carrying loads. If you cannot hold on to the load, you cannot lift it, or carry it, and if you can't hold your own bodyweight you won't be able to perform even a single repetition of a pull-up. No matter how strong you make your biceps or back muscles, if you cannot hold on to the pull-up bars, it doesn't matter.

For many years trainers used a hand-grip dynamometer to test grip strength, as an indication of overall strength. A lot of experts criticised this tool, as did I, citing that there must be limited correlation between grip strength and other compound strength tests, like the deadlift or pull up, but with more research it seems that there is some validity to using it.

In addition, many strength coaches are using this test as an indication of short-term overreaching and potential long-term overtraining. There are lots of indicators that trainers can use. Some will say that if your heart rate is 5bpm above or below what it normally is, then make your training session easier, and if it is 10bpm from the normal, then you haven't recovered adequately from the previous session and should take a day off. If your grip strength (as shown by the test) is below what it should be, this would be an indication, just like an elevated heart rate, that you should take a rest day rather than train.

If you see individuals in the gym using straps religiously for lifting exercises, then this is the type of person who would definitely benefit from grip strength, grip endurance, wrist stability and forearm strength training. There are lots of supplementary exercises that will help to achieve this, in addition to fat grip bars or using Fat Gripz™ (see page 41).

18. ENSURE THE CORRECT FOUNDATION IS DEVELOPED FOR EACH MOVEMENT PATTERN, PRIOR TO TRAINING FUNCTIONAL APPLIED STRENGTH OR RANGE.

Strength, like a building, must be built upon a solid foundation, or it will be limited in its potential. Prior to commencing phases of hypertrophy, strength or power there must be a period of training, which develops all of the foundations to each movement pattern. Strength coaches will call this a general adaptation phase, or general preparation phase, and it should work on achieving optimal mobility, stability, skill and connective tissue strength. For training to have maximum benefit, these phases must be undertaken or the potential for functional strength, range or capacity will be limited. General preparation or foundation training usually then will involve basic strength exercises (some bodyweight, some freeweight, some fixed path), as well as postural correction exercises, core strength and stability work, and flexibility work with stretching and foam rollers. This will address the common issues beginners present with and will form a foundation of ability to progress from with later phases of training (hypertrophy, strength, power, etc).

19. FITNESS IS MOVEMENT PATTERN-SPECIFIC.

This is essentially the principle of specificity. If we know that the human movement patterns are the basis of all the tasks we perform, then we should train this way. Many trainers look to use 'cardiovascular exercises' such as running and swimming to improve aerobic and anaerobic fitness. However, if your sport or job requires that you lift repeatedly, then these activities will not have the carryover that you require. Resistance exercises like squats and deadlifts can be used to improve cardiovascular (CV) fitness, without the need for CV machines. Perform the following sequence of exercises, and realise the impact that these exercises can have on the cardiovascular system:

A1	Squats	60s	Rest 60s
A2	Bench press	60s	Rest 60s
A3	Deadlifts	60s	Rest 60s
A4	Pull-ups	60s	Rest 60s
And repeat x 5			

Gait and locomotion, which includes walking, running and swimming, is only one of the human movement patterns, and if your sport or job requires 'fitness' in other movement patterns, it is essential that you train these sufficiently as well.

20. THE DEVELOPMENT OF STRENGTH IS HIGHLY TRAINABLE AND HAS A HIGH DEGREE OF TRANSFER.

'Strength is an essential component of all human performance and its formal development can no longer be neglected in the preparation of any athlete.'

Siff, Mel, 2004

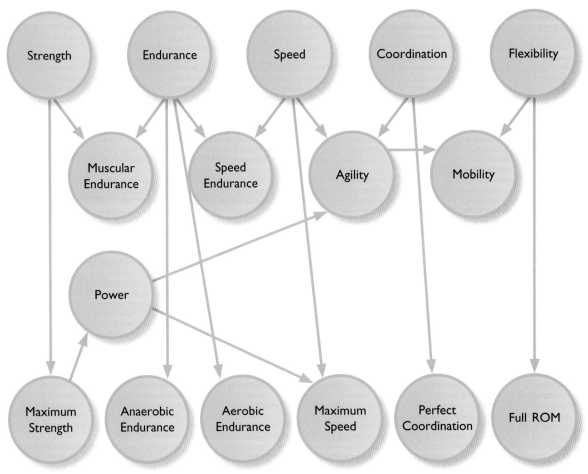

Figure 1.12 The relationship between strength and other biomotor abilities, adapted from Bompa, (1999).

Some trainers or individuals may question the importance of focusing training on the improvement of strength, but not only does it have a high correlation to other facets of fitness, there is also much research to show how to improve it. It is important to realise how the different bio-motor abilities (or facets of fitness) are related to each other, and how a foundation of strength is correlated with other facets of fitness, such as power, agility and speed. According to Bompa (1999) strength training can improve:

- Maximum strength
- Muscular endurance
- Power
- Maximum speed
- Agility

The image above shows how these facets of fitness are interrelated.

When evaluating the strength requirements for the individual, we can choose from the following categories of strength:

Type of strength	Sub-category	Example
Table 1.3	**Categories of strength**	
Maximal strength	Concentric	The ability to generate maximal force when the muscle is shortening.
	Eccentric	The ability to generate maximal force when the muscle is lengthening.
	Isometric	The ability to generate maximal force when the muscle does not change length or a position is held.
	Relative	The ability to generate maximal force in relation to your bodyweight.
	Absolute	The ability to generate maximal force irrespective of your bodyweight.
Speed-strength	Starting strength	The ability to produce maximal force at the beginning of a contraction (Poliquin, 2004). This is a key determinant of successful performance in sports that require high initial speed and where the external load to overcome is relatively light, such as in tennis or boxing.
	Explosive strength	The ability to produce maximal force once movement has already been initiated (Poliquin, 2004). In sports where the external resistance is great, such as wrestling and rugby, the quicker the rate that an athlete can reach maximal force production, the better the performance.
	Reactive strength	The ability to change quickly and efficiently from an eccentric to a concentric contraction (Poliquin, 2004). The more efficient the athlete can utilise the forces thrusting the body in one direction, to change and accelerate the body in another direction, the higher they will be able to jump, bound and run, and the more agile they will be.
Strength endurance		The ability of the neuromuscular system to produce sustained contractions of consistent force output for longer durations.
	Short	Short duration is from 40s–2 mins.
	Moderate	Moderate duration is from 2–5 mins.
	Long	Long duration is from over 6–10 mins

All of these factors can be improved with different types of strength training. For example, if your sport or occupation requires reactive strength (the ability to move between an eccentric and concentric contraction efficiently, utilising the stretch-shortening cycle) then plyometric training would be more beneficial than lateral sled pulls, whereas if you need lateral speed and agility, that would be the most appropriate tool and exercise to select.

The tool, the exercises and the type of training all need to be selected specifically to achieve the end result of gaining very specific adaptations that will transfer to increased performance and injury resilience in your daily tasks, occupation or sport.

FUNCTIONAL TRAINING EQUIPMENT AND METHODS

Any tool can be functional or non-functional depending on its use or application. These pages will try to highlight the correct application of different equipment.

KETTLEBELLS

Kettlebells are an excellent addition to the arsenal of different tools that a trainer can use with their clients. They have been used to develop strength for over a hundred years, and have more recently received somewhat of a revival. As a variation to a dumbbell, they alter the strength curve (because the point where the muscle is overloaded is different – the bell hangs below the handle) when used for exercises like a bicep curl. They are most often used for dynamic, rhythmical exercises (such as the swing) that are continuous and will overload the cardio-respiratory system as much as the muscular system, leading to a high energy expenditure, metabolic acceleration and fat loss and increased strength-endurance and power-endurance.

Kettlebell training exercises will help to broaden the functional range (or breadth of functional ability), more than increasing pure strength, and are best applied with heavier strength exercises, such as barbell squats or deadlifts, to improve

Figure 1.13 Kettlebells are more comfortable than dumbbells when performing certain exercises.

Figure 1.14 Suspension training systems

the body's ability to apply that strength at speed and for prolonged periods, with a lower weight than would be used in something like a deadlift.

SUSPENSION SYSTEM TRAINING

Suspension systems, such as the MiloKit from SAQ® International or the Jungle Gym XT from LifeLines USA have become popular pieces of equipment in health clubs, performance training facilities and group exercise environments, but, again, they are not entirely new products. Athletes have used gymnastic rings and ropes to manipulate their body for improved athletic performance for many years; gymnasts who train on rings have sculpted, strong and toned physiques.

The modern systems, unlike the gymnastic rings or basic ropes, have integrated foot straps to allow for a multitude of upper body, lower body and core-specific drills. With a little training, suspension systems can be very easy to use and they allow not only some isolated muscle recruitment, but also complex, dynamic, multi-planar drills. There are hundreds of exercise variations, which manipulate the bodyweight (to make

the exercises easier or harder) and can be easily progressed or regressed to vary the intensity.

Suspension systems are best applied when strength levels are on the lower side (as with most gym users) and when the individual has been using fixed path machines excessively. These individuals will undoubtedly have weaker core and stabiliser muscles, which can be improved using suspension systems to correct the agonist-synergist strength balance.

When heavy strength training is sought this piece of equipment may not be the best choice as it is difficult to apply heavy loads alongside it.

Figure 1.15 Using a suspension training system

Figure 1.16 (a) An early dumbbell, (b) A handmade dumbbell, (c) A modern dumbbell

DUMBBELLS

Dumbbells are another piece of training equipment that have been around for hundreds of years. 'Dumbbell' as a word originated in Tudor England – athletes used hand-held church bells, which ranged in weight from a few ounces to many pounds, to develop the upper body and arms. They made a great deal of noise, so athletes would take out the clappers to enable them to practise quietly; hence the name dumb- (or quiet) -bell.

When strongmen started to make their own equipment, they kept the name, even though the shape changed. During the time of Vintage Training in the 1800s and 1900s, the familiar shape of the dumbbell, with two equal weights attached to a handle, had appeared.

Nowadays dumbbells can be manufactured at home (as in figure 1.15(b), taken by the author on a holiday to Indonesia), or more commonly by manufacturers with more commercial and durable materials.

Dumbbells can be used individually or in pairs to train either functional strength or with lighter loads for functional range. Even the loads used for functional strength are normally at least 10 per cent less when using two dumbbells, as opposed to a more stable single barbell. However, the benefit of using two independent dumbbells over a single barbell is that it can help to correct bilateral differences. Dumbbells are one of the most versatile pieces of training equipment for compound functional strength/range exercises, or for supplementary exercises.

BARBELLS

Barbells are essentially elongated dumbbells, with weights at either end, and have been used traditionally in weightlifting for many years. They can be fixed barbells (a certain weight that cannot be altered), or they can be plate loaded, making it easier to vary the load applied to a certain exercise. Although the exercise selection is more limited, they are most effectively used to increase functional strength and power because a greater

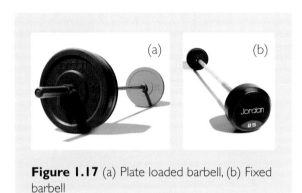

Figure 1.17 (a) Plate loaded barbell, (b) Fixed barbell

Figure 1.18 An overhead squat using a barbell

load or intensity can be used than with kettlebells, dumbbells or cables.

Strongman used barbells to perform one-handed exercises, the benefits being the increase in grip strength, wrist stability, core and hip stability and shoulder stability. However, it is quite uncommon to see modern gym users performing drills with one hand, since the single hand feats of strength like the side press, bent press, clean and jerk and snatch have been replaced by the more stable two hand variations where possible. It is not that single hand drills should always be performed over two hand variations, but (as Vintage Strongmen did) a combination of both should be incorporated within the training programme.

MEDICINE AND TORNADO BALLS

The medicine ball is one of the oldest pieces of freeweight training equipment, pre-dating both barbells and dumbbells. Training with this tool has come a long way since animal-based medicine balls were first used by the Romans and Greeks centuries ago.

Medicine balls commonly come in weights of up to 10kg, so are very light in comparison with dumbbells, kettlebells and barbells. They are therefore best used for multi-planar exercises, such as a lunge with overhead reach or rotation, or for rebounding exercises, such as rotation throws against a wall or chest throws onto a rebounder.

Medicine balls can be also be used in the development of basic bio-motor abilities with clients new to resistance training, who may find it difficult or uncomfortable to use dumbbells or barbells. One of its prominent uses is in the field of athletic development, where most upper body plyometric training drills utilise the versatility of the medicine ball.

Figure 1.19 Different types of medicine balls

There are a number of different types of medicine balls and accessory equipment including semi-bouncing medicine balls, medicine balls with handles, tornado balls (roped medicine balls) and medicine ball rebounders.

Figure 1.20 Stability ball training

STABILITY BALLS

Stability balls (also known as fit balls, physio balls or Swiss balls) are commonly pushed as one of the most 'functional' tools available to fitness enthusiasts. They were originally used by Swiss physiotherapists in the 1960s to help improve function with stroke victims and other patients with certain neuromuscular issues. They found that performing certain exercises on an unstable surface helped to train neuromuscular pathways that had been inhibited.

The stability ball can be used for a variety of unstable training exercises, utilising bodyweight, freeweights and cables, but usually the load is quite low. This may help to provide foundations for functional capacity or to train functional range, but the load must always be above the overload threshold to ensure adaptations are occurring.

FOAM ROLLERS

The foam roller is a long cylindrical-shaped foam piece, available as half round and full round. Self-myofascial release (SMFR) on a foam roller is effectively another form of flexibility training that focuses on the fascial system. SMFR is a great technique used by many trainers to improve flexibility, function, performance and reduce injuries with their clients by inhibiting overactive

Figure 1.21 Using a foam roller

muscles. SMFR techniques, although not new, have become more and more prominent among athletes, fitness enthusiasts and those seeking a healthier well-being.

This form of stretching utilises the concept of autogenic inhibition (developing excessive tension in a muscle to cause a reflex inhibition of the muscle and to decrease muscle tension) to improve soft tissue extensibility (the ability of the muscle to stretch and return), thus relaxing the muscle and allowing the activation of the antagonist muscle. Foam rollers offer many of the same benefits as a sports massage, but at a much cheaper price. The foam roller not only stretches muscles and tendons but it also breaks down soft tissue adhesions and scar tissue. By using your own body weight and a cylindrical foam roller, you can perform a self-massage or myofascial release, break up trigger points, and soothe tight fascia while increasing blood flow and circulation to the soft tissues.

UNSTABLE SURFACE TRAINING
Stability discs, BOSU® and wobble boards all form part of this group (foam rollers and stability balls can also fall into this category). As mentioned on page 34, the load is quite low,

Figure 1.22 Unstable surface training using a wobble board

which for prehabilitation or rehabilitation is very important. They can help to provide foundations for functional capacity or to train functional range, but the load used should (for non-injured training) be above the overload threshold to ensure strength adaptations are occurring.

For rehabilitation, these tools excel for developing proprioception, strength and stability in injured joints, such as after foot, ankle and knee injuries.

AGILITY LADDERS AND HURDLES
Agility ladders and hurdles are used to improve running technique, develop first step quickness and for plyometrics. They are used by many strength and conditioning coaches from numerous sports, including football, rugby, hockey, netball and basketball. They are best applied in the gait and locomotion movement pattern, to

Figure 1.23 Using hurdles

develop efficiency and speed, alongside the development of strength and power using barbells, dumbbells and sled work, to name a few of the commonly used tools.

WEIGHTED VESTS

Weighted vests are an excellent functional training tool as a progression to bodyweight exercises, with blocks of bags of weights able to be inserted into the vest to gradually load the exercise. This piece of equipment is great used in exercises such as press-ups, dips and pull-ups to increase the load, where holding on to a plate, dumbbell or barbell is either impractical or impossible. You can hold a dumbbell between the feet when performing a pull-up, but it will affect the optimal biomechanics and is awkward to perform. You can

attach a plate to a weights belt for a dip, but this will likely pull the pelvis forward into an anterior pelvic tilt, affecting your posture and potentially compromising safety.

Weighted vests can also be used for plyometric training, such as jumps, hops and bounds, or for weighted running or quadruped drills. Because you don't have to hold on to the load, this leaves the hands free to move normally and unrestricted, mimicking the normal movement pattern more closely and thus having a greater potential for carryover. Vests can also help to replicate the additional load of protective clothing in sports such as rugby league, American football, ice hockey, or in occupational roles such as firefighters, SWAT teams or soldiers.

The downside to using weighted vests is the limitation on the amount of load that can be applied. Commonly the maximum load is about 40lbs, which when compared with the loads attained with a barbell is pretty low.

Figure 1.24 Using a weighted vest

RESISTANCE BANDS

Elastic or resistance bands have been used for many years in a number of capacities for exercise and performance training. They have been used extensively for low load rehabilitation exercises, for rotator cuff work, for example, after a shoulder dislocation, or for isolated resistance drills after a sprained ankle. These bands are also used for exercises such as bicep curls, lateral raises or rows, commonly where other equipment is not available, such as in circuits classes, at home or when travelling.

Thick resistance bands are being used more frequently as a method of performing resisted running, crawling or quadruped movements. Equipment like the Flexi-Cord from SAQ® allows you to attach one end of the band to an anchor, or for a partner to hold, while you perform multiple sprints, trying to accelerate away as the tension increases, or a lateral crossover step, or lunges. The band allows the vector of resistance to be more horizontal, rather than the typical vertical vector associated with gravity and traditional weighted exercises.

The main downsides to resistance band work are the low levels of resistance that they provide and also the fact that the tension increases as you move through the range of motion (rather than it being constant as with freeweights).

Strangely enough what is commonly described as a negative with resistance band training can also be turned into a positive method of varying the stimulus on the body during exercise. For several decades some powerlifting clubs, such as Westside Barbell Club, have

been using thick bands with their freeweights. This system of progressive resistance training, also known as linear variable resistance training (LVRT) is one that encompasses lifting chains and resistance bands, and essentially provides a means of progressively adding more load throughout a range of motion while you are performing an individual repetition. The bands are connected to the ends of the barbell and anchor points near the floor, and would be used with exercises such as the squat, deadlift and bench press. As you perform the bench press, for example, the tension would be decreased at the start of the concentric phase, when the band is slack, and increases at the end of the concentric phase (the lockout). Alternatively the bands can be attached to high anchor points to again overload the final phase of the bench press; at the start of the concentric phase the tension on the bands is high, assisting the lift, and slackens at the end of the concentric phase, increasing the tension. The second technique is usually applied with a supramaximal weight, i.e. a weight that is more than you

Figure 1.25 Using a resistance band

could usually bench press, but is assisted in the first phase, as if being helped by a training partner.

LIFTING CHAINS

Chains also form part of the system of LVRT alongside resistance bands. They can be added to an Olympic bar, EZ bar, triceps bar or hex bar in addition to the standard weight plates or even instead of them. Connecting chains means that as you lift, the weight of the chain progressively increases as more and more of the chain lifts off the floor. The weight you are lifting progressively becomes heavier, providing maximum muscular stimulation throughout the entire range of motion. For example, as you perform a back squat with a barbell and plates, the exercise is hardest in the bottom range of motion, and gets easier in the final phase of the exercise. Using chains with this exercise means that the end range can be overloaded sufficiently to improve strength with more load than is needed to overload the body in the bottom position.

Progressive resistance training has been used by powerlifters for decades because it is fantastic for improving strength and power. Now athletes, bodybuilders and everyday clients are embracing this training tool as a

Figure 1.26 Using chains

Figure 1.27 The Alpha Strong bag

complement to traditional freeweights, such as barbells, dumbbells and kettlebells. They are also being used as part of unconventional training techniques, as a way of stimulating the body in unusual and unique ways. For example, performing overhead barbell walks with chains causes the chains to swing (if off the floor) or drag (if long enough to touch the floor) which stimulates the core muscles to have to stabilise more than if simply walking with just a weighted barbell.

SANDBAGS AND POWERBAG™

Sandbags, like the Alpha Strong bag shown in figure 1.26, are bags of sand encased in heavy duty fabric, used for more unconventional style training where you want the bag to roll, shift and collapse as you lift it. It makes exercising much more challenging, and with the heavy duty fabric construction is more suited to extreme use, such as being thrown.

Figure 1.28 The Powerbag™

The Powerbag™ is a type of sandbag, again with handles, but unlike a normal sandbag, while it is being lifted, squatted, pressed, caught and rotated it will retain its tubular shape and the contents will shift to provide the challenge to the body's stabilisers, especially the core.

Sandbags and the Powerbag™ provide a crossover between Olympic lifting, medicine ball work and core stability training. Using these tools incorporates all the benefits of a power-based lifting programme with the flexibility offered through sport-specific movement-based training and throwing drills. Over the last five years or so the popularity of extreme metabolic training, such as the Crossfit style of training, has dramatically increased, as well as unconventional style of training, and both tools can be used extensively with these training methodologies.

The sandball

The sandball is effectively a cross between a sandbag and a medicine ball or kettlebell. It is still filled with sand and can be used with many of the extreme exercises, like the sandbag, but can also be used for numerous medicine ball throwing, catching and single hand drills. One-hand snatches, cleans, swings and other drills can also be performed with this versatile piece of kit.

Sandbags and the Powerbag™ are the epitome of tools that improve functional range and are best combined with more stable tools like a barbell. For example, a barbell clean will help develop strength and power in a stable sagittal plane, while a diagonal sandbag or Powerbag™ clean will challenge the body in the transverse plane, and frontal planes as well, and with the inherent instability and movement of the contents, will mimic everyday life and sports more closely than the barbell variation alone.

SLEDS

Westside Barbell Gym (a popular and progressive training facility for powerlifters) training methods, such as progressive resistance using chains and bands, have gradually seeped into the fitness from the strength and conditioning world. Another of their fantastic tools, which has become hugely popular in recent years, is the sled. Sled training is an incredible way to train for athletic speed and improved performance, but also for the

Figure 1.29 Using a sled to train

everyday person to improve functional strength, fitness and achieve fat loss. They are easy to use and, unlike some freeweights, which many females believe will bulk them up, clients have no preconceptions about them, and they can be used indoors or outdoors, with individuals or for group training. Strongmen, combat fighters, rugby and football players, and any athlete interested in improving speed, power, strength and stability can use sled training within their strength and conditioning programme. Exercises like the sled pull through are commonly cited as being a key exercise for the improvement of explosive hip extension, and to improve the ability to accelerate quickly or jump higher.

TYRES AND HAMMERS

Another form of unconventional training that has increased in popularity is the use of tyres and hammers. Tyre flipping, dragging and pushing has become the norm with many strength and conditioning coaches as a progression or variation from Olympic lifting, sled dragging and bench press respectively.

These unconventional tools are excellent for the development of truly functional applied strength, and are best used once strength has been developed with the more stable, and less proprioceptively-challenging gym-based barbell exercise versions of these movement patterns. They are cheap, versatile and are excellent to develop resilience to injury, which translates to the real world or sports field.

Figure 1.30 Using tyres in training

CONDITIONING ROPES

Conditioning ropes are somewhat of a recent training tool, and can be used for pulling, climbing or for undulating training, which is simply a method of making waves with the ropes in a continuous, rhythmical fashion for upper body anaerobic conditioning. Good for grip and forearm work, as well as rotator cuff development, it is a fun, challenging and dynamic form of exercise that can be used to maintain strength and fitness during rehabilitation; with uninjured athletes to improve cardiovascular fitness, shoulder strength and endurance; or for core training.

Figure 1.31 Using conditioning ropes for undulating training

FAT GRIPZ™

Fat Gripz™ were invented a number of years ago and are a fantastic training tool, designed to fit around most grips on freeweights and machines to convert a standard grip into a thicker 'fatter' grip. This has the effect of increasing recruitment of the hand, wrist and forearm musculature. Thick bar training with Fat Gripz™ immediately targets the body's weak links, helping to address the agonist-synergist strength balance.

While there are also Fat Grip cable attachment handles, dumbbells, EZ bars, Olympic bars and other bars, Fat Gripz™ can be used with any standard variations of these, making them

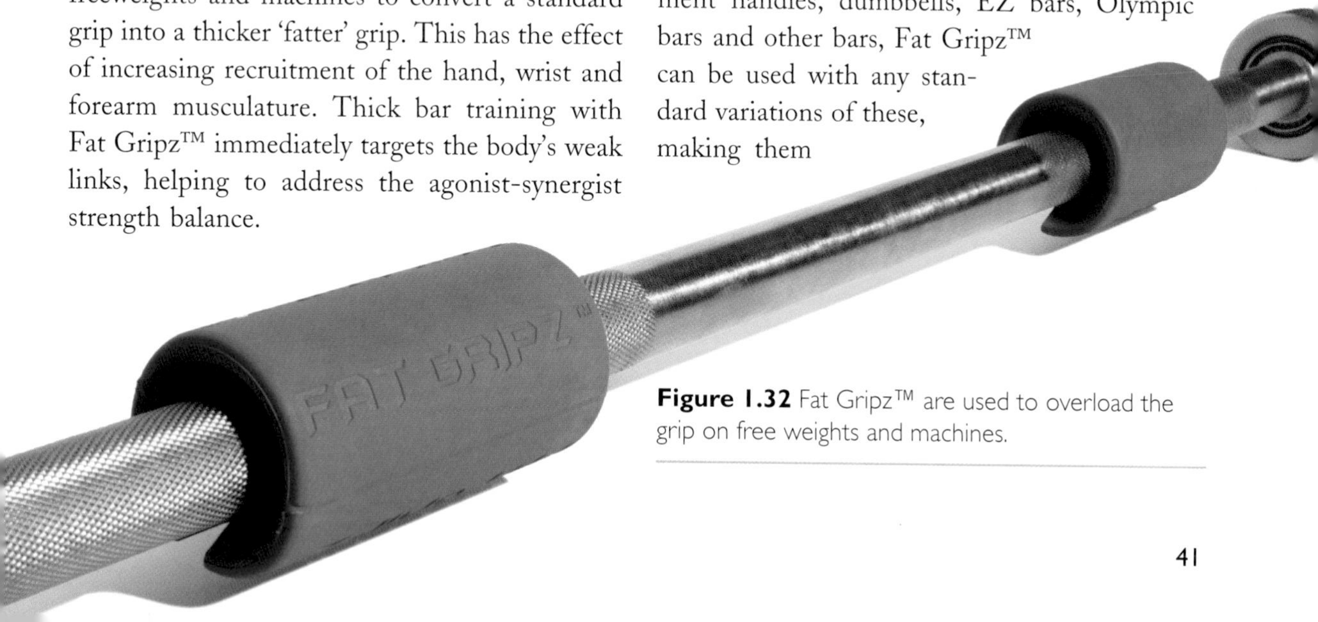

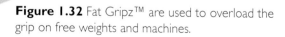

Figure 1.32 Fat Gripz™ are used to overload the grip on free weights and machines.

much more affordable for the average trainer or individual. Although not commonly seen in many gyms, there are strongly advocated by anyone that uses them.

CABLES

Cable columns have been used for many years to supplement training and today they form an integral part of most fitness training facilities. Many individuals use them for biceps curls, triceps pushdowns and cable crossovers, but not much else. They are probably one of the best training tools to work the rotation and smash patterns, as well as a plethora of supplementary exercises.

They can be used with a variety of attachments, including ropes, long bars, waist belts and vests, and can be used to train virtually every one of the human movement patterns. The downside is the potential to overload the agonist muscles. Santana, Vera-Garcia & McGill (2007) showed that the potential weight on the stack would be limited to about 40 per cent of the individual's mass for a one-handed chest press. They are, however, a great method to teach the stabilisation and integration of the core and lower body when performing an upper body push or pull. They are best applied in the functional preparation phase of training (the initial phases of training where a variety of fitness issues are addressed) to improve functional range.

CORE PLATE

The core plate, or land mine as it also known, is a nice tool to work the body in the transverse plane and for many pressing and pulling variations. A bar is fed into the sleeve and the core plate allows a three-dimensional movement to occur. While limited to about half of the human movement

Figure 1.33 A core plate

patterns, it does provide a nice variation for many of the common tools used, and it is this variation that can allow the continued overload and subsequent adaptations to occur.

FIXED PATH MACHINES

Fixed path machines can have a place within a fully comprehensive and integrated approach to training. For those that wish to develop hypertrophy, they work well to provide an overload on certain muscles as they are isolated. But, rather than a replacement to, they are best integrated with large compound freeweight exercises such as the squat or deadlift.

Many fixed path machines would mostly come under the supplementary category of exercises, to prepare the individual for the more proprioceptively challenging freeweight exercises, or to complement them. Excessive utilisation of fixed path machines, over the more 'functional' tools described, will lead to less carryover in functional applied strength, range or capacity.

In the end, it's not so much which functional training tool is 'better', but rather ensuring that you use the right tool for the right job!

SQUAT PATTERN

2

The squat movement pattern is one of the most versatile of all the human movement patterns, and can be defined as a sitting motion. It involves moving from a standing upright position to a position where the knees are partially or fully bent. In general terms the word 'squat' is synonymous with the rear end being lowered, whether it is the squat effect in hydrodynamics, or the pitching motion of cars during acceleration. In humans, the squat pattern has been used since primal times as a resting position, the hips resting on the heels or lower leg, and has also been adopted as a position for urination, defecation and childbirth. In the modern world, squatting to a full depth is more common in Asian cultures.

The squat pattern in functional exercise involves the following different movements or positions – the standard parallel stance squat, the split stance squat, the lunge, the single leg squat, the step-up, the jump, the landing and the hop. It primarily works the muscles of the legs and hips (the quadriceps, hamstrings, gluteals) as well as the plantarflexors of the lower leg and stabilisers of the ankles, knees and hips. The core musculature and muscles of the upper body are also recruited during certain drills for lumbo-pelvic-hip stabilisation (such as during a lunge

Figure 2.1 The squat pattern is used frequently in everyday life

and rotation), to stabilise an external load (such as during a front squat) or for additional propulsion (such as during a vertical jump).

The squat pattern is used extensively by strength and conditioning specialists and health practitioners because of its carryover to running and jumping (Dunn et al, 1984 & Escamilla et al, 1998). This movement pattern and the exercises that are classified under this pattern are integral to lower extremity strength, power and endurance enhancement, as well as for rehabilitation of lower body injuries (Shelbourne & Nitz, 1990; Fu, Woo & Irrgang, 1992; Bynum, Barrack & Alexander, 1995).

> The International Powerlifting Federation (IPF) world record for the squat in powerlifting currently stands at 457.5kg.

TERMINOLOGY AND SUBCATEGORIES OF THE SQUAT

It is important to know the terminology used to describe the squat and also what each of the squat subcategories actually refer to to avoid any confusion. The terminology described by Chandler et al (Chandler, Wilson & Stone, 1989) will be used to define many of the squat exercises and variations (see table 2.1).

FUNCTIONS AND IMPORTANCE OF THE SQUAT PATTERN

Many strength coaches consider the squat exercise essential for the full development of athletic potential (Fleck & Kraemer, 1987; Stone, Byrd, Tew & Wood, 1980). The squat pattern should be included within a functional training programme for the following reasons:

IT PROMOTES OPTIMAL RANGE OF MOTION (ROM) IN THE LOWER BODY

Many individuals will present with limited mobility in ankle dorsiflexion and hip flexion and extension. Performing split stance squats with the front foot elevated and focusing on driving the knee forward will help to mobilise the plantarflexors. Performing a split stance squat with the rear leg elevated (commonly called a Bulgarian split squat) will help to mobilise the hip flexors.

IT IMPROVES SPORTS PERFORMANCE THAT REQUIRES SPEED AND ACCELERATION

Because squats have a good correlation with 30m and 60m times (Poliquin, 2006), it is logical to deduce that improved squat performance will translate to improved acceleration and speed, which will help with performance in sports that have speed as a crucial facet. For rugby, football, hockey, netball, basketball and many, many others, increasing squat ability can translate to improved performance and success.

IT IMPROVES SPORTS PERFORMANCE THAT REQUIRE POWER AND JUMPING ABILITY

Poliquin (2006) has shown that increases in full squat strength have a higher correlation with increases in vertical jump and penta jumps (five successive long jumps) over training with half squats. For sports that require the athlete to jump high or jump far, training to increase full squat

Table 2.1	Squat terminology (Chandler, Wilson & Stone, 1989)
Terminology	**Description**
Back squat	Squatting with the bar positioned behind the neck on the upper back
Front squat	Squatting with the bar positioned in front of the neck on the shoulders
Overhead squat	Squatting with the bar held above the head, with the arms extended
Parallel stance	Feet positioned next to each other, usually about hip to shoulder width apart
Split stance	Feet positioned with one forward, usually about the distance of twice the length of the tibia
Lunge	A dynamic split stance squat, where the individual steps into and out of the split stance squat
Rack position	The bar is held on the anterior deltoids and clavicles, with the wrists extended and the elbows flexed so that the upper arms are parallel to the floor
Quarter squat	Squatting to a point of full extension minus 30 degrees of knee flexion
Half squat	Squatting to a point of full extension minus 60 degrees of knee flexion
Bench squat	Squatting to a bench at approximately knee height
Parallel squat	Squatting to the point where the femur is parallel with the floor
Deep squat	Squatting to the point where the distal portion (furthest end) of the hamstrings touches the proximal portion (closest end) of the gastrocnemius muscle
Full squat	Sometimes used to describe a parallel squat or a deep squat. For the purposes of this book it will be used to describe the latter.

SQUAT PATTERN

strength will help with their performance of that action in their sport.

IT IMPROVES STRENGTH AND HYPERTROPHY

As a big, compound exercise that utilises a large amount of muscle mass and loads the axial spine, the stress that a squat causes on the body will assist with other types of strength or hypertrophy training. It is commonly advised that if you want to increase the efficiency of your hypertrophy arm sessions, then include squats and deadlifts within your programme, as they will increase the release of growth hormone, improving your anabolic potential.

IT IS USED FOR BOTH PREHABILITATION AND REHABILITATION

According to data collected on seven Canadian national teams preparing for the Albertville,

Lillehammer and Nagano Winter Olympics (Poliquin, 2006), all of the following are benefits of performing full squats over half squats in relation to injuries:

- A reduction in groin pulls and tears
- A reduction in lower back injuries
- A reduction in hamstring pulls and tears (900 per cent)
- A reduction in knee surgeries
- Increases in knee stability (improvements in 17 out of 23 measures of knee stability)
- Improvement in hamstring: quadriceps strength ratio from 58 per cent to 78 per cent in 11 weeks (the hamstring:quadriceps ratio being a predictor of prevention of anterior cruciate ligament (ACL) injuries)

Full squats are beneficial for lower body rehabilitation because they can strengthen the quadriceps and hamstrings in a closed chain format, balance the quad:hamstring strength ratio and also strengthen the vastus medilias obliques (VMO), all improving knee stability.

Lower extremity sports

Squats are perhaps the best exercise for preparing the lower extremities for ground-based sports. Moreover, they are thought to produce a complete training stimulus due to the balance, coordination, and activation of the lower extremity musculature involved in completing the exercise.

FULL SQUAT DEBATE AND RESEARCH

Historically, the squat has been an exercise surrounded by controversy. Research conducted in the 1960s (Klein, 1962) showed that training with full squats had a number of potential negative issues:

- Deep-squat exercises have a detrimental effect on the medial and lateral collateral ligaments and the anterior cruciate ligaments.
- Deep squatting tends to weaken the ligaments and hence make the knee more vulnerable to injury.
- Internal derangements, osteoarthritis and the like may be more frequent.

Since this research was published in 1962, many other authors and experts have come forward to propose the negative impact of squats:

'Squatting is a basic component of many disciplines and sports ... Hence, the avoidance of squatting is virtually impossible. However, squatting exercises should be avoided by laypeople, especially the middle-aged or elderly.'

Alter (2004)

Many fitness professionals today have the following concerns related to squats:

- Squats can promote knee injuries.
- The squat exercise is detrimental to knee joint stability.
- Squatting results in high forces on the back, increasing injury potential.
- The squat exercise could damage connective

tissue, including muscles, bones, ligaments and tendons.

- Bouncing in the bottom position of a squat to help initiate ascent increases mechanical loads on the knee joint.

These concerns have resulted in three main recommendations when performing a squat exercise:

- Hold on to something for support or squat with your back against a wall.
- Reduce the depth of the descent by squatting to only a 90 degree angle at the knee (the knee should remain over the long axis of the foot).
- Keep the knee behind the toes, so as to limit potential stress on the knee joint.

These recommendations are commonly advocated, but unfortunately the initial studies have since been shown to have produced less than reliable results and conclusions.

KLEIN'S RESEARCH
Karl Klein published a number of studies and articles in the early 1960s (Klein, 1961, 1962). He examined the knees of competitive weightlifters using standard assessments and self-developed tests of medial and lateral knee stability. These results showed that 'Squats have a debilitative effect on the ligament structures of the knee…' and that there was greater MCL (medial collateral ligament) and LCL (lateral collateral ligament) instability in weightlifters when compared to controls. He concluded that deep knee squats stretched the ligaments and caused increased instability of the knee, and he advised that parallel squats should be used in place of deep squats.

SUBSEQUENT RESEARCH
Since Klein's work in the 1960s, there has been a significant amount of research in the area of squatting, the results of which bring into question both the reliability of Klein's work and the conclusions proposed:

- Knee ligament injuries were the same in loose and tight knee joints using objective measures of the knee (Kalenak and Morehouse, 1975).
- A 10 week programme of deep squats did not affect the stability of the knee (Karpovich et al, 1970).
- Meyers, using Klein's assessment equipment, did not find any differences between collateral ligament stability, quadriceps strength or knee flexibility with subjects that performed half or full squats (Meyers, 1971).
- An eight week full squat programme did not result in increased instability (Chandler et al, 1989).
- Knee stress (assessed by peak knee extensor moment, patellofemoral joint reaction force and patellofemoral joint stress) did not vary significantly between three squatting trials – 70 degrees (above parallel), 90 degrees (at parallel) and 110 degrees (below parallel) of knee flexion (Salem and Powers, 2001).

This leads us to question several of the conclusions or recommendations previously highlighted.

Keep the shins vertical and the knees behind the toes
During a squat the load or stress should be equally distributed throughout the joints that perform this movement pattern. If one joint has less stress placed upon it, then the other joints will have to undergo

more stress to compensate. For example, if the knees are deliberately kept back and knee flexion is restricted then the body will flex more from the hips and the upper torso will lean further forward to maintain balance over the base of support. This may cause less stress to be placed upon the knee, but will cause more load and stress on the spine and the structures and tissue that support it.

Keeping the shins perpendicular has been shown to increase the stress on the lower back near ten-fold (Fry et al, 2003). This can be seen in figure 2.2, where the athlete must lean further

Figure 2.2 Example of a restricted knee squat

forward to maintain their balance over their feet. The athlete will either lean forward with a flat back or rounded spine, but this position will increase the load on the spine, as the position technically becomes more of a good morning exercise (see page 98).

To optimally distribute the load between the knees, hips and spine, the torso and the shins should be roughly parallel with each other throughout the movement. Avoid deliberately keeping the knees back and the question of whether the knees should move beyond the toes or not will depend on the individual's biomechanics, such as the length of their tibia and the size of their feet.

Only squat down to 90 degrees

There is no reason why an athlete cannot squat down through a full range of motion in the squat. Apart from the exceptions of plyometrics, limited mobility, (which compromises optimal technique), or some pre-existing conditions, there is no valid reason why the squat differs from any other exercise where fitness professionals advise to 'always work through a full range of motion'. Today, a number of authors actively advise that full squats should be trained over half squats because of the increased activation of the vastus medialis obliquus (VMO) at full flexion (Kinakin, 2004). The VMO is a major knee stabiliser and full squats may therefore improve the medial to lateral quad strength balance, potentially helping to prevent lateral tracking (the patella being pulled outward during a normal knee bend or straightening) and improving knee stability.

There is inherently no reason why an individual cannot undertake full depth squats, including loaded, unless that individual experiences pain or has pre-existing conditions that may inhibit them, or that could be worsened with this exercise. If the individual cannot maintain a neutral spine position or a flat back throughout the range without rounding over, then the range of motion should be reduced to allow for optimal technique.

CURRENT RECOMMENDATIONS

In the US, the National Strength and Conditioning Association (NSCA) released a position statement in 1991 with nine points regarding the squat exercise in athletic conditioning:

1. Squats, when performed correctly and with appropriate supervision, are not only safe, but may be a significant deterrent to knee injuries.
2. The squat exercise can be an important component of a training programme to improve the athlete's ability to forcefully extend the knees and hips, and can considerably enhance performance in many sports.
3. Excessive training, overuse injuries and fatigue-related problems do occur with squats. The likelihood of such injuries and problems is substantially diminished by adherence to established principles of exercise programme design.
4. The squat exercise is not detrimental to knee joint stability when performed correctly.
5. Weight training, including the squat exercise, strengthens connective tissue, including muscles, bones, ligaments and tendons.
6. Proper form depends on the style of the squat and the muscles to be conditioned. Bouncing in the bottom position of a squat to help initiate ascent increases mechanical loads on the knee joint and is therefore contraindicated (not advised).

7. While squatting results in high forces on the back, injury potential is low with appropriate technique and supervision.
8. Conflicting reports exist as to the type, frequency and severity of weight training injuries. Some reports of high injury rate may be based on biased samples. Others have attributed injuries to weight training, including the squat, which could have been caused by other factors.
9. Injuries attributed to the squat may result not from the exercise itself, but from improper technique, pre-existing structural abnormalities, other physical activities, fatigue or excessive training.

LIMITING FACTORS FOR THE SQUAT PATTERN

Limiting factors are potential causes for decreased functional strength, range or capacity when performing the different movement patterns. Identifying and correcting these issues or dysfunctions will improve an individual's ability to perform that movement pattern, such as the squat, lift, press, etc. The following list highlights the five common limiting factors for the squat movement pattern:

1. Immobile foot or ankle
2. Immobile hip
3. Weak lower back
4. Weak knee stabilisers
5. Mobility issues at the wrist or shoulder

1. IMMOBILE FOOT OR ANKLE

For the knee to move forward, to keep the torso and shin approximately parallel, the foot and

ankle must be mobile. If there is any restriction at the ankle joint, such as tight plantarflexors (gastrocnemius and soleus, for example) or adhesions on the Achilles tendon, this will limit ankle dorsiflexion, and subsequently the squat technique and depth.

In order for the ankle to dorsiflex optimally there must also be sufficient mobility at the foot.

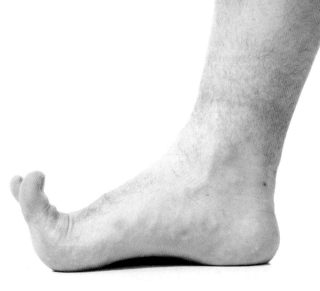

Figure 2.4 Big toe dorsiflexion

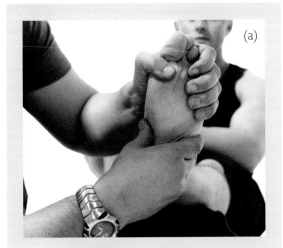
(a)

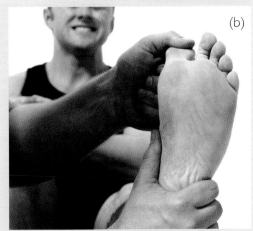
(b)

Figure 2.3 Foot mobilising techniques (a) medial arch plantarfascia, (b) hallux mobilisation

Mobility release work on the foot and plantarfascia can be very helpful in improving this mobility (see figure 2.3). Gary Gray has developed a number of techniques, which are useful in the pursuit of this.

In addition, an immobile big toe may be indicative of restrictions in the lower limb. It is common to see those individuals that cannot dorsiflex their big toe to approximately 60 degrees finding that they have limited dorsiflexion at the ankle as well.

2. IMMOBILE HIP

Tightness around the hip is a common reason for many individuals being unable to squat to a full depth with good technique. Figure 2.5 demonstrates how to assess hip rotation mobility with an individual.

Have the individual adopt a supine position with their legs together. Lift the near leg up, with the knee bent so that the femur is vertical above the hip (a). Place your foot on the far side of their other leg to ensure the hips do not move

(a)

(b)

Figure 2.5 Assessing hip rotation mobility

To correct this lack of mobility, perform self-myofascial release (SMFR) and developmental stretches on the rotators of the hip, including the piriformis.

3. WEAK LOWER BACK

For many individuals that are trying to develop their squatting strength, a weak lower back can cause a plateauing effect, despite an otherwise effective programme. The body will limit the weight lifted in certain movement patterns if the fixators (muscles that hold another bone or joint in place) cannot tolerate these loads. The lower back muscles for example are used in a squat to maintain an upright torso position, and a weak lower back will cause the torso to flex under load. Improving lifting strength with deadlifts, good mornings and kettlebell swings can help to address this agonist-synergist strength imbalance.

4. WEAK KNEE STABILISERS

The VMO is one of the major knee stabilisers. When the knees buckle in during a squat, step-up, jump, hop or landing, this is indicative of a lack of strength at the VMO to be able to control and correct the pronation effect. This pronation effect should 'switch on' the VMO to maintain the position of the knees over the second or third toe. Having the knee cave in means that the VMO is either not activating or is too weak to control the forces.

Training the VMO with Peterson step-ups or sled drags and ensuring deep (full flexion) squats are performed will help to improve its strength. The VMO muscle is mainly made up of fast-twitch fibres so multiple sets (5–10) of lower rep ranges (6–8) are best for VMO hypertrophy. Pausing in the bottom position of the squats will

as you rotate the leg. Rotate the leg so that the shin moves towards the midline and further (b). The optimal range of motion should allow the lower leg to be in a horizontal position across the hips. Less than 90 degrees of motion would be indicative of mobility restrictions. Also assess for any bilateral differences or variations in mobility between one side and the other.

increase the time under tension and decrease the elastic component, thus helping to ensure greater muscle activation and strengthening.

Figure 2.6 Example of pronation pattern squat

5. MOBILITY ISSUES AT THE WRIST OR SHOULDER

Many individuals will struggle with the barbell front or back squat because they are simply unable to get the bar into the correct position comfortably. When performing the back squat, there must be sufficient mobility in the medial rotators of the shoulder to move the hand back to hold the bar, while keeping the forearms vertical. Tight medial rotators will cause the elbow to flare back, making it difficult to generate force through the arms and limiting the load squatted. This will be the same for the overhead squat, where tight medial rotators will cause the bar to be forward of the feet, making it very difficult, if not impossible, to perform correctly.

When performing the front squat there must be adequate mobility at the shoulders and wrist to hold the bar on the anterior deltoids and across the clavicles in the barbell rack position. If you cannot get your upper arms near horizontal when holding the barbell, then it is likely you have restrictions at the shoulder and/or wrist. Adhesions in the muscles that affect these joints are commonly to blame for the described lack of mobility.

OVERHEAD SQUAT TEST

The overhead squat is commonly used as a test of upper and lower body mobility, and is a good test to perform prior to loading an individual in the squat pattern with significant weight. The weight does not have to be a 20kg Olympic bar, but could be a fit bar or even an adjustable studio barbell. The additional challenge of holding a bar above the head and keeping the bar over the feet requires optimal mobility in the hips and shoulders and helps to show if the upper torso is leaning too far forward. The hands should be positioned shoulder width apart on the bar or slightly further. Squat down as low as possible to evaluate how the body undertakes this task.

- If the heels lift up, this indicates restrictions in the foot or ankle and limited dorsiflexion.
- Knees caving in indicates poor knee or hip stability.
- Being unable to achieve a full range of motion (full squat) indicates limitations in the foot, ankle or hips.
- The bar coming forward of the toes indicates either limited thoracic mobility, tight shoulders (particularly the muscles that medially rotate the shoulder) or restrictions in the foot, ankle or hip causing issues further up the kinetic chain.

Common advice is that individuals should be able to successfully complete this test or exercise before undertaking certain drills, such as overhead pressing. If the thoracic mobility is limited, then that individual will struggle to get the arms straight up above the head without having to compensate somewhere else, such as anteriorly tilting the pelvis forward and overarching the lumbar spine (lower back).

Other common dysfunctions that will be seen during a squat include the following:

- If the individual cannot go below 90 degrees, then that is usually indicative of a tight piriformis. This can also be seen by the feet rotating out (one or both feet).
- If the individual leans forward with perpendicular shins, then that usually indicates tight hip flexors or limited foot/ankle mobility.

Figure 2.7 Performing the overhead squat test

- If the individual's back rounds over, this is either indicative of weak erector spinae or a limited ankle mobility, where they lean forward to maintain their balance.
- Adhesions between the medial hamstring and adductor magnus will cause a sideways twitch at about 90 degrees of extension (on the concentric phase). This is due to the adductor becoming 'stuck' on the way up.
- If the individual's elbows rotate back during a back squat, then this is due to a tight subscapularis.

SQUAT PATTERN EXERCISES

Exercise 2.1 Back squat – parallel stance

(a)

(b)

Equipment
Barbell (variations: chains, Powerbag™, sandbags)

Aim
To work the squat pattern muscles, specifically the quads, hamstrings, glutes and calves, in a stable position to handle heavy loads.

Set-up
- Stand in front of a squat rack with the barbell set up on it.
- Duck underneath the bar and place the thickest area of the upper back muscle (the trapezius) in contact with the bar.
- Hands should be as close as possible to the outside of the shoulders. Elbows should be pushed forward so that they are aligned right under the bar.
- Stand with feet hip to shoulder width apart with the feet pointing forwards or rotated out to a maximum of 30 degrees.
- Stand upright by straightening the legs and take one step back per foot to clear the racks.
- Take a breath in and brace the core.

Execution
- Push the knees forward and bend forward from the waist to lower the hips towards the heels.
- Squat down as low as possible, keeping the chest up, the spine neutral or flat and the feet flat on the ground.
- Keep the lower body under control until the hamstrings come into contact with the calves.
- Push the hips forward to straighten the knees

and hips and drive through the feet to press the body back up to the start position.

- The knees should be travelling forward and over your toes throughout the descent.
- Focus on slowly descending and accelerating through the ascent.

Technical considerations

- The feet can be rotated up to approximately 30 degrees, but anything more than that will usually be indicative of tight hip rotators, either on one or both feet, depending on what is seen.
- There should be a conscious effort to keep the elbows under the bar throughout the movement.
- The trunk should be as erect as possible throughout the movement.
- Ensure the knees track over the second or third toe.
- Do not bounce in the bottom position.
- Tight quadriceps, psoas or tight Achilles tendons can cause a compensatory forward bending or rounding of the spine.
- Do not fatigue the lower back and abdominals before doing squats.
- Do not squat to a bench or box.
- Variations include using chains (see figures) or back squat with Powerbag™/sandbags.

Exercise 2.2 Squat – sumo stance

(a)

(b)

Equipment
Kettlebells (variations: barbell, Powerbag™, sandbag)

Aim
To work the squat pattern muscles in a sumo or wide stance which will recruit the adductors and the quadriceps and will require a more upright torso than the standard squat.

Set-up
- Lift two kettlebells up from the floor and hold in a double kettlebell rack position.
- Adopt a wide stance with the feet pointing out at approximately 45 degrees.
- Take a breath in and brace the core.

Execution
- Push the knees outwards over the toes and lower the hips towards the floor.
- Squat down as low as possible, keeping the chest up, the spine neutral or flat and the feet flat on the ground.
- Straighten the knees and hips and drive through the feet to press the body back up to the start position.
- Focus on slowly descending and accelerating through the ascent.

Technical considerations
- The sumo stance squat is good for those with limited ankle dorsiflexion.
- The trunk should be as erect as possible throughout the movement.
- Ensure the knees track over the second or third toe.
- Do not bounce in the bottom position.
- Variations include barbell sumo back squat, barbell sumo front squat, single kettlebell sumo squat, and sumo back squat with Powerbag™/sandbag.

Exercise 2.3 Front squat

(a)

(b)

Equipment
Barbell with chains (variation: heavy bands)

Aim
To work the squat pattern muscles with the load on the front of the body, to target the quadriceps, more than the back squat position.

Set-up
- The chains are attached to the barbell, usually outside of any plates being used.
- The barbell can be cleaned up to the rack position or taken from a squat rack.

Set-up from clean
- Approach the barbell as if performing a deadlift.
- Adopt a slightly wider than shoulder width grip on the bar, with a hook grip (a pronated grip with the thumb positioned underneath the index and middle fingers).
- Shoulders positioned over or in front of the bar, chest up and core braced.
- Perform a clean and catch the bar on the anterior deltoids in the barbell rack position.

Set-up from rack
- Approach the barbell, which should be set in the squat rack at about chest height.
- Dip under the bar so that is rests across the anterior deltoids in the barbell rack position. Holding the bar with the hands outside the shoulders, squat up to lift the bar from the rack and step back.
- The wrists are extended, with the hand open and the barbell held on the fingers.
- The hands should be wider than the shoulders and the elbows lifted high, so that the arm is horizontal.
- The feet should be flat, between hip and shoulder width apart.

Execution

- Take a breath in and brace the core.
- Flex at the knees maximally, keeping the heels down and the torso upright.
- Squat down so that the thighs go below parallel and ideally so that the distal hamstrings touch the proximal calves.
- Push the elbows up during the descent to ensure correct torso and arm position, and to prevent the bar from 'pulling' the body down and forward.
- Pause briefly at the bottom, then push the floor away by extending the legs, particularly through the heels, keeping the hips forward and the torso upright.

Technical considerations

- The front squat requires a near vertical position of the torso, unlike the back squat, which can afford more of a forward lean without compromising technique.
- The chains provide a method of progressively increasing the load during the ascent so that there is more load in the upright position than in the bottom position.
- The trunk should be as erect as possible throughout the movement
- Ensure the knees track over the second or third toe.
- Do not bounce in the bottom position.
- Variations include barbell front sumo squat with chains, barbell back squat with chains, and barbell front squat with heavy bands.

Exercise 2.4 Split stance squat – front foot raised on step

(a)

(b)

Equipment
Dumbbells, step

Aim
To work the squat pattern muscles in a split stance, with the front foot elevated to help mobilise the

ankle plantarflexors and to help activate the VMO at the knee.

Set-up

- Adopt an exaggerated stance, with the lead foot on the step and the rear foot up on the toes.
- Although apart, the feet should still be between hip and shoulder width apart.
- The front foot should be flat on the step.
- Take hold of two dumbbells, one in each hand.

Execution

- Inhale and brace the core.
- Sit down and forward onto the lead leg.
- Keep the lead foot flat on the step and drive the knee forward in line with the second or third toe (or the shoelaces).
- Flex the knee maximally until the distal hamstrings touches the proximal calf.
- Pause briefly at the bottom, then push back up to the starting point, pressing through the heel until the leg is extended.
- Focus on the contraction of the VMO and gluteal muscles of the lead leg throughout the exercise.
- Keep the hips facing forward throughout to effectively mobilise the rear hip flexors.

Technical considerations

- This is a fantastic drill to mobilise the foot and ankle in the sagittal plane to help promote a greater range of motion for those with limited dorsiflexion.
- If the rear foot is too close to the step (short stance) then many will find it difficult to achieve maximum knee flexion because of mobility restrictions in the foot and ankle. Many adopt too short a stance because of mobility restrictions in the rear hip flexor.
- If the rear foot is too far away from the step (long stance) then it will also make it difficult to achieve maximal knee flexion. This is because the foot is in front of the knee, which cannot move forward.
- If the rear leg externally rotates (seen as the knee or foot rotated out rather than pointing straight down), this again would indicate mobility issues with the rear hip flexor. The body moves the femur into hip abduction rather than taking it behind into extension.
- Variations include barbell split squat and cable split squat with contralateral grip.

Exercise 2.5 Overhead Bulgarian split stance squat

(a)

(b)

Equipment
Barbell (variation: dumbbells)

Aim
To work the squat pattern muscles in a split stance, with the rear foot elevated to help mobilise the hip flexors.

Set-up
- Adopt an exaggerated stance, with the rear foot on the step and the front foot flat on the floor.
- Although apart, the feet should still be between hip and shoulder width apart.
- The rear foot should be on the toes on top of the step.
- Hold the barbell overhead, with the arms locked.

Execution
- Inhale and brace the core.
- Squat down and forward onto the lead leg.
- Keep the lead foot flat on the floor and drive the knee forward in line with the second or third toe (or the shoelaces).
- Flex the knee maximally, although it will be difficult to reach a full range of motion.
- Pause briefly at the bottom, then push back up to the starting point, pressing through the heel until the leg is extended.
- Focus on the contraction of the VMO and gluteal muscles of the lead leg throughout.
- Keep the hips facing forward throughout to also effectively mobilise the rear hip flexors.

Technical considerations
- Having the bar held overhead will help to mobilise the anterior chain of muscles, of which the hip flexor is a part.
- It will also fatigue the shoulders and upper back, so the reps should be kept on the low side.
- If the rear leg externally rotates (the knee or foot rotated out) this would indicate mobility issues with the rear hip flexor. The body moves the femur into hip abduction rather than taking it behind into extension.
- Variations include barbell back Bulgarian split squat and dumbbell Bulgarian split squat.

Exercise 2.6 Front squat kettlebell one hand

(a)   (b)

Equipment
Kettlebell

Aim
To work the squat pattern muscles with the load on the front of the body, to target the quadriceps, more than the back squat position. Holding the kettlebell on one side of the body will stimulate the lateral core and hip stabilisers.

Set-up
- Lift up one kettlebell and hold in one hand in the kettlebell rack position.
- The chest should be high with the spine in a neutral position.
- The feet should be flat, between hip and shoulder width apart.

Execution
- Brace the core to stabilise and protect the back.
- Push the knees forward and drop into a deep squat using the hip flexors to 'pull' you into position.
- Keep the torso as vertical as possible.
- Squat down until the distal hamstrings touch the proximal calves, or until technique falters.
- Ensure the knees and toes are in alignment (patella tracking over the second or third toe) throughout the descent.
- Hold the position for 1–3 seconds without losing tension or relaxing.
- From the deep squat position push the hips forward and drive out of the position, releasing the air from the lungs during the ascent.
- Extend the knees and hips to return to the standing start position and repeat.

Technical considerations
- The front squat requires a near vertical position of the torso, unlike the back squat, which can afford more of a forward lean without compromising technique.
- Use the hip flexors to 'pull' you into position.
- Push the hips forward to start the concentric phase.
- Keep the feet flat and knees aligned over toes throughout both the descent and ascent.
- Do not bounce in the bottom position.
- Variations include double kettlebell front squat, and kettlebell one hand overhead squat.

Exercise 2.7 Vintage front squat

(a)

(b)

Equipment
Barbell (variation: dumbbells)

Aim
To work the squat pattern muscles in a vintage style with a narrow stance, specifically the quads, hamstrings, glutes and calves, without restriction from the lower limbs.

Set-up
- Attach an appropriate load to a bar or select a suitably heavy barbell.
- Place the bar on the upper back and unrack the bar if required.
- Adopt a stance with the heels together and the feet rotated out.

Execution
- Take a breath in and brace the core. Lift the heels off the ground and flex maximally at the knees.
- Keep the torso vertical and bend down until the hamstrings touch the calves.
- Briefly hold in the bottom position then stand back up to the start position.
- You can either press the heels down on the ascent, or maintain the heels' raised position throughout.
- Allow the knees to track over the second or third toe (knees will move out at the same angle as the feet).

Technical considerations
- Push up with the arms to help with the ascent and to ensure an efficient transfer of force from the lower body, through the core to the bar.
- This technique will allow for a good activation of the VMO, without limitations of a restrictive foot or ankle joint or tight plantarflexion.
- Variations include vintage barbell front squat (in rack), vintage overhead squat or vintage dumbbell squat (held in both hands in a vertical position).

Exercise 2.8 Pistol squat with suspension system

(a)

(b)

Equipment
Suspension strap system, bodyweight (variations: dumbbell, kettlebell)

Aim
To work the squat pattern muscles in a single leg stance, specifically the quads, hamstrings, glutes and calves.

Set-up
- Connect the two-strap suspension system to the anchor points, ideally at least 6ft high and about shoulder width apart.
- Stand facing the anchor points and hold one handle in each hand or with just one hand (as shown)
- Brace the core and lean back so that the arm is extended and the body is straight and rigid.
- Move the feet forward or backwards to achieve the optimal level of intensity.
- Lift one leg up and forward and hold that position.

Execution
- Squat downwards keeping the foot flat, with the knee in line with the second-third toes.
- Squat down until the distal portion of the hamstring touches the proximal part of the calf.
- Allow the knee to move forward and do not attempt to keep shin vertical.
- Pause briefly at the bottom then push back up to the start position.
- Keep the 'free' leg extended in front and off the ground throughout the exercise.
- Try to maintain as upright a torso position as possible.

Technical considerations
- Pull with the arm to decrease the load on the lower body as required.
- Having the foot closer to the anchor point will allow a greater lean backwards and therefore less dorsiflexion at the ankle.
- Variations include single leg squat with posterior reach, or pistol squat holding dumbbell or kettlebell by side or in rack.

Exercise 2.9 Pistol squat with kettlebell

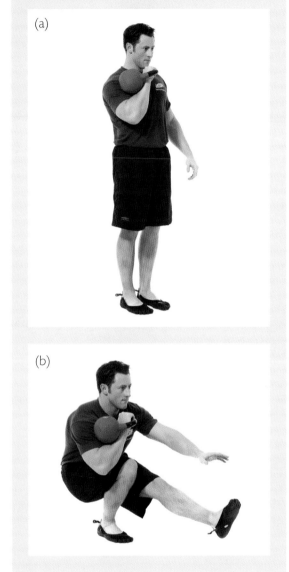

(a)

(b)

Equipment
Kettlebell (variations: bodyweight, plyometric platform)

Aim
To work the squat pattern muscles in a single leg stance, specifically the quads, hamstrings, glutes and calves.

Set-up
• Start by cleaning a single kettlebell to the rack position.
• Stand on one leg with the other leg forwards off the ground.
• The front leg will help you to counterbalance, and can be placed just a few inches above the floor.
• The second arm can be placed on the hip or out at the side to be used for balance.

Execution
• Squat downwards keeping the foot flat, with the knee in line with the second-third toes.
• Squat down until the distal portion of the hamstring touches the proximal part of the calf.
• Keep the heel firmly fixed on the floor, maintaining the position of the front leg straight in front of you, and keeping the chest and back upright throughout.
• Ensure that the hips move backwards as the knee simultaneously moves forwards over the toe of the standing leg.
• Pause briefly at the bottom then press the heel down into the floor and contract the glute and thigh of the working leg to drive back up to the start position.
• Keep the 'free' leg extended in front and off the ground throughout the exercise.
• Try to maintain as upright a torso position as possible.

Technical considerations

- A pistol squat is a challenging asymmetrical exercise that overloads the muscles of the legs. As with other types of squat, the ideal ROM is to full depth – with the hamstring touching the calf – but for beginners a smaller ROM can be used initially as balance and leg strength will increase with practice.
- Variations include bodyweight pistol squat or perform on a plyometric platform.

Exercise 2.10 Overhead squat, two hands, parallel stance

(a)　　　　　(b)

Equipment

Barbell (variations: dumbbell, kettlebell, Powerbag™, sandbag)

Aim

To work the squat pattern muscles, while stabilising a load overhead in two hands. This will also mobilise the upper body, and promote shoulder and scapula stability.

Set-up

- Take hold of the barbell in a wide grip and lift above the head.
- Arms should be fully extended with the bar above the head.

- Stand with feet hip to shoulder width apart with the feet pointing forwards or rotated out to a maximum of 30 degrees.
- Take a breath in and brace the core.

Execution

- Push the knees forward and bend forward from the waist to lower the hips towards the heels.
- Squat down as low as possible, keeping the chest up, the spine neutral or flat and the feet flat on the ground.
- Lower body under control until the hamstrings come into contact with the calves.
- Push the hips forward to straighten the knees and hips and drive through the feet to press the body back up to the start position.
- The knees should be travelling forward and over your toes throughout the descent.
- Focus on slowly descending and accelerating through the ascent.
- Push upwards with the arms throughout the exercise.

Technical considerations

- Keep the repetitions low – between 1 and 3.
- Keep the bar positioned over the feet throughout the movement.
- Trunk should be as erect as possible throughout the movement.
- Ensure the knees track over the second or third toe.
- Variations include single arm overhead squat with dumbbell/kettlebell/barbell/Powerbag™/sandbag.

Exercise 2.11 One hand overhead squat

(a)

(b)

Equipment
Barbell (variations: dumbbell, kettlebell, sandbag)

Aim
To work the squat pattern muscles, while stabilising a load overhead in one hand. This will also mobilise the upper body and promote shoulder and scapula stability.

Set-up
*   Take hold of the barbell with one hand in centre of bar and lift above the head.
*   Arm should be fully extended with the bar above the head.
*   Stand with feet hip to shoulder width apart with the feet pointing forwards or rotated out to a maximum of 30 degrees.
*   Take a breath in and brace the core.

Execution
*   Push the knees forward and bend forward from the waist to lower the hips towards the heels.
*   Squat down as low as possible, keeping the chest up, the spine neutral or flat and the feet flat on the ground.
*   Lower body under control until the hamstrings come into contact with the calves.
*   Push the hips forward to straighten the knees and hips and drive through the feet to press the body back up to the start position.
*   The knees should be travelling forward and over your toes throughout the descent.
*   Focus on slowly descending and accelerating through the ascent.
*   Push upwards with the arm throughout the exercise.

Technical considerations
*   Watch the barbell throughout.
*   Keep the repetitions low – between 1 and 3.
*   Keep the bar positioned over the feet throughout the movement.
*   Trunk should be as erect as possible throughout the movement.
*   Ensure the knees track over the second or third toe.
*   Variations include single arm overhead squat with dumbbell/kettlebell/sandbag, two hands anyhow with barbell and kettlebell.

Exercise 2.12 Zercher front squat

(a) (b)

Equipment

Sandbag (variations: barbell, Powerbag™)

Aim

To work the squat pattern muscles with the load on the front of the body, to target the quadriceps, more than the back squat position.

Set-up

- Lift up the sandbag and hold in the crutch of the elbows, with arms bent and crossed.
- The chest should be high with the spine in a neutral position.
- The feet should be flat, between hip and shoulder width apart.

Execution

- Brace the core to stabilise and protect the back.
- Push the knees forward and drop into a deep squat using the hip flexors to 'pull' you into position.
- Keep the torso as vertical as possible.
- Squat down until the distal hamstrings touch the proximal calves, or until technique falters.
- Ensure the knees and toes are in alignment (patella tracking over the second or third toe) throughout the descent.
- Hold the position briefly without losing tension or relaxing.
- From the deep squat position push the hips forward and drive out of the position.
- Extend the knees and hips to return to the standing start position and repeat.

Technical considerations

- The front squat requires a near vertical position of the torso, unlike the back squat, which can afford more of a forward lean without compromising technique.
- Use the hip flexors to 'pull' you into position.
- Push the hips forward to start the concentric phase.
- Keep the feet flat and knees aligned over toes throughout both the descent and ascent.
- Do not bounce in the bottom position.
- Variations include Powerbag™ zercher squat and barbell zercher squat.

Exercise 2.13 Forward lunge

(a)   (b)

Equipment
Dumbbells (variation: barbell)

Aim
To work the squat pattern muscles in a dynamic lunge, to target the quadriceps, hamstrings, glutes and hip stabilisers.

Set-up
* Lift up the dumbbells and hold by the sides of the body.
* The chest should be high with the spine in a neutral position.
* Stand with the feet about hip width apart.

Execution
* Brace the core to stabilise and protect the back.
* Take an exaggerated step forward, allowing the rear heel to lift off the ground.
* Keep the torso as vertical as possible.

* Move forwards until the distal hamstrings touch the proximal calves, or until technique falters.
* Ensure the front knee and toes are in alignment (patella tracking over the second or third toe) throughout the descent.
* Without holding the position, push down with the front foot and drive out of the position.
* Extend the knee and hips to return to the standing start position and repeat on both sides.

Technical considerations
* Focus on keeping the front foot always pointing forwards and the hips level.
* Do not step across with the front foot – maintain a hip-width distance apart.
* Maintain a fluid and controlled movement as much as possible.
* Variations include barbell back squat forward lunge and barbell overhead forward lunge.

Exercise 2.14 Reverse crossover lunge, two kettlebells racked

(a)   (b)

Equipment

Kettlebells (variation: one kettlebell)

Aim

To work the squat pattern muscles in a dynamic lunge pattern in the frontal plane; to target the hip abductors, quadriceps, glutes and hip stabilisers.

Set-up

- Lift up the kettlebells and hold in a double rack position.
- The chest should be high with the spine in a neutral position.
- Stand with the feet about hip width apart.

Execution

- Brace the core to stabilise and protect the back.
- Take a step back and across with the left leg.
- Keep the hips facing forwards.
- Squat down as low as possible on the right leg.
- Ensure the front knee and toes are in alignment (patella tracking over the second or third toe) throughout the descent.
- Without holding the position, push off with the left leg and extend the right leg.
- Extend the knee and hips to return to the standing start position and repeat on both sides.

Technical considerations

- The hips should tilt to load the hip abductors, but should always face forwards.
- Maintain as fluid and controlled a movement as possible.
- Variations include one kettlebell in rack and one held by the hips on the contralateral side – the benefit of this is a greater increase in the activation of the abductors on the hips.

Exercise 2.15 Single leg squat and reverse crossover reach with a suspension system

(a)   (b)

Equipment
Two-strap suspension system (variations: single strap, kettlebell, dumbbells)

Aim
To work the squat pattern muscles in a single leg stance, specifically the quads and glutes, and to emphasise the hip abductors.

Set-up
- Connect the two-strap suspension system to the anchor points, ideally at least 6ft high and about shoulder width apart.
- Stand facing the anchor points and hold one handle in each hand, with a semi-supinated grip (palms facing inwards).
- Brace the core and lean back so that the arms are extended and the body is straight and rigid.

- Move the feet forward or backwards to achieve the optimal level of intensity.
- Lift one foot off the ground by bending the knee and hold that position.

Execution
- Reach the non-stance leg behind and across the body, past the stance leg.
- Squat downwards on the stance leg keeping the foot flat, with the knee in line with the second-third toes.
- Keep the torso upright and focus on flexing the knee.
- Pause briefly at the bottom then push back up to the start position, driving the knee up on the non-stance leg.

Technical considerations
- Pull with the arms to decrease the load on the lower body.
- Standing too far from the anchor point will cause an excessive forward lean of the torso and poor squat mechanics in the lower body.
- Variations include single strap for increased instability, or holding a dumbbell or kettlebell by side or in rack.

Exercise 2.16 Lateral lunge

(a)

(b)

Aim
To work the squat pattern muscles in a dynamic lunge pattern in the frontal plane, to target the hip abductors, quadriceps, glutes and hip stabilisers.

Set-up
- Lift up the weight plate and hold in the front of the body with both hands.
- The chest should be high with the spine in a neutral position.
- Stand with the feet about hip width apart.

Execution
- Brace the core to stabilise and protect the back.
- Keeping the hips square to the front, take a big step out to the side allowing the foot to naturally turn out.
- Keep the hips facing forwards.
- Lunge down into the working leg, keeping the other leg straight with both feet flat on the floor.
- Ensure the front knee and toes are in alignment (patella tracking over the second or third toe) throughout the descent.
- Extend the working leg strongly to bring the two feet back together.
- This can be performed by alternating the right and left leg or as a single set all on one side.

Technical considerations
- Maintain as fluid and controlled a movement as possible.
- Variations include lateral lunge with lateral overhead reach (medicine ball), or lateral lunge off step.

Equipment
Weight plate (variations: medicine ball, step)

Exercise 2.17 Lunge and overhead reach

(a)   (b)

Equipment
Two-strap suspension system (variations: single strap, dumbbells, Powerbag™, fit bar)

Aim
To work the squat pattern muscles in a dynamic split stance, specifically the quads, glutes and hamstrings and to stimulate the anterior core muscles (rectus abdominis).

Set-up
- Connect the two-strap suspension system to the anchor points, ideally at least 6ft high and about shoulder width apart.
- Stand facing away from the anchor points and hold one handle in each hand.
- Hold with a pronated grip (palms facing downwards) with arms extended at about chest height.

- Move the feet forward or backwards to achieve the optimal position when dropping into the lunge and overhead reach position.

Execution
- Take a larger than normal step forward, without coming in or out from the hip-width position.
- Lunge downwards on the lead leg keeping the foot flat, with the knee in line with the second/third toes.
- Allow the rear heel to come off the ground and keep the rear knee off the ground.

Figure 2.8 Variation with Powerbag™

73

- During the lunge, reach both hands upwards and backwards, maintaining the tension on the straps throughout.
- Extend the lead leg and push back to the start position, and at the same time press downwards on the straps.

Technical considerations

- Keep hips facing forwards throughout the drill.
- Drop into the end lunge and overhead reach position to start with, to ensure that the optimal position is achieved at the end of the descent and no injury occurs.
- Standing too far from the anchor point will cause an excessive stretch on the anterior core or hip flexor muscles.
- Press down more with the arms and lift the foot rather than lunging back, to achieve a greater activation of the core flexors.
- Variations include single strap with two hands, single strap with one hand and holding a dumbbell or kettlebell by side or in rack. This can also be performed with a Powerbag™ (see figure 2.8) or fit bar.

Exercise 2.18 Lunge and rotate

(a)　　(b)

Equipment

Powerbag™ (variations: kettlebells, medicine ball, weights)

Aims

To work the squat pattern muscles in a dynamic lunge; to target the quadriceps, hamstrings, glutes and hip stabilisers and to load the core in a rotation pattern.

Set-up

- Lift up the Powerbag™ and hold in front of the body with two hands.
- The chest should be high with the spine in a neutral position.
- Stand with the feet about hip width apart.

Execution

- Brace the core to stabilise and protect the back.
- Take an exaggerated step forward, allowing the rear heel to lift off the ground.
- Keep the torso as vertical as possible.
- Squat down until the distal hamstrings touch the proximal calves, or until technique falters.
- As soon as you step forward start to rotate to the same side as the lead leg.
- The lunge and rotation should terminate at the same time.
- Ensure the front knee and toes are in alignment throughout the descent.
- Without holding the position, push down with the front foot and drive out of the position, rotating the body back to facing forwards.
- Return to the standing start position and repeat on both sides.

Technical considerations

- Focus on keeping the front foot always pointing forwards and the hips level.
- Do not step across with the front foot – maintain a hip-width distance apart.
- Maintain as fluid and controlled a movement as possible.
- Variations include with kettlebells in rack position, medicine ball or weights plate.

Exercise 2.19 Squat jump

(a)   (b)

Equipment

Powerbag™ (variations: step)

Aim

To work the squat pattern muscles in an explosive, dynamic manner to develop reactive strength and to challenge the lower body stabilisers.

Set-up

- Lift up the Powerbag™ and hold across the upper back with two hands.
- The chest should be high with the spine in a neutral position.
- Stand with the feet about hip width apart.

Execution

- Brace the core to stabilise and protect the back.
- Push the knees forward and drop into a semi-squat position.

- Keep the torso as vertical as possible.
- Without pausing, immediately drive upwards into the air, so that the feet leave the ground.
- The legs should be fully extended.
- Land softly, flexing at the ankles, knees and hips back into a semi-squat position.
- Ensure the knees and toes are in alignment during the landing/descent.
- Load the lower body again and repeat.

Technical considerations

- The squat jump makes use of the elastic energy generated in the stretch shortening cycle and is used to improve reactive strength.
- Holding the Powerbag™ should be used as a progression from a bodyweight squat jump.
- Variations include Powerbag™ squat jump onto step, squat jump with horizontal movement or squat jump with lateral movement.

Exercise 2.20 Hop over hurdle

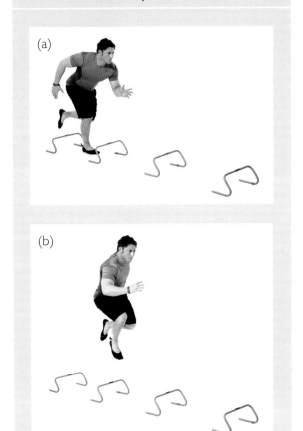

(a)

(b)

Equipment

Hurdles, bodyweight

Aim

To work the squat pattern muscles in a single leg explosive and dynamic manner to develop reactive strength and to challenge the lower body stabilisers.

Set-up

- Stand on one leg facing a series of hurdles.

- The chest should be high with the spine in a neutral position.

Execution
- Brace the core to stabilise and protect the back.
- Push the free leg backwards and drop into a semi-squat position on the stance leg.
- Keep the torso as vertical as possible.
- Without pausing, immediately drive the free leg forwards and upwards.
- Use the force to help drive off the stance leg so that the body leaves the ground.
- Jump over the hurdle and land softly on the same leg, flexing at the ankle, knee and hips back into a semi-squat position.
- Ensure the knees and toes are in alignment during the landing/descent.
- Load the lower body again and repeat.

Technical considerations
- The hop makes use of the elastic energy generated in the stretch shortening cycle and is used to improve reactive strength.
- Hops (or same-side single leg jumps) challenge the stabilisers of the lower body more than two footed jumps.
- Focus on landing in a balanced position.
- Land quietly and softly.
- Use the opposite knee for propulsion.
- Variations include hurdle hops with stabilisation pauses with each landing, lateral frontal hurdle hops or medial frontal hurdle hops.

Exercise 2.21 Jump onto step

(a)

(b)

Equipment
Step, bodyweight

Aim
To work the squat pattern muscles in an explosive and dynamic manner to develop reactive strength and to teach a correct landing position.

Set-up
- Stand with feet hip-width apart facing a step between 4 and 30in high.
- The chest should be high with the spine in a neutral position.

Execution

- Brace the core to stabilise and protect the back.
- Quickly drop into a semi-squat position, and throw the arms back.
- Keep the torso as vertical as possible.
- Without pausing immediately extend the ankles, knees and hips and throw the arms forward. Use the force to project the body forwards and upwards so that it leaves the ground.
- Jump onto the step and land softly on both feet, flexing at the ankles, knees and hips back into a semi-squat position.
- Ensure the knees and toes are in alignment during the landing/descent.
- Step back down onto the floor and repeat.

Technical considerations

- The jump helps to teach a correct landing position, while limiting the eccentric forces.
- Squat depth should be the same on take-off and landing.
- Focus on landing in a balanced position.
- Land quietly and softly.
- Use the arms for propulsion.
- Variations include tuck jump onto step, or jumps onto multiple steps.

Exercise 2.22 Forward step-up

(a)

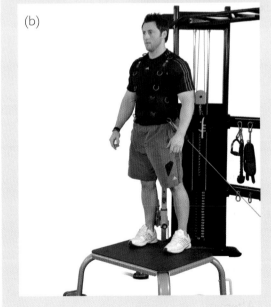

(b)

Equipment

Cable attachment, step (variations: barbell, dumb-bell, kettlebell, sandbag)

Aim

To work the squat pattern muscles in a step-up, targeting the quadriceps and gluteals. Attaching the load from a cable to a waist or vest attachment will keep the arms free, but allows significant load to be applied.

Set-up

- Attach a low cable to a waist or vest attachment on the back.
- Stand facing away from the cable column, with a step in front of you.
- The chest should be high with the spine in a neutral position.
- The feet should be flat, between hip and shoulder width apart.

Execution

- Brace the core to stabilise and protect the back.
- Place one foot flat on the step and shift the weight forwards.
- Keep the torso as vertical as possible.
- Drive upwards onto the step, using the lead leg for propulsion.
- Ensure the knee and toes are in alignment (patella tracking over the second or third toe) throughout the ascent.
- Stand up on the step with the rear leg on the step as well.
- Hold briefly then step back with the rear leg and control the descent with the lead leg.
- Return to the start position and repeat set on the same side.
- Alternate sides with each set.

Technical considerations

- Step-ups are a functional exercise that allows loading of the legs in a dynamic way, while recruiting the core muscles by the same means as daily movement patterns such as walking or climbing stairs.
- The intensity of the exercise can be increased by introducing a much higher step or more load.
- Variations include step up with barbell/dumbbell/kettlebell/sandbag with the load held on the chest/back/one shoulder/by the sides/overhead.

SQUAT PATTERN

Exercise 2.23 Lateral step-up

(a)

(b)

Equipment

Barbell, step (variations: dumbbell, kettlebell, sandbag)

Aim

To work the squat pattern muscles in a step-up, targeting the quadriceps, gluteals, adductors and abductors.

Set-up

- Hold a barbell on your back.
- Stand with a step to the side of you.
- The chest should be high with the spine in a neutral position.
- The feet should be flat, between hip and shoulder width apart.

Execution

- Brace the core to stabilise and protect the back.
- Place the near foot flat on the step and shift the weight sideways.
- Keep the torso as vertical as possible.
- Drive upwards onto the step, using the near leg for propulsion.
- Ensure the knee and toes are in alignment (patella tracking over the second or third toe) throughout the ascent.
- Stand up on the step with the far leg off the step.
- Hold briefly then step back down with the far leg and control the descent with the near leg.
- Return to the start position and repeat set on the same side.
- Alternate sides with each set.

Technical considerations

- Lateral step-ups challenge the body in the frontal plane and will therefore work the hip adductors and abductors and hip stabilisers.
- The intensity of the exercise can be increased by introducing a much higher step or more load.
- Variations include lateral step up with dumbbell/kettlebell/sandbag with the load held on the chest/one shoulder/by the sides/overhead.

Exercise 2.24 Crossover lateral step-up

(a)

(b)

Equipment

Resistance band, step (variations: dumbbell, barbell, kettlebell, sandbag)

Aim

To work the squat pattern muscles in a step-up, targeting the quadriceps, gluteals, adductors and abductors.

Set-up

- Attach a resistance band around the waist, pulling from the side.
- Stand with a step to the side of you.
- The chest should be high with the spine in a neutral position.
- The feet should be flat, between hip and shoulder width apart.

Execution

- Brace the core to stabilise and protect the back.
- Place the far foot flat on the step and shift the weight sideways.
- Keep the torso as vertical as possible.
- Drive upwards onto the step, using the far leg for propulsion.
- Ensure the knee and toes are in alignment (patella tracking over the second or third toe) throughout the ascent.
- Stand up on the step with both feet.
- Hold briefly then step back down with the near leg and control the descent with the far leg.
- Return to the start position and repeat set on the same side.
- Alternate sides with each set.

Technical considerations

- Crossover lateral step-ups challenge the body in the frontal plane, and will therefore work the hip adductors and abductors and hip stabilisers.
- The intensity of the exercise can be increased by introducing a much higher step or more load.
- Variations include crossover lateral step-up with dumbbell/barbell/kettlebell/sandbag with the load held on the chest/one shoulder/by the sides/overhead.

Exercise 2.25 Lateral box drive

(a)

(b)

Equipment
Bodyweight, step

Aim
To work the squat pattern muscles in a step-up, in an explosive and dynamic manner to develop reactive strength and to challenge the lower body stabilisers.

Set-up
* Stand with a step to the side of you.
* The chest should be high with the spine in a neutral position.
* The feet should be flat, between hip and shoulder width apart.

Execution
* Brace the core to stabilise and protect the back.
* Place the near foot flat on the step and shift the weight sideways.
* Keep the torso as vertical as possible.
* Drive explosively upwards onto the step, using the near leg for propulsion.
* The body should leave the step as you drive into the air.
* Land on the nearside leg, and control the descent until the far leg touches the floor.
* Without pausing, drive back up and repeat set on the same side.
* Alternate sides with each set.

Technical considerations
* The intensity of the exercise can be increased by introducing a higher step, by adding load or by extending the duration of the set.
* Variations include box drives facing the step, alternating box drives facing the step.

OTHER SQUAT PATTERN EXERCISES
Back squat – barbell with heels raised on wedge

The squat can be performed with the heels raised on a wedge. This can be used for two reasons – to accommodate limited foot/ankle mobility, or simply for variation. Placing a wedge under the heels will mean that the individual can squat through a greater range of motion to full depth, while keeping a better technique and posture. While this can help to activate the VMO at the knees because of the greater knee flexion achieved, it is a 'get-around' for the limited foot or ankle mobility. The individual should also seek to achieve optimal range of motion in the lower leg so that full squats can be performed on a flat surface. If you do have optimal ROM then the wedge can be used as a variation, just like varying the width of the stance or the position of the load.

Peterson step-up

The Peterson step-up is effectively a shallower style lateral step-up (see page 80), performed with the heel elevated on the step at the start, rather than the flat foot start position. This is used to focus on the VMO at the knee and can be performed either with bodyweight or a barbell/dumbbells. Place the leg closest to a platform (about 4–8in high) so that the back of the heel is in line with the front of the foot of the trailing leg, and lift the heel of the top leg off the step. The working leg on the step should be rotated out to about 30 degrees. Straighten the leg by pressing your heel down and lift the other leg off the ground. Lifting the toes of your non-working leg during push off will place more emphasis on the working leg because there will be no force generated by the non-working leg.

Peterson drag

Face the sled holding onto the handles, or with the straps attached to a waist. Position the right ball of the foot just behind the left heel such that there is a slight bend in the right leg at the knee, and the right leg should be rotated out slightly. Press the heel downward and extend the knee and foot. When the foot is flat with the leg straight, adopt the start position with the left leg and repeat on that side. Do not take large steps, as this will nullify the benefits. Keep the trunk upright throughout the exercise, otherwise other muscles will be recruited or the resistance is too heavy.

Kettlebell front squat push press

This variation combines a front squat (see page 57) and an overhead press (see page 121). The benefit of this drill is the demand placed on the cardiovascular system, as it is a large compound movement, which requires a high energy (and thus calorie) expenditure. Holding the bell in the rack position, as you perform the squat pattern and begin to push into the heels to return to a standing position, simultaneously press the kettlebell overhead (as you would with a standard one hand overhead press). As you begin to bend the legs, simultaneously lower the kettlebell back to the rack position.

LIFT
// PATTERN

3

The lift pattern is probably one of the most, if not the most important movement patterns. Humans use this movement repeatedly on a daily basis; it

Figure 3.1 Deadlift technique with a sandbag

allows us to pick up our children, to help move articles from one place to another, or to throw an object up in the air or behind you.

In relation to an exercise programme, every time a dumbbell, barbell or kettlebell is taken from the rack or floor the lift pattern is performed. The deadlift, the exercise that is the epitome of lifting strength, is one of the three events in competitive powerlifting. It is also an integral exercise in preparation for, and as an assistant exercise to, the Olympic lifts – the snatch, clean and jerk.

The lift pattern is a hip dominant movement that utilises the hip extensor muscles (the hamstrings and the gluteals) and the spinal erectors. The hip extension motion is caused by the integration of two groups of muscles, also referred to as myofascial meridians. The first is the posterior oblique system or Back Functional Line – the gluteus maximus muscle and the opposite latissimus dorsi, linked by the thora-

World record

The world record for a raw deadlift currently stands at 461kg (1017lbs).

Figure 3.2 Deadlift technique with neutral spine

FUNCTIONS AND IMPORTANCE OF THE LIFT PATTERN

The benefits of the deadlift for a power or strength building programme are innumerable. As a compound exercise, it contains movements spanning three joints with concentric extension and stabilisation occurring at the hip, knee and ankle joints. For athletes, multi-joint exercises have greater specificity transfer than single joint exercises (Fleck & Kraemer, 1997) so strength gains will aid performance.

For weight management, calorific expenditure will be greater because compound movements involve a greater number of muscle groups, due to the additional synergistic and stabilising control. For time efficiency you can also load several muscle groups with a single exercise, which can reduce the time it would otherwise take to load each muscle separately with an isolation exercise. It is also the precursor to such fantastic power exercises as the power clean and the snatch, an essential aspect of an athlete's programmed power phase.

ART OF THE FLAT BACK

In the early 1900s, weight training was developing into popular culture. The 'art of the flat back' (or being able to flex and extend at the hips, without flexing or rounding the back) was akin to the concept of the neutral spine in today's fitness industry. Whereas the barbell two hand deadlift and the kettlebell continuous swing are two of the most popular lift pattern exercises today, a hundred years ago it was exercises like the dumbbell dead swing (see figure 3.3).

columbar fascia. The second is the superficial Back Line – the gastrocnemius, the hamstrings and the erector spinae. The superficial back line is the pure group of muscles that produces extension, while the back functional line produces a rotational extension force. When both back functional lines contract, the rotational aspects of each are cancelled out, producing a purer sagittal plane extension movement.

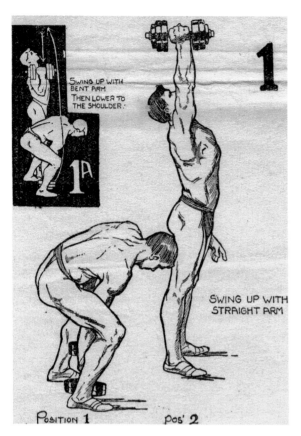

SWING UP WITH
BENT ARM
THEN LOWER TO
THE SHOULDER.

SWING UP WITH
STRAIGHT ARM

POSITION 1   POS' 2

Figure 3.3 The dumbbell dead swing

With the modern concepts of functional training presented in this book, both modern lift pattern exercises and vintage exercises can be combined in the pursuit of optimal performance. In addition, heavy slow tempo deadlifts, high speed power snatches, kettlebell swings and the dumbbell step and reach can all fit together within the functional lift continuum. It is important to know which exercises will promote strength, which are best to develop power, which will develop grip, which will promote bilateral strength balance, which will improve power-endurance and which will be suitable for improving muscle activation.

LIMITING FACTORS FOR THE LIFT PATTERN

The following list highlights the five common limiting factors for the lift movement pattern:

1. Poor hip–back dissociation
2. Sciatic nerve in spasm
3. Weak lower back (strength or endurance)
4. Weak grip
5. Weak glutes or hamstrings

To improve the function of the lift pattern, these limiting factors should be addressed, in addition to improving the strength of the lift and the range of lifting ability. For this movement pattern, this would also include integrating the lift pattern with the rotation and pull patterns.

1. POOR HIP-BACK DISSOCIATION

The key factor in the performance of a lift pattern is whether an individual can differentiate between spinal flexion (rounding the back) and hip flexion (pivoting from the waist). For any fitness professional that has ever tried to teach a client how to perform a deadlift, a squat, or a bent over row, to name but a few, they will appreciate that many individuals will round their backs over when performing these techniques. To optimally perform a lift pattern, the hips flex as the torso leans over, but the lower back is kept in a neutral or flat position. This is achieved by anteriorly tilting the pelvis at the same time as the torso leans forward.

Not tilting the pelvis forward, allowing the sternum to drop and allowing the subsequent rounding of the back to occur may expose the lifter to a greater risk of injury. With the lower back in a flexed, loaded position, the risk of

Figure 3.4 Lifting with flexed spine

it is important to learn, or to teach others, how to pivot from the hips and maintain an optimal back position as well as how to activate the core muscles correctly.

2. SCIATIC NERVE TENSION

The sciatic nerve is a large nerve fibre that originates in the lower back and runs through the glutes and down the lower limb. It supplies the lifting muscles (hamstrings, glutes, calves) with nervous activation and issues with it may cause pain and limit strength when lifting.

The following assessment can be used to assess for adverse nerve tension in the sciatic nerve. Indications to perform the test would be previous hamstring tears, excessive hamstring tension, gluteal or lower back pain, tingling or numbness in the lower leg, or pain shooting down the back of the leg. This test was taught to me by physiotherapist and biomechanics expert Martin Haines and, alongside the subsequent mobilising drill, has been really effective in improving lifting function:

Straight leg raise test

Position the client in a supine position on the floor or a massage couch, with their legs together. Place one hand underneath the lower calf, and the other hand above the knee to ensure a straight leg position throughout (a).

Slowly lift the leg into flexion, until a point where the client feels a sensation (b). This could be a stretch, pain, tingling, numbness or tension. Note the angle (the ideal should be about 70 degrees or more) to assess for any bilateral differences and to monitor improvement (if you can take a photo that is even better). At this point of sensation, move the leg across the midline into an

posterior migration of the intervertebral discs will increase, which may cause a posterior bulging or even a prolapse of the discs, commonly referred to as a slipped disc. This bulging or prolapse can press on the nerves causing pain, functional restriction and even weakening the muscles that straighten the spine (spinal erectors) over a period of time.

Many clients that present with this limiting factor may only realise this poor level of proprioception when shown a video or through watching themselves in the mirror – their body awareness being very poor in relation to maintaining an optimal hip and spine position. To help prevent this,

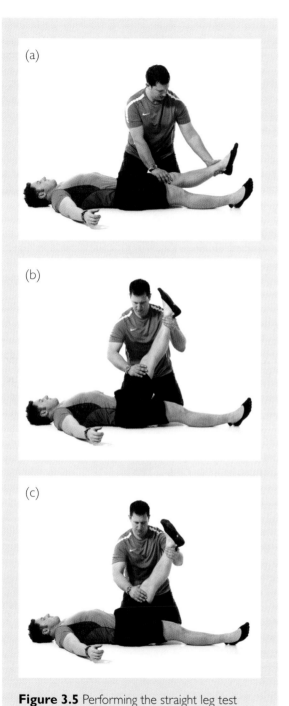

(a)

(b)

(c)

Figure 3.5 Performing the straight leg test

adducted position (c). Any increase in sensation indicates a positive test for adverse nerve tension, and the following mobilising technique would be indicated.

Slump mobilising drill

This drill can be used when a positive straight lat raise test result has been demonstrated to help decrease the symptoms and improve function. Sit on the end of a wall, bench or couch. A chair can be used (see figure 3.6(a)) but it is better if both

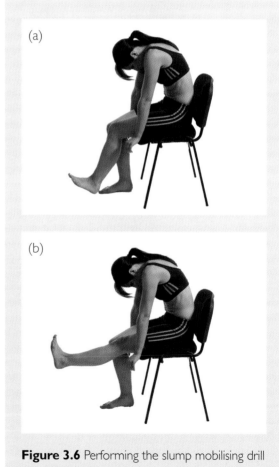

(a)

(b)

Figure 3.6 Performing the slump mobilising drill

legs are hanging down and not touching the floor. Place the chin on the chest and slump the upper body over as far as possible. On the left leg, pull the toes to the shin (dorsiflexion) and then, holding that position at the ankle, perform a leg extension and straighten the leg at the knee. Stop at the point of tension. Then bend the knee slightly, enough to take the tension off, and straighten again. Perform 10–15 repetitions then change legs. Repeat 3–4 times on each leg, 4 times a day (including before and after any exercise session).

For some individuals with an irritated sciatic nerve, this mobilisation technique may aggravate symptoms, in which case cease the drill. However, most coaches that use this technique do find it to be very effective for the majority of clients that present with the issues mentioned above or that have a positive test on the straight leg raise test (sciatic nerve).

3. WEAK LOWER BACK

The lower back must work efficiently with the agonist muscles (hamstrings and glutes) to stabilise the spine, while the hips are flexing and extending. The stabilisation will not only help to protect the structures of the spine, but will also help to efficiently transmit the forces being generated by the agonists through the upper torso to the load being held in the hands. Weak back extensor muscles, both in strength and strength-endurance, can be a limiting factor and an indicator of potential issues in the future. The Biering-Sørensen back extension test is an endurance test for these muscles to hold the upper torso in a neutral position for maximum duration. It is common to see those with current and previous back problems have decreased absolute and relative scores in the extensor test, even when symptoms (of back pain) have resolved (McGill, 2002).

Biering-Sørensen back extension test

The client adopts a prone position, with the upper body cantilevered out over the bench, with the pelvis, hips and knees supported. The arms are held across the chest, the legs are secured and the body is in a straight line.

Figure 3.7 Biering-Sørensen back extension test

The client holds this horizontal, isometric position for maximum duration until the upper body drops from the horizontal. It should also be noted if the position changes (the pelvis drops into an anterior tilt, but the body compensates by overarching the back to keep the shoulders up). The optimal scores for this test (collected from healthy young individuals) are 161 seconds for males and 185 seconds for females (McGill, 2002). Scores less than this would be indicative of poor extensor endurance. In addition the lateral endurance test (side plank) should be at 40–42 per cent (females) or 58–61 per cent (males) of this score for optimal core function.

4. WEAK GRIP

The grip is probably one of the most commonly seen limiting factors for the lift pattern. Many individuals will find that it is their grip, rather then weak legs and hips, which fails when they are deadlifting. They are either unable to lift the bar (grip strength) or to hold on to the bar for the duration of the set (grip endurance). This is usually significantly worse when asked to perform a lift with an increased grip emphasis, such as single hand barbell lifting, wide grip lifting or fat grip lifting. Many individuals will complain that the grip gives out, when they feel they could lift much heavier loads. As the body is only as strong as the weakest link, if the glutes and hamstrings can lift 200kgs, but the grip muscles can only hold on to 150kg, then 150kg will be the maximum you can lift. That is unless you utilise lifting straps, which negates this weakness. However, with prolonged use this strength imbalance between the agonists and the synergist (the grip) will only increase and worsen if excessive use of the straps is advocated.

Using a fat bar or utilising Fat Gripz™ will help to address this strength deficit. Submaximal loads will be used as the weak grip is strengthened, so there will be less overload on the agonists for a period of time, but in the long run optimal agonist-synergist strength balance will be achieved leading to improved applied strength.

5. WEAK GLUTES OR HAMSTRINGS

As with every movement pattern, improving the agonist strength should help to improve the applied strength within this pattern. Physiotherapists will advise that poor gluteal function is a common trait with many of their patients. This may be due to extended periods in a seated position (seen extensively in the modern world), overactive hip flexors or a number of other interrelated factors. Isolation exercises, such as a supine bodyweight bridge, or a prone bent leg kick-up are examples of how the glutes can be activated in an isolated way before applying that activation or strength in a lift pattern exercise.

In addition to this, poor hamstring strength is a common trait with many clients and athletes. In particular there may also be an imbalance between the medial and lateral hamstring muscles. This will also limit overall hamstring strength and its applied strength within a lift pattern. Turning the feet inwards or outwards will allow for greater lateral or medial hamstring activation respectively during traiing exercises.

LIFT PATTERN EXERCISES

Exercise 3.1 Two hand snatch grip deadlift

(a)

(b)

Equipment
Barbell

Aim
A lift pattern exercise to work the posterior chain (hamstrings, glutes and erector spinae), the scapula stabilisers and the grip muscles.

Set-up
- Set up an Olympic barbell with a submaximal load (to your standard deadlift) and ensure that the clips are attached to the bar ends.
- Position the bar over your feet, with your feet in a hip/shoulder width stance, feet pointing forwards.
- Bend down and grip the bar with a pronated grip, with a wide grip (approximately one and a half arm lengths).
- Lift the chest up to achieve an optimal back position and brace the core.

Execution
- Extend the legs and hips and push the feet through the floor.
- Keep upper back tight and try to squeeze the shoulder blades together.
- Stand up in an upright position with the shoulders pulled back and the hips fully extended.
- Pause briefly then slowly lower the bar to the floor by pushing the hips back and bending the knees.
- Reset the core and repeat for the prescribed number of repetitions.

Technical considerations
- You shouldn't be able to actually squeeze the shoulder blades together if the weight is correct, but it helps to prime the correct muscles.
- Focus on keeping the core braced and the spine neutral throughout the exercise.
- Variations include a deadlift with a hook-pronated grip, a deadlift with a split grip (the best for lifting heaviest weights) or a deadlift with a fat grip.

Exercise 3.2 Two hand Romanian deadlift

(a)

(b)

Equipment
Barbell (variation: dumbbells)

Aim
A lift pattern exercise to work the posterior chain (hamstrings, glutes and erector spinae).

Set-up
- Select an appropriate weight for a barbell or load an Olympic bar.
- Ensure that the clips are attached to the bar if using plates.
- Grip the bar with a pronated grip, just wider than shoulder width apart.
- Lift the bar off a rack or lift from the floor and hold with arms extended at about hip height.
- Ensure feet are about hip width apart, no wider.
- Lift the chest up to achieve an optimal back position and brace the core.

Execution
- Push the hips back and lean forward, maintaining an optimal back position and avoid rounding over.
- Lower the bar to approximately mid-shin height or as far as possible with good technique.
- Pause briefly then squeeze the glutes and pull the hips forward to lift the bar back to the start position.
- Pause briefly at the top as well then reset the core and repeat for the prescribed number of repetitions.

Technical considerations
- The loaded Romanian deadlift should be preceded with the bodyweight Romanian deadlift, also known as the hip hinge or waiters bow.
- An individual should be able to 'hinge' at the hips and have what some authors refer to as hip–back disassociation. This means that they

can flex or bend at the hips, while not flexing or bending at the spine and maintaining a normal lumbar curvature (neutral spine) or flat back.

- If the individual rounds the back, then this has the potential to excessively load the structures of the spine and could cause injury.
- The shins should be vertical throughout the movement. This is the difference between the Romanian deadlift and the stiff leg deadlift (SLDL), keeping the shins vertical causes a slight (approximately 20–30 degree) knee bend. This causes the stress of the exercise to be felt slightly higher up the hamstrings, more in the belly of the muscle, unlike the SLDL, which is felt more towards the distal end at the knee.
- The name originates from Romanian weightlifters who felt that this variation had a better carryover to the clean and snatch exercises than the SLDL variation.
- Variations include snatch grip RDL, suitcase grip RDL, single leg RDL, RDL with dumbbells, or RDL with calf raise and shrug.

Exercise 3.3 Two hand deadlift uneven load

(a)

(b)

Equipment
Barbell

Aim
A lift pattern exercise to work the posterior chain (hamstrings, glutes and erector spinae), knee extensors and core muscles, which stabilise rotation and lateral flexion.

Set-up
- Attach an unevenly distributed load to an Olympic bar (one plate to one side of a barbell, or a heavier plate on one side and a lighter plate on the other).
- Ensure that the clips are attached to the bar as well.
- Position the bar over the mid-foot and bend down to grip it with a pronated grip, just wider than shoulder width apart.
- Lift the chest up to achieve an optimal back position and brace the core.

Execution
- Extend the legs and hips and push the feet through the floor.
- Keep the bar horizontal throughout the lift and control the urge to lift one side of the bar more than the other.
- Stand up to an upright position with the shoulders pulled back and the hips fully extended.
- Pause briefly then slowly lower the bar to the floor by pushing the hips back and bending the knees.
- Reset the core and repeat for the prescribed number of repetitions.

Technical considerations
- Focus on keeping the core braced and the spine neutral throughout the exercise.
- Maintain a level horizontal position of the bar, using the core and hip stabilisers.
- Variations include uneven load snatch grip deadlift, offset grip deadlift or suitcase deadlift.

Exercise 3.4 Two hand deadlift offset grip

(a)

(b)

Equipment
Barbell

Aim
A lift pattern exercise to work the posterior chain (hamstrings, glutes and erector spinae), knee extensors and core muscles, that stabilise rotation and lateral flexion.

Set-up
- Selectc a barbell with a submaximal load and ensure that the clips are attached to the bar ends if using plates.
- Position yourself at the bar, but off centre or towards one end.
- Bend down and grip the bar with a pronated grip, just wider than shoulder width apart.
- Lift the chest up to achieve an optimal back position and brace the core.

Execution
- Extend the legs and hips and push the feet through the floor.
- Keep the bar horizontal throughout the lift and control the urge to lift one side of the bar more than the other.
- Stand up to an upright position with the shoulders pulled back and the hips fully extended.
- Pause briefly then slowly lower the bar to the floor by pushing the hips back and bending the knees.
- Reset the core and repeat for the prescribed number of repetitions.

Technical considerations
- Focus on keeping the core braced and the spine neutral throughout the exercise.
- Maintain a level horizontal position of the bar, using the core and hip stabilisers.
- Variations include uneven load snatch grip deadlift or suitcase deadlift.

Exercise 3.5 One hand deadlift

(a)

(b)

Equipment
Barbell

Aim
A lift pattern exercise to work the posterior chain (hamstrings, glutes and erector spinae) and the grip muscles.

Set-up
- Set up an Olympic barbell with a submaximal load and ensure that the clips are attached to the bar ends.
- Position the bar over your feet, with your feet in a mid or wide stance, turned out slightly.
- Bend down and grip the bar with a single hand pronated grip in the centre of the bar.
- Lift the chest up to achieve an optimal back position and brace the core.

Execution
- Extend the legs and hips and push the feet through the floor.
- Keep the shoulder levels and the chest up.
- Keep the bar horizontal throughout the lift and control any tilting forces, by gripping the bar hard.
- Stand up to an upright position with the shoulders pulled back and the hips fully extended.
- Pause briefly then slowly lower the bar to the floor by pushing the hips back and bending the knees.
- Change hands and reset the core and repeat for the prescribed number of repetitions.

Technical considerations
- Perform multiple repetitions (or the whole set) to significantly overload the grip.
- Focus on keeping the core braced and the spine neutral throughout the exercise.
- Variations include a one hand sumo deadlift with a fat grip or a straddle stance one hand sumo deadlift (with the bar between the legs).

Exercise 3.6 One hand suitcase grip Romanian deadlift

(a) (b)

Equipment
Barbell (variations: core plate, dumbbell, cable)

Aim
A lift pattern exercise to work the posterior chain (hamstrings, glutes and erector spinae), the grip muscles and the core muscles, which stabilise rotation and lateral flexion.

Set-up
- Select a barbell with a submaximal load and ensure that the clips are attached to the bar ends if using plates.
- Position the bar to one side so that the centre of the bar is about level with the front of the ankle.
- Have your feet in a narrow stance, about hip width apart.
- Bend down and grip the bar with a single hand grip (palm facing the leg) in the centre of the bar.

- Extend the knees slightly so that the shins are vertical, lift the chest up to achieve an optimal back position and brace the core.

Execution
- Extend the hips forward and push the feet through the floor.
- Keep the shoulders level and the chest up, maintaining a normal Romanian deadlift technique, despite the unilateral load.
- Keep the bar horizontal throughout the lift and control any tilting forces by gripping the bar hard.
- Stand up to an upright position with the shoulders pulled back and the hips fully extended.
- Pause briefly then slowly lower the bar down by pushing the hips back and bending the knees slightly, keeping the shins vertical.
- Reset the core and repeat for the prescribed number of repetitions on the same side.

Technical considerations
- Change sides with each set.
- Keep the shins vertical and allow a slight knee bend (you should feel the stress towards the middle of the hamstrings).
- Focus on keeping the core braced and the spine neutral throughout the exercise.
- Variations include performing the exercise with one end of the barbell in a core plate, or using a dumbbell or cable.

Exercise 3.7 Good morning

(a) (b)

Equipment

Barbell (variations: chains, Powerbag™/sandbag)

Aim

This is a lift pattern exercise to work the posterior chain (hamstrings, glutes and erector spinae), specifically overloading the spinal erectors more than some of the other lift variations.

Set-up

- Select an appropriate weight for a barbell or load an Olympic bar on a squat rack.
- Ensure that the clips are attached to the bar if using plates.
- Position the bar across the upper back muscles and posterior deltoid (not the neck).
- Grip the bar with both hands, outside of the shoulders.
- Lift the bar off the rack and step back.
- Ensure feet are about hip width apart.
- Lift the chest up to achieve an optimal back position and brace the core.

Execution

- Push the hips back and lean forward, maintaining an optimal back position and avoid rounding over.
- Lower the torso to horizontal, or as far as possible, with good technique.
- Pause briefly then squeeze the glutes and pull the hips forward to lift the bar back to the start position.
- Pause briefly at the top as well then reset the core and repeat for the prescribed number of repetitions.

Technical considerations

- The good morning will overload the spinal erectors more than a deadlift with the same load because the lever arm is greater.
- Keep the core braced throughout the exercise to develop sufficient intra-abdominal pressure to protect the spine.
- Variations include barbell good morning with chains, barbell seated good morning or Powerbag™/sandbag good morning.

Exercise 3.8 Single leg Romanian deadlift

(a)

(b)

(c)

Equipment
Barbell

Aim
This is a lift pattern exercise that works the posterior chain (hamstrings, glutes and erector spinae) and challenges the hip stabilisers in a single leg stance.

Set-up
- Select an appropriate submaximal weight.
- Grip the bar with a pronated grip, shoulder width or wider if you wish to incur more upper back recruitment.
- Lift the bar off a rack or lift from the floor and hold with the arms extended at about hip height.
- Stand on one leg, with the lifted leg ready to move backwards.
- Lift the chest up to achieve an optimal back position and brace the core.

Execution
- Push the hips back and lean forward maintaining an optimal back position and allowing the free leg to extend behind to aid balance.
- Lower the bar to approximately mid-shin height or as far as possible with good technique.
- Pause briefly then squeeze the glute and pull the hips forward to lift the bar back up to the start position.
- Pause briefly at the top as well then reset the core and repeat for the prescribed number of repetitions all on the same leg.
- Change legs with each set.

Technical considerations
- Keep the shin vertical throughout the movement.
- If using a heavy load, change legs between each repetition.
- Variations include snatch grip single leg RDL, dumbbell single leg RDL or single leg RDL with calf raise and shrug.

Exercise 3.9 Step and reach

(a)   (b)

Equipment
Dumbbells

Aim
This is a lift pattern exercise to work the posterior chain (hamstrings, glutes and erector spinae) and to stimulate the muscle spindles for greater muscular activation in a split stance.

Set-up
- Select an appropriate submaximal pair of dumbbells.
- Hold the dumbbells by the hips at the sides or just in front.
- Stand with feet about hip width apart with some space in front of you.
- Lift the chest up to achieve an optimal back position and brace the core.

Execution
- Take a small step forward (about half a lunge) and shift weight onto the lead leg.
- Keep the rear foot on the floor for balance, but allow heel to rise.
- Reach the dumbbells forwards and downwards as if placing either side of the lead foot.
- Keep the lead shin vertical and do not allow knee to excessively bend or the stimulation on the hamstrings will be negated.
- Maintain a high chest position and do not allow the back to round.
- As the dumbbells reach mid-low shin, do not pause and push straight back to the start position using the hip extensors.
- Pause briefly and repeat for the prescribed number of repetitions.

Technical considerations
- It is critical to keep the lead shin vertical throughout the descent.
- Imagine you are reaching over a small fence to pick something up.
- Complete the whole set on the same leg or alternate legs with each repetition.
- Variations include medial hamstring emphasis (reaching to the inside of the leg), lateral hamstring emphasis (reaching to the outside of the leg) or reaching forward.

Exercise 3.10 Vintage swing

(a)

(b)

(c)

Equipment
Dumbbell

Aim
This is a lift pattern exercise to work the posterior chain (hamstrings, glutes and erector spinae) from a dead start position, and to teach a single arm ballistic lifting technique.

Set-up
- Stand with feet approximately shoulder width apart or slightly more.
- Place the dumbbell between the feet lengthways, with the front bell level with the heels.
- Bend forward by pushing the hips back, keeping the spine neutral, and grip the handle with one hand.

- The hips should go back, to keep the weight on the heels and mid-foot, and position the upper torso near horizontal with the shins vertical.
- Tilt the dumbbell so that the rear bell is lifted off the ground.
- Lift the chest up to achieve an optimal back position and brace the core.

Execution
- Extend the legs and hips forcefully to drive the dumbbell forwards and upwards in an arc.
- Catch the dumbbell above the head with the arm extended and stabilise.
- The hand should be a semi-supinated position.
- Lower the dumbbell to the shoulder, then place back between the feet in the start position.
- Reset the core and repeat for the prescribed number of repetitions.

Technical considerations
- Use the hips to provide the force to drive the dumbbell upwards.
- The dumbbell should drive up in an arc (hence the name swing), rather than a vertical trajectory (which would be a snatch).
- If the arm bends slightly during the swing, that is fine, but do not actively pull up using the upper body.
- Complete the whole set on the same side or alternate with each repetition.
- This is classic vintage strength test, comparable with a modern two hand barbell power snatch. It requires powerful hip extensors, good core stability to transmit the force to the dumbbell, co-ordination and upper body mobility and stability to catch the dumbbell.
- Add a fat grip to the dumbbell to overload the hand and forearm musculature.

Exercise 3.11 Two hand swing

(a)

(b)

Equipment
Kettlebells

Aims
To work the posterior (extensor) chain muscles in a lifting pattern, to teach a ballistic lifting technique, and to stimulate the muscle spindles for greater muscular activation over prolonged periods.

Set-up
* Position the body with feet about shoulder width apart and the kettlebell facing forward on a position in line with the heels.
* Take hold of the handle with both hands and gently grip.
* The chest should be high with the spine in a neutral position or flat.
* The shins should be vertical and there should be a reasonable degree of tension in the hamstrings and glutes.

Execution
* Take a breath in, hold it and brace your core muscles.
* Contract the muscles of the glutes and hamstrings to quickly bring the hips forward to a fully extended (upright) position.
* This movement should drive the kettlebell upwards towards about shoulder chest or shoulder height.
* At this point the body position should look like an upside-down 'L', with the legs and upper torso in a vertical straight line and the arms forming the horizontal line.
* As the kettlebell drops, guide it back towards the groin and between the legs, hinging the hips back.

- Keep the hands close to the groin, but avoid touching the forearms on the insides of the thighs.
- As the hands reach backwards and behind, getting into a similar 'lift position' as at the start, the kettlebell will become weightless again.
- At this second transition point contract the glutes and hamstrings ballistically and repeat.

Technical considerations
- Focus on keeping the glutes taut throughout each and every repetition.
- Keep the back flat or neutral; avoid rounding the back as you reach between the legs and avoid overarching the back when stood upright.
- The weight should be on your heels and mid-foot.
- The hips, core and arms should work as a single unit, transmitting force efficiently through to the bell to lift it.
- Limit knee bend to effectively load and work the posterior chain and posterior sling muscles.
- The top position should look like an upside-down 'L'.
- The kettlebell should always be an extension of the arms, not flicking up or sagging during the swing.
- Try to keep the shins vertical and limit knee bend; flexing or bending the knees will recruit more of the quadriceps or thigh muscles and will diminish the activation of the hamstrings and glutes at the back.
- Variations include one hand kettlebell swing, hand-to-hand kettlebell swings or two single hand kettlebell swings.

Exercise 3.12 One hand swing

(a)   (b)

Equipment
Kettlebells

Aims
To work the posterior (extensor) chain muscles in a lifting pattern, to progress from the two hand swing and to stimulate the muscle spindles for greater muscular activation in a unilateral lifting pattern.

Set-up
- Position the body with feet about shoulder width apart and the kettlebell facing forward on a position in line with the heels.
- Take hold of the handle with one hand and gently grip.
- The chest should be high with the spine in a neutral position or flat.
- The shins should be vertical and there should be a reasonable degree of tension in the hamstrings and glutes.

Execution

- Take a breath in, hold it and brace your core muscles.
- Contract the muscles of the glutes and hamstrings to quickly bring the hips forward to a fully extended (upright) position.
- This movement should drive the kettlebell upwards towards about chest or shoulder height.
- At this point the body position should look like an upside-down 'L', with the legs and upper torso in a vertical straight line and the arms forming the horizontal line.
- As the kettlebell drops, guide it back towards the groin and between the legs, hinging the hips back.
- Keep the hand close to the groin, but avoid touching the forearm on the insides of the thighs.
- As the hand reaches backwards and behind, getting into a similar 'lift position' as at the start, the kettlebell will become weightless again.
- At this second transition point contract the glutes and hamstrings ballistically and repeat.
- Use the other arm to help generate force with the hips, just as you would in a vertical jump.
- As the hand holding the kettlebell reaches between the legs, the other arm should be reaching back as well. As the hips extend this arm comes forward to level with the body.

Technical considerations

- Focus on keeping the glutes taut throughout each and every repetition.
- Keep the back flat or neutral; avoiding rounding the back as you reach between your legs and avoid overarching the back when stood upright.
- The weight should be on your heels and mid-foot.
- Use the hips, core and arms as a single unit, transmitting force efficiently through to the bell to lift it.
- Draw the shoulder back into the socket when lifting the kettlebell.
- The bell should extend out as a continuation of the arm.
- Variations include one hand kettlebell swing with release and catch, hand-to-hand kettlebell swings or two kettlebell swings in one hand.

Exercise 3.13 Two hand lift overhead

(a)

(b)

Equipment
Sandbag

Aim
This is a lift pattern exercise to work the posterior chain (hamstrings, glutes and erector spinae) from a dead start position, with a dynamic, unstable object.

Set-up
- Stand with feet approximately shoulder width apart or slightly more.
- Place the sandbag just in front of the feet.
- Bend forward by pushing the hips back, keeping the spine neutral, and grip the bag with two hands.
- Position the upper torso near horizontal with the shins vertical.
- Lift the chest up to achieve an optimal back position and brace the core.

Execution
- Extend the legs and hips forcefully to drive the sandbag upwards.
- Catch the sandbag above the head with the arms extended and brace to stabilise the bag as it shifts.
- Lower the bag to the shoulders, then place back in front of the feet in the start position.
- Reset the core and repeat for the prescribed number of repetitions.

Technical considerations
- Use the hips to provide the force to drive the sandbag upwards.
- Use a Powerbag™ instead of a sandbag if you prefer the bag to retain its shape. The contents should still shift to provide a challenge for the stabilisers.
- Use a sandball if you wish to perform a single arm variation.
- To gain maximum benefit on power production throw the sandbag upwards and behind in a sandbag backwards throw, rather than decelerating the load as you would in the overhead lift.

Exercise 3.14 Two hand lift to alternating shoulder

(a) (b)

Equipment
Powerbag™

Aim
This is a lift pattern exercise to work the posterior chain (hamstrings, glutes and erector spinae) in a dead start position, with a dynamic, unstable object, and to overload the grip muscles.

Set-up
- Stand with feet approximately shoulder width apart or slightly more.
- Place the Powerbag™ lengthways between the feet.
- Bend forward by pushing the hips back, keeping the spine neutral, and squeeze grip the Powerbag™ on the sides with both hands.

- Position the upper torso near horizontal, with the shins vertical.
- Lift the chest up to achieve an optimal back position and brace the core.

Execution
- Extend the legs and hips forcefully to drive the Powerbag™ upwards and to one side.
- Catch the Powerbag™ on one shoulder and stabilise with the arms.
- Lower the Powerbag™ back to the start position then forcefully lift to the other shoulder.
- Repeat for the prescribed number of repetitions or time period.

Technical considerations
- Use the hips to provide the force to drive the Powerbag™ upwards.
- Do not drop the Powerbag™ on the floor after each lift. Ensure the eccentric phase is performed as well.
- A squat can be added between each repetition, as the Powerbag™ is on the shoulder, for an added metabolic challenge and to link movement patterns.
- Using the squeeze grip will cause an overload on the grip muscles of the hand and forearm. To maximise overload on this area do not allow the Powerbag™ to touch the floor between each repetition, but stop 1in off the ground before lifting again. With heavier loads and to avoid challenging the grip endurance, allow the hands to release the bag when it's placed on the floor.

Exercise 3.15 Two hand diagonal hang clean

(a)   (b)

Equipment

Sandbag (variation: Powerbag™)

Aim

This is a lift and pull pattern exercise to work the posterior chain (hamstrings, glutes and erector spinae), the biceps, shoulders and upper back muscles, as well as the posterior rotational muscles (glutes and lats).

Set-up

- Stand with feet approximately hip shoulder width apart.
- Place the sandbag on the floor at an angle of about 45 degrees to the side of the feet.
- Bend forward and to the side and grip the bag with two hands on the handles.
- Brace the core and lift the sandbag upwards, so it is held level with the hips on one side.

Execution

- Dip down to lower the sandbag to about low thigh/knee height.
- Without pausing explosively extend the hips and pull the bag diagonally upwards to the centre line.
- Roll the hands quickly underneath the sandbag and catch it in a rack position with the bag resting on the chest and upper arms.
- As you catch the bag, drop down in a shallow front squat position to help absorb the load.
- Stand up and roll the sandbag off the arms and to the other side to drop into the next repetition.
- Repeat for the prescribed number of repetitions, pausing in the rack position (not the hang position) if required.

Technical considerations

- Use the hips to provide the force to drive the sandbag upwards.
- Use the pull to help guide the sandbag to the rack position.
- The rack position with a sandbag (or Powerbag™) is much easier for most people to master than a barbell rack.
- To add more of a metabolic challenge include a squat push press between each repetition, when the bag has been caught in the rack position.
- Variations include the sandbag/Powerbag™ diagonal high pull or the sandbag/Powerbag™ diagonal clean from the floor.

OTHER LIFT EXERCISES
Barbell sumo deadlift

This is one of the most commonly performed and important variations of the conventional deadlift. In the sumo style, the grip is medial, or on the inside, of the legs. Many would argue that this is more of a functional exercise for everyday life than the conventional technique, since we would predominantly position our feet to the outside of an object, such as a TV. The sumo style utilises a slightly wider stance than the conventional method, and the feet are at an approximate 45 degree angle pointing outwards. This would cause greater knee flexion (thus more stress on the quadriceps) and activation of hip adductors. This style has gained a reputation as decreasing the stress placed on L4/L5 (the joint between the fourth and fifth lumbar vertebrae) by as much as 10 per cent when compared to the conventional deadlift (Escamilla et al, 2000).

This technique may be favoured by those with longer than average torsos, since the sumo style requires less hip flexion and a more upright trunk position (Escamilla et al, 2000; McGuigan & Wilson, 1996). The sumo style of deadlift offers a significant mechanical advantage over the conventional method (25–40 per cent less work! (Escamilla et al, 2000)), a 10–15 per cent shorter lifting distance (Escamilla et al, 2001), and by reducing the shear forces on the spine, indicates that it could be a safer lifting style than the conventional method (Escamilla et al, 2000; McGuigan & Wilson, 1996).

Barbell partial deadlift

Many clients will be unable to perform a complete deadlift from the floor due to restrictions in flexibility, usually around the hamstrings, or motor skills (Chek, 2001). In this instance there are a couple of options: either to limit the range of motion (ROM) thus enabling perfect technique throughout; or to try a different style, such as the sumo deadlift.

With the partial deadlift, we limit the ROM by placing the bar on adjustable blocks and increasing the starting height, thus eradicating the initial, poorly performed lift from the floor. Restrictions, however, should be addressed and not simply bypassed.

Barbell deadlift with calf raise and shrug

This is one of the first progressions when learning the Olympic weightlifting exercises (the clean and the snatch). Initially it is performed with just a single addition to the deadlift exercise – deadlift with calf raise or deadlift with shrug. The calf raise or shrug action is initiated just as the bar reaches the end point of the concentric phase of the deadlift. When these have been mastered separately, integrate them together.

This can be performed with a clean width or a snatch width grip. It is also commonly performed with a hook grip (a pronated grip with the thumb pinned under the first two fingers) to acclimatise the athlete to this grip, which is used for both the clean and snatch.

Barbell power clean

The barbell power clean is described in the pull section of this book (see page 159), but is a combination exercise consisting of the lift, pull and squat patterns. The weight is lifted from the floor, or an elevated or hang position, to the barbell rack position on the chest/shoulders in a front squat position. It is an excellent exercise to improve strength-speed.

Barbell power snatch

This is described in the pull section of this book (see page 160–1), but is a combination exercise consisting of the lift, pull and squat patterns. The weight is lifted from the floor, or an elevated or hang position, to an overhead squat position. It is an excellent exercise to improve speed-strength. The power clean will focus more on the strength side of power development, while the power snatch will improve more on the speed side of power development.

Kettlebell (swing) snatch

The kettlebell (swing) snatch is usually performed with a single kettlebell in one hand, and is a combined lift and pull pattern exercise, described in more detail in the pull section of this book (see page 153). It is swung between the legs then projected upwards to be caught above the head.

While similar to the barbell snatch, it does not usually involve a squat pattern catch position and is performed more for strength-endurance (high repetitions) rather than the relative strength range used for the barbell clean or snatch (less than 6 reps). It can be performed from the floor (kettlebell dead snatch), from a hang position, with different catch positions, or with two kettlebells.

Kettlebell (swing) clean

The kettlebell (swing) clean is commonly performed with one or two kettlebells, is a combined lift and pull pattern exercise, and involves lifting the load from the floor or between the legs to the kettlebell rack position on the chest. It forms one of the events in kettlebell competitions, alongside the jerk and snatch.

Just as with the kettlebell snatch, there are many variations of this drill including bottoms-up clean (pistol grip) or flipped clean.

Dumbbell vintage clean

The dumbbell vintage clean is almost like a combined lift and bicep curl exercise. The dumbbell is lifted from a dead position on the floor, to a dumbbell rack position, with the forearm vertical as if resting at the top of a hammer curl (semi-supinated grip biceps curl). From this position the dumbbell can be pressed upwards or jerked above the head, for vintage exercises like the windmill or overhead squat. Alternatively it was pressed upwards using a side press or bent press technique, both common vintage exercises, but performed infrequently today.

Barbell/kettlebell/dumbbell stiff leg deadlift

Many people are unsure of the differences between the straight leg deadlift, the stiff leg deadlift and the Romanian deadlift. Essentially the main difference is the knee position: a straight leg deadlift has the knee locked, the stiff leg deadlift is straight but not locked, and the Romanian deadlift has about a 30 degree knee bend and a vertical shin position. The stiff leg deadlift is felt more distally than the Romanian deadlift, closer to the knee. It seems to be more popular with bodybuilders, while the Romanian deadlift is preferred by weightlifters.

Barbell/kettlebell/dumbbell split stance Romanian deadlift

This variation is somewhat of a happy medium between the parallel two leg exercise, which is typically performed, and the more unstable one leg Romanian deadlift. In this exercise the effort is taken on the lead leg, but the other leg is placed on the toes behind to aid balance. It is essentially a 'slightly stabilised' one leg Romanian deadlift.

Barbell snatch grip deadlift on step

The snatch grip deadlift can be performed on a step to increase the range of the exercise. This will have the impact of increasing the strength through a greater range, and will incur greater energy expenditure, which will be helpful for body composition changes. Ensure a good back position is maintained through the new range.

Barbell snatch grip deadlift with chains

Adding chains to the end of the barbell will change the force curve, as the load will increase during the concentric phase. This is commonly used to help improve strength for powerlifters performing this exercise, particularly when they are weak at lockout.

Barbell walking dead lift

This is an excellent combination of a lift and moving/carrying load exercise, perfect for improving grip endurance and for body composition. It requires some space in front of the lifting area for you to walk into. To perform, deadlift the barbell using whatever technique you prefer (Romanian deadlift, sumo, conventional, snatch grip, etc.) then walk two to three paces forwards. Lower the bar and lift back up, then take two to three paces back to the start position and repeat for the prescribed number of repetitions or duration.

Barbell pop up to deadlift

This variation entails performing a pop-up from a kneeling position while holding the bar between deadlifting reps. Adopt a kneeling position while holding the barbell. Pop up and then lift the bar with minimal delay. Lower the bar, adopt the kneeling position again and repeat. It is a very good exercise for incorporating an additional metabolic challenge to the lift exercise.

Barbell Fat Gripz™ Deadlift

Using a fat bar or attaching Fat Gripz™ to a barbell will challenge the gripping muscles of the hand and forearm. For many people the grip is a weak link in their lifting kinetic chain, which limits the overload possible on the agonist muscles. Spending six to eight weeks lifting a submaximal load with a fat grip will help to rebalance this muscle imbalance. It may mean less overload in the short term, but will allow for greater loads to be lifted and higher levels of strength to be developed in the long run.

Barbell deadlift alternating stance (conventional, sumo)

This is less of an exercise variation, and more of a way of manipulating the training stimulus. Within a single set both the sumo and conventional deadlift techniques are used, alternating one repetition of each style. This is nice way of ensuring both techniques are improved, and a good way to overload different motor units of the lifting muscles.

PRESS PATTERN

4

The press pattern is an upper body movement pattern that is characterised by a movement of the hands away from the shoulders. It usually involves pressing an object away from the body, or the body away from a solid object.

The press pattern is an antagonistic pattern to the pull pattern and in everyday life it is used to push the torso off the ground in a prone position to get to a standing position, to move an object from the chest or shoulders to a position overhead or to push the body up when climbing over a wall. It is used to push an opponent away in sports like rugby, or in a fight, and is involved in the generation of force in straight punches (jab and cross).

The press pattern can be broken down into three primary groups:

1. Vertical upwards press (lifting a weight above the head)
2. Vertical downwards press (pushing the body up over a wall)
3. Horizontal press (pushing someone away from you)

There are of course the diagonal downwards, diagonal upwards and the intermediary angles of press as well, but we tend to usually limit the classification to one of the three primary groups.

It is important that all three of these movements are trained within the press pattern, as different muscle groups and motor units will be activated depending on the vector. For example, the horizontal press may use the sternal fibres of the pectorals, while the diagonal upwards press will use the clavicular fibres of the pectorals (an incline of 30 degrees or more is needed to stress

Figure 4.1 The shot putt is a dynamic press pattern

111

the upper chest fibres). The deltoids and upper back muscles will take over in a more vertical upwards press.

Many individuals will predominantly perform the horizontal press exercise – the barbell bench press – with maybe some diagonal upwards, seated shoulder presses, as their press pattern exercises. Overdevelopment in a single plane will likely cause issues in this pattern and in the joints used, potentially leading to dysfunction and injury. In a muscle dysfunction, any exercise that stresses that muscle through one plane will cause pain. In a joint dysfunction, any exercise that stresses that joint through various planes of motion will cause pain. For example, if a person has pain in the shoulder when bench pressing but not overhead shoulder pressing, the rotator cuff muscles may

not be functioning optimally, and the pectoral muscles may also be dysfunctional. If there is pain during both bench pressing and overhead shoulder pressing, there may be a joint dysfunction that may need rehabilitation or treatment. If the primary problem is joint dysfunction, there may be a secondary problem of muscle dysfunction.

FUNCTIONS AND IMPORTANCE OF THE PRESS PATTERN

The press pattern is a fantastic way to improve upper body strength of the chest, shoulders and arms and, if correctly selected exercise are chosen, core and hip stability. Lifting appropriately heavy loads above the head can also stimulate muscle growth for hypertrophy, which can be beneficial for contact sports like rugby, to act as an additional layer of protection for the body. It is also used to push opponents away, to pop up off the ground or on a surfboard to get up to standing position, and to press the body up when climbing over a wall. Strength on the press pattern is also essential for the jerk exercise in Olympic weightlifting and competitive kettlebell lifting. Although this exercise uses the power of the hips and lower body to project the load upwards, the press pattern muscles must be strong enough to catch and stabilise the load overhead. This is why the standing shoulder press is used as an assistant exercise for Olympic lifters.

Indeed the ability to press a load overhead in a standing position was used to test upper body strength throughout the late 1800s and early 1900s and was only surpassed by the bench press as powerlifting became popular. However, in many circles, like strongman competitions, it is still the preferred method of assessing upper body strength

Figure 4.2 Overhead pressing is commonly underdeveloped in lieu of horizontal pressing

to press the load overhead. Unlike a stable supine press, the standing press requires concurrent hip and core stability, shoulder and thoracic mobility and scapula and shoulder stability, in addition to the strength of the pressing muscles.

LIMITING FACTORS FOR THE PRESS PATTERN

The following list highlights the five common limiting factors for the press movement pattern:

1. Poor upper body strength balance
2. Poor connection with core
3. Poor exercise selection
4. Shoulder and scapula dysfunction
5. Weak elbow extensors

To improve the function of the press pattern, these limiting factors should be addressed, in addition to improving the strength of the press and the range of pressing ability. For this movement pattern, this would also include integrating the press pattern with the squat and rotation patterns, and ensuring frontal plane stability for single arm pressing.

1. POOR UPPER BODY STRENGTH BALANCE

To improve the ability of the body to press, there are several areas which should be evaluated for weakness. These may be indicators that the body will limit the weight you can lift or indicators that too much time is being spent on certain press movements and not enough on others.

To begin with, what is the strength-balance between the horizontal press and the vertical press patterns? Using Poliquin's upper body structural balance scores (2006) the press pattern can be evaluated using the ratios in taable 4.1.

The barbell bench press is used as the reference lift (hence 100%), against which all of the other exercises are compared for weakness or strength deficits. If an individual could perform the bench press with 100kg for 1RM, then this would be the standard for the horizontal press and would provide a reference for the vertical and diagonal pressing motions. If they cannot perform a body-weight dip (plus any external load) for a total of 117kg for 1RM (or 117% of the Bench Press), then they would be weak in the vertical downward press pattern. If they couldn't perform a 91kg barbell inclined press (at 45 degrees) or a behind

Table 4.1	Poliquin's upper body structural balance scores (2006)		
Exercise		**Intensity**	**Relative Score**
Biacromial grip width barbell bench press (reference lift)		1RM	100%
Dips (bodyweight and additional load)		1RM	117%
Biacromial grip width barbell inclined bench press		1RM	91%
Seated barbell behind the neck press		1RM	66%
Seated dumbbell overhead press		8RM	29% per DB

the neck press with 66kg for 1RM, then they would be weak in the diagonal upward press or vertical upwards press patterns respectively. The seated dumbbell overhead press provides another method for evaluating the vertical upwards press pattern, and if they could not perform this drill with a pair of 29kg dumbbells for 8RM, then more emphasis should be placed on working the overhead pattern in this manner. Poliquin (2006) also believes that seated dumbbell external rotations 8RM should be around 10 per cent of the bench press 1RM, which would provide an indication of the shoulder internal-external strength balance.

Many individuals may not be able to perform the barbell behind the neck press because of thoracic mobility, rotator cuff adhesions or shoulder rotation mobility. Performing this exercise without addressing these issues may cause pain, inflammation or damage to the structures of the shoulder. Poliquin (2006) believes that this exercise is inherently fine if you have optimal shoulder mechanics, and as a baseline an individual should be able to perform this lift with a minimum load of 80 per cent of their bodyweight for 1RM, with Olympic athletes scoring up to 143 per cent.

Weak pulling muscles may also limit the ability of the body to press in different planes, because of the agonist-antagonist strength balance. The brain will limit the load lifted because it recognises the inherent instability this strength imbalance will cause at the related joints – the shoulder. The optimal press to pull ratio (Poliquin, 2006) can be calculated using the supinated grip chin-up and should be 87 per cent of the load for the Bench Press (weight calculated as bodyweight plus external load).

Boyle (2004) on the other hand believes that the maximum number of press ups is 'a much more accurate test for larger athletes than bench press numbers' for assessing functional upper-body strength. Males should be able to achieve 25+reps (high school level), with 35+ a collegiate level, 42+ being national calibre and 50+ scoring world class. For females a score of 12 minimum is ideal (high school level), with 20+ a collegiate level, 27+ being national calibre and 35+ scoring world class. For the average athlete or person this may be fine, but for strength and power athletes, they may not be able to demonstrate strength-endurance (maximum reps) in the press pattern, but could demonstrate huge relative strength scores when loaded on exercises like the bench press.

Weaknesses in the chest and shoulder muscles will present as (Kinakin, 2004):

- Pain on overhead pressing
- Limited range of motion in shoulder abduction or flexion (tight sternal or clavicular pectoral fibres)
- Arm in an internally rotated position when relaxed (tight pectoralis major)
- Winging of the scapula and the shoulder drawn forward (tight pectoralis minor)

2. POOR CONNECTION WITH CORE (WEAK LIFTING MUSCLES)

For many of the pressing exercises described later in this chapter it is important that there is sufficient strength or strength-endurance in the stabilising muscles of the core to maintain an optimal posture, technique or position. When the body is loaded in the squat or lift position, the tendency is for the load to want to collapse into flexion, thus the core extensors are hard at work to prevent this accessory movement. When pressing overhead, the tendency is for the body to want to move into a hyperextended position at the spine, thus the flexors of the core must contract to stabilise and prevent this movement.

When pressing a unilateral load overhead, such as a dumbbell held in one hand, there is also a tremendous amount of frontal plane stability required at the hips and lateral core to provide a stable base for the agonists to generate force. In earlier days, this strength and stability was developed using exercises like the windmill, which has been lost over the last hundred years as an effective method of preparation. The stability of the lateral core muscles can be assessed using the lateral musculature test below, as described in McGill (2002).

Position

The client adopts a full side plank position, with the top foot placed in front of the lower foot for stability, and the torso supported on one elbow/forearm. The client lifts the hips off the ground so the body is in a straight line and places the other hand on the opposite shoulder.

Assessment

The client holds the position for maximum duration until the straight back posture is lost and the hip returns to the floor.

Figure 4.3 Performing the lateral musculature test

Scores

The following scores are collected from healthy young individuals (McGill, 2002).

Having a right hand side/left hand side bridge endurance difference greater than 5 per cent would indicate unbalanced endurance.

For the two hand overhead press exercises it is important to have both posterior and anterior core stability, since the force of the load above the head can cause the body to be bent into a flexed or extended position. To stop the body being forced into a hyperextended position the anterior core contracts to maintain the neutral position. Hence, before lifting significant loads overhead, the individual should develop lateral core stability (for one hand pressing) and anterior core stability (for heavier two hand pressing). A weak lower

Table 4.2	Scores for performing the lateral musculature test – all scores are time in seconds					
	Men		**Women**		**All**	
Task	Mean	SD (standard deviation)	Mean	SD (standard deviation)	Mean	SD (standard deviation)
Right hand side	95	32	75	32	83	33
Left hand side	99	37	78	32	86	36

back (maybe because of excessive supine bench pressing) will also limit overhead pressing ability, and exercises such as the Romanian deadlift, good mornings and reverse hyperextensions should help to correct this.

3. POOR EXERCISE SELECTION

There are a few areas of issue with the press pattern exercise selection. The first is the over-emphasis on the barbell bench press. As discussed previously, the popularity of the bench press increased in the mid 1900s as powerlifting become more prominent. Today extremely heavy loads are lifted off the rack and pressed in the horizontal plane in a very stable supine position.

One of the potential problems with the bench press is that high levels of strength can be developed in a very narrow plane. With the overhead press you need to be able to lift and pull the load up onto the shoulders or chest before pressing it above the head. This means that you only press what you can get to that position. In the bench press you can develop pressing strength without the concurrent lifting and pulling strength, which has the potential to cause movement pattern strength imbalances.

Another area of concern is the biomechanics of the barbell bench press. Whenever a press pattern motion is occurring at the shoulder (glenohumeral) joint there is also a concurrent motion occurring at the scapula (referred to as scapula-humeral rhythm). The scapula must retract (or come together) during the eccentric phase of a high elbow horizontal press to accommodate the horizontal extension at the shoulder. When performing a supine bridge press, a vintage single arm press or a standing cable press the scapula is free to move, as it should do normally. However,

when performing a barbell bench press, the load of the bar will push the torso onto the bench, pinning down the scapula and limiting the normal scapula-humeral rhythm. This means that more stress is placed on the glenohumeral joint, as the normal mobility is limited. This is exacerbated by the very heavy loads used in the barbell bench press, and the fact that the movement of the arms is more limited and restricted than if a pair of dumbbells was being used. This can be offset by using a biacromial distance grip, rather than a wide grip, so the arms are in flexion-extension rather than horizontal flexion-extension.

I am of the opinion that the barbell bench press is a good exercise to lift heavy loads in the horizontal plane, but it is far too overused. The issues mentioned above can be overcome by following the following guidelines:

- Perform a powerlifting style barbell bench press only if you are a powerlifter.
- Perform the barbell bench press with a biacromial grip – not only will it be less stressful on the shoulder joint, it will improve shoulder stability and triceps strength.
- Vary the angle of the barbell bench press frequently.
- Perform a dumbbell bench press frequently rather than just the barbell version.
- Perform standing cable press exercises frequently to balance out the agonist to core strength.
- Perform overhead pressing exercises frequently, if not more so, than horizontal pressing exercises.
- Perform bodyweight dips frequently to train the entire spectrum of pressing angles.
- Ensure adequate shoulder mobility and stability, and antagonist strength with a variety of supplementary exercises.

4. SHOULDER AND SCAPULA DYSFUNCTION

To perform the press pattern correctly the shoulder and scapula stabilisers must be functioning optimally. This means that a client should have optimal shoulder mobility (in internal and external rotation) and thoracic mobility for flexion and extension. The muscles around the scapula must function well to allow the scapula to move (upwards, downwards or rotationally) to accommodate the movement at the glenohumeral joint.

The rotator cuff comprises four muscles: the subscapularis, infraspinatus, teres minor and supraspinatus. Their role is to internally and externally rotate the shoulder, to assist in abduction and to stabilise the head of the humerus. Weakness in the pressing muscles may be due to the following factors:

- Weakness in the external rotators due to adhesions in the muscles. The amount of force that a contracting muscle can produce will be partially dictated by how much the antagonistic muscle can relax and elongate.
- Adhesions in the subscapularis muscle from excessive bench pressing (Kinakin, 2004). This is often felt as pain during bench pressing, as the subscapularis becomes stressed at the end of the eccentric phase, causing inflammation and subsequent adhesions and scar tissue.

In addition to adhesions within the rotator cuff, weakened trapezius or rhomboids will limit ideal scapula movements and can lead to inflammation or impingement at the shoulder joint. Isolated strengthening work of any weak areas with supplementary exercises, as well as myofascial release work, using a foam roller or tennis ball, or by a therapist, will help to limit these common issues.

An inability to flatten and extend the thoracic spine will limit normal mobility at the shoulder joint, and the arm will struggle to reach full flexion when pressing a load overhead. As a result it is common for an individual to subconsciously tilt the pelvis forward and overarch the lower back to compensate for this lack of mobility further up the kinetic chain. This commonly causes tension or pain in the lumbar erectors, which is what many individuals complain of when performing standing overhead presses.

5. WEAK ELBOW EXTENSORS

The elbow extensors must be strong enough to assist in moving the hands away from the shoulders, in whichever plane the press is occurring. The triceps brachii is made up of three heads – the long head, the lateral head and the medial head. Although the medial head is active in all elbow extension, the lateral and long head have minimal recruitment except when the load is heavy (8RM or heavier).

Weakness in the triceps can cause problems with locking out on the bench press or overhead shoulder press (Kinakin, 2004). Triceps extension strength is greater with the arm below the shoulder than above it, and if the shoulders are healthy enough to perform dips then it is an excellent exercise to work this muscle. Supplementary exercises, such as the supine EZ triceps extension, standing triceps cable pushdown or dumbbell triceps kickback, will allow a greater neural drive to these muscles, increasing the overload and subsequent strength adaptations. These strength increases can then be applied back into the 'more functional' press pattern exercises.

PRESS PATTERN EXERCISES
VERTICAL PRESS UPWARDS
EXERCISES

Exercise 4.1 Shoulder to shoulder press

(a)   (b)

Equipment
Powerbag™ (variation: sandbag)

Aim
This is a press pattern exercise to work the upwards-pressing muscles (deltoids, upper trapezius and elbow extensors).

Set-up
- Assume a standing position, feet hip width apart.
- Hold the Powerbag™ in a position on one shoulder and held in both hands in a 'squeeze grip' (for an image of this please see the starting position for exercise 3.14, p.106).
- Have the elbows tucked in and close to the chest.
- Lift the chest to ensure a good back position and brace the core.

Execution
- Press the Powerbag™ to a position directly overhead, with the arms fully extended.
- Keep the lower body still and do not use the legs for propulsion.
- Lower the Powerbag™ to the other shoulder.
- Briefly pause then repeat in the opposite direction for the prescribed number of repetitions or duration.

Technical considerations
- The Powerbag™ will be an unusual load to lift overhead and will require more grip emphasis than a barbell or dumbbell press, but the load lifted will be lower.
- Variations include sandbag shoulder to shoulder press, or adding a lift to shoulder with each repetition.

Exercise 4.2 Single arm press

(a) (b)

Equipment

Kettlebell (variation: sandbag)

Aim

This is a press pattern exercise to work the upwards-pressing muscles (deltoids, upper trapezius and elbow extensors) and lateral core muscles.

Set-up

- Assume a standing position, feet hip width apart.
- Hold the kettlebell with one hand in the rack position.
- Have the elbow tucked in and close to the hip.
- Lift the chest to ensure a good back position and brace the core.

Execution

- Press the kettlebell straight upwards, rotating the arm during the movement to finish with the palm facing forwards.
- Hold at the top with the arm locked and the handle, not the kettlebell, positioned over the shoulder and hip.
- The kettlebell should sit slightly behind the body.
- Lower back to the start position and repeat.

Technical considerations

- This is the same trajectory used during the push press and jerk, and is similar to the dumbbell Arnold press.
- For this strict variation of the press exercise, limit any lateral hip movement and avoid stabilising the hips with the other hand.
- It keeps the bell closer to the mid-line, requires slightly less lateral stability of the core, but will be challenging on the anterior deltoid and thoracic mobility.
- Variations include bottoms-up kettlebell press, or double kettlebell see-saw press.

Exercise 4.3 Behind the neck press

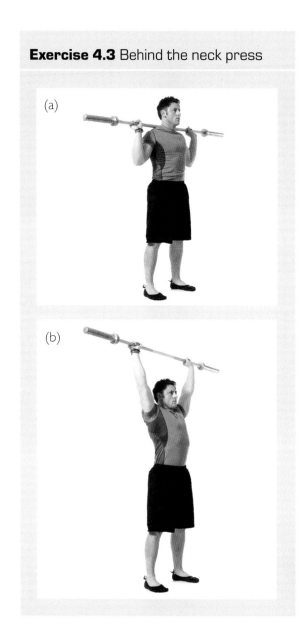

(a)

(b)

Equipment
Barbell (variation: chains)

Aim
This is a press pattern exercise to work the upwards-pressing muscles (deltoids, upper trapezius and elbow extensors) and to maintain mobility at the shoulder joint.

Set-up
- Assume a standing position, feet hip width apart.
- Hold the bar across the upper back with both hands.
- Have the elbows tucked in and positioned under the bar.
- Lift the chest to ensure a good back position and brace the core.

Execution
- Press the bar to a position directly over the head.
- Hold at the top with the arms locked.
- Keep the head up and do not allow the head to poke forward.
- Maintain an optimal position of the lower back and do not overarch to accommodate the movement.
- Slowly lower back to the start position and repeat.

Technical considerations
- Keep the load light to begin with to ensure adequate mobility and that no excessive stress is placed on the anterior shoulder.
- Many individuals will not be able to perform this exercise because of shoulder or thoracic mobility issues. These should be addressed otherwise there will be potential damage caused to the shoulder joint or lower back.
- Do not use the legs at all to move the bar off the upper trapezius.
- Variations include seated (unsupported) behind the neck press, behind the neck press with chains, or behind the neck power jerk.

Exercise 4.4 Overhead press

(a)

(b)

Equipment
Barbell with chains

Aim
This is a press pattern exercise to work the upwards-pressing muscles (deltoids, upper trapezius and elbow extensors) with a progressive resistance load.

Set-up
- Assume a standing position, feet hip width apart.
- Attach the chains to the outside of any plates or collars.
- Lift bar up to rack position, with bar resting across collar bone/anterior deltoids.
- Hold the bar wider than shoulder width apart and have the elbows tucked in and positioned under the bar.
- Lift the chest to ensure a good back position and brace the core.

Execution
- Press the bar to a position directly over the head.
- Hold at the top with the arms locked.
- Keep the head up and do not allow the head to poke forward.
- Maintain an optimal position of the lower back and do not overarch to accommodate the movement.
- Slowly lower back to the start position and repeat.

Technical considerations
- Chains added to the sides of the bar increase tension on the concentric phase with progressive resistance.
- Do not use the legs at all to move the bar off the upper trapezius.
- Variations include seated (unsupported) barbell press with chains, push press with chains, or barbell jerk with chains.

Exercise 4.5 Push press

(a)

(b)

Equipment
Barbell with chains

Aim
This is a press pattern exercise to work the upwards-pressing muscles (deltoids, upper trapezius and elbow extensors) with a progressive resistance load, heavier than could be lifted by strict technique alone.

Set-up
- Assume a standing position, feet hip width apart (see exercise 4.4, p.121).
- Attach the chains to the outside of any plates or collars.
- Lift bar up to rack position, with bar resting across collar bone/anterior deltoids.
- Hold the bar wider than shoulder width apart and have the elbows tucked in and positioned under the bar.
- Lift the chest to ensure a good back position.

Execution
- Brace the core and keeping feet flat and torso upright, squat downwards to quarter depth.
- Drive through the heels to stand back up and use momentum to push the bar off the shoulders.
- Press the bar to lockout to a position directly over the head.
- Hold at the top with the arms locked.
- Keep the head up and do not allow the head to poke forward.
- Do not overarch the lower back.
- Lower back to the start position and repeat.

Technical considerations
- Chains increase tension on the concentric phase with progressive resistance.
- The legs are used to initiate the movement of the bar off the upper trapezius, and the pressing muscles are used for the final phase to achieve lockout.
- More load should be used for the push press than a strict press exercise.
- Variations include barbell jerk with chains or barbell snatch balance with chains.

Exercise 4.6 Power jerk

(a)

(b)

Equipment
Barbell with chains

Aim
This is a press pattern exercise to work the upwards-pressing muscles (deltoids, upper trapezius and elbow extensors) with a progressive resistance load, heavier than could be lifted by push press or strict press techniques alone.

Set-up
- Assume a standing position, feet hip width apart (see exercise 4.4, p.121).
- Attach the chains to the outside of any plates or collars.
- Lift bar up to rack position, with bar resting across collar bone/anterior deltoids.
- Hold the bar wider than shoulder width apart and have the elbows tucked in and positioned under the bar.
- Lift the chest to ensure a good back position.

Execution
- Brace the core and keeping feet flat and torso upright, squat downwards to quarter depth.
- Drive through heels to stand back up and use momentum to push bar off shoulders.
- Drop the body down into an overhead squat position to catch the bar overhead with arms locked.
- Stand up, keeping arms extended.
- Do not overarch the lower back.
- Drop the bar back down to the start position and repeat.
- Do not try to slowly eccentrically lower the bar, as the load should be too heavy to do that.

Technical considerations
- Chains added to the sides of the bar increase tension on the concentric phase with progressive resistance.
- The pressing muscles are used to stabilise the load overhead.
- More load should be used for the jerk than with a push press or strict press exercise.
- Variations include the barbell split jerk with chains.

Exercise 4.7 Split kneeling single arm press

(a) (b)

Equipment
Sandbag

Aim
This is a press pattern exercise to work the upwards-pressing muscles (deltoids, upper trapezius and elbow extensors) and lateral core muscles in a split stance position with an unconventional load.

Set-up
- Assume a split kneeling position.
- Hold the sandbag with the opposite hand to the lead leg in a rack position.
- Have the elbow tucked in and close to the torso.
- Lift the chest to ensure a good back position and brace the core.

Execution
- Press the sandbag straight upwards, keeping the hand in a semi-supinated position throughout.
- Hold at the top with the arm locked and the hand positioned over the shoulder and hip.
- Lower back to the start position and repeat for the rest of the set on the same side.
- Repeat on the other side.

Technical considerations
- Although the load will be lower than a single arm standing press, it will cause a greater overload on the lateral core muscles to stabilise.
- Variations include sandbag two hand split kneel press or split kneeling shoulder to shoulder press.

Exercise 4.8 Standing single arm press

(a)   (b)

Execution
- Press the sandbag straight upwards, keeping the hand in a semi-supinated position throughout.
- Hold at the top with the arm locked and the hand positioned over the shoulder and hip.
- Lower back to the start position and repeat for the rest of the set on the same side.
- Repeat on the other side.

Technical considerations
- A standing sandbag press requires slightly less lateral stability of the core, but will be challenging on the anterior deltoid and thoracic mobility.
- Variations include standing sandbag shoulder to shoulder press, and sandbag single arm push press or jerk.

Equipment
Sandbag

Aim
This is a press pattern exercise to work the upwards-pressing muscles (deltoids, upper trapezius and elbow extensors) and lateral core muscles with an unconventional load.

Set-up
- Assume a standing position, feet hip width apart.
- Hold the sandbag with one hand in the rack position.
- Have the elbow tucked in and close to the hip.
- Lift the chest to ensure a good back position and brace the core.

Exercise 4.9 Standing See Saw press

(a) (b)

Equipment

Kettlebells

Aim

This is a press pattern exercise to work the upwards-pressing muscles (deltoids, upper trapezius and elbow extensors), the lateral core muscles and the cardio respiratory system.

Set-up

- Assume a standing position, feet hip width apart.
- Hold the kettlebells, one in each hand, in the double kettlebell rack position.
- Have the elbows tucked in and close to the hips.
- Lift the chest to ensure a good back position and brace the core.

Execution

- Press one of the kettlebells straight upwards, rotating the arm during the movement to finish with the palm facing forwards.
- Hold at the top with the arm locked and the handle, not the bell, positioned over the shoulder and hip.
- The bell should sit slightly behind the body.
- As you lower that kettlebell, press the other one overhead in the same technique.
- Repeat this continuous alternating pressing action.

Technical considerations

- This will be a great overload on the cardio-vascular system and will create a high demand on the core muscles to stabilise in an asymmetrical movement pattern at a dynamic pace.
- Variations include alternately pressing the kettlebells overhead one at a time, fully re-racking one kettlebell before beginning the press action of the other arm.

Exercise 4.10 Vintage standing press

(a)

(b)

(c)

(d)

Equipment
Dumbbell

Aim
This is a vertical press pattern exercise to work the shoulder and triceps muscles in a standing position, with lateral hip movement to integrate the lateral core and hips with the pressing muscles.

Set-up
• Clean a single dumbbell with one hand up to shoulder height on the right hand side.

• Pull the forearm back and out to the side, until the palm is facing forwards.
• The dumbbell should be at shoulder height, the forearm vertical and the feet hip width apart.
• Take a breath in and brace the core.

Execution
• Push the hips out to the left so the torso laterally flexes to the right to initiate the movement.
• Without pausing, push the hips out to the right and at the same time initiate the upward press.
• Imagine pressing the torso laterally underneath the body.
• As the elbow goes past 90 degrees, pull the hips and torso back to an upright position, which should help to snap the arm into full extension.
• Briefly hold this pressed position, then lower the dumbbell back to the shoulder and repeat.
• Perform an equal number of sets of both sides.

Technical considerations
• This is the equivalent of the push press, using the hips to initiate the upward press movement. However, in this variation the first movement occurs not in the sagittal plane (like the push press) but in the frontal plane, and solely from the hips and not the knees.
• The load should be heavy enough so that body is forced to use this 'adapted' press technique.
• Keep the repetitions on the low side – 12 or less.
• Variations include side press or using a kettlebell or barbell.

Exercise 4.11 Bent press

(a)

(b)

(c)

Equipment
Dumbbell

Aim
This is a press pattern exercise to work the upwards-pressing muscles (deltoids, upper trapezius and elbow extensors) and to integrate the core and hips to be able to lift heavy loads.

Set-up
* Clean a single dumbbell with one hand up to shoulder height on the right hand side.
* Pull the forearm back and out to the side, until the palm is facing forwards.
* The dumbbell should be at shoulder height, the forearm vertical and the feet hip width apart.
* Take a breath in and brace the core.

Execution
* Press the body downwards underneath the load, not directly forwards nor sideways, but towards the left knee.
* Keep the right elbow placed on the hips for as long as possible.
* Support the left hand or arm on the left thigh.
* Swell the right latissimus dorsi muscle and press the load upwards.
* Try to keep hand pointing forwards throughout.
* Bend the right leg and lock out the right arm then stand upwards.
* Lower the weight and repeat on the other side.

Technical considerations
* This was traditionally performed with a very heavy barbell or dumbbell (as shown in figure 4.4). Strongmen knew that for heavy loads to be lifted overhead, the strict press technique

was not the most efficient way to do this. The core and legs had to be integrated with the pressing muscles – just as with the push press, the jerk, the side press or the vintage press.

- Keep the repetitions very low and the load heavy.
- Variations include side press and two hands anyhow.

Figure 4.4 Arthur Saxon, a British strongman, still holds the record for the bent press at 370lbs.

HORIZONTAL PRESS EXERCISES

Exercise 4.12 Bench press biacromial pronated grip

(a)

(b)

Equipment
Barbell (variations: chains, bands)

Aim
This is a press pattern exercise to work the horizontal pressing muscles (pectorals, deltoids and triceps).

Set-up
- Adopt a supine position on a bench (or similar to position in photos).
- Place the feet flat on the ground or slightly elevated on a step.
- Lift a barbell off a rack or have it handed to you.
- Hold the bar with arms extended straight up above the shoulders in a pronated grip equivalent to the distance between your two acromion processes.
- Take a breath in and brace the core.

Execution
- Slowly lower the bar towards the lower sternum, taking 3–4 seconds to do so.
- Pause briefly when the bar reaches the sternum, without losing tension.
- Press the bar upward back to the start position.
- Focus on accelerating the bar on the concentric phase.
- Repeat for the prescribed number of repetitions.

Technical considerations
- Keep elbows close to sides and forearms vertical.
- Keep the core braced and hips on the bench.
- Variations include barbell inclined bench press, dumbbell close grip press with rotation, or adding chains or bands for progressive resistance.

Exercise 4.13 Plyometric press-up

(a)

(b)

Equipment
Bodyweight (variation: weighted vest)

Aim
This is a press pattern exercise to work the horizontal pressing muscles (pectorals, deltoids and triceps) and integrating the core to improve pressing reactive strength.

Set-up
- Adopt a prone plank position on the floor with the arms extended.
- Hands should be about shoulder width apart.
- Feet should be about hip width apart.
- Take a breath in and brace the core.

Execution
- Quickly lower the body into a partial press-up – about one-quarter of the full depth.
- Without pausing immediately press through the floor and accelerate your body upwards.
- Extend the arms fully, and allow the momentum to lift the hands off the floor.
- Extend the arms to land in the start position, drop straight into the next rep and repeat.
- Repeat for the prescribed number of repetitions.

Technical considerations
- You can perform a clap after the hands have left the ground between each press up (b).
- Keep the core braced throughout.
- Focus on accelerating through the concentric phase.
- Keep the repetitions low and the quality high.
- Variations include Spiderman plyometric press-ups or plyo press-ups wearing a weights vest.

Exercise 4.14 Spiderman press-up

(a)

(b)

Execution
- Slowly lower the body into a press-up.
- At the same time look to one side. On the same side lift the foot off the ground and bring up the same side elbow.
- Briefly hold in the press-up position, then press up and bring the foot back to the start position.
- Repeat, alternating sides, for the prescribed number of repetitions.

Technical considerations
- Keep the core braced throughout.
- Focus on controlled eccentric lowering and accelerating through the concentric phase.
- Variations include Spiderman plyometric press-ups and Spiderman crawls.

Equipment
Bodyweight

Aim
This is a press pattern exercise to work the horizontal pressing muscles (pectorals, deltoids and triceps) and integrating the core.

Set-up
- Adopt a prone plank position on the floor with the arms extended.
- Hands should be about shoulder width apart.
- Feet should be about hip width apart.
- Breathe in and brace the core.

Exercise 4.15 Single arm chest press on stability ball

(a)

(b)

Equipment
Dumbbell and stability ball

Aim
This is a press pattern exercise to work the horizontal pressing muscles (pectorals, deltoids and triceps) and to integrate the core and hips on an unstable surface.

Set-up
- Sit on top of a stability ball.
- Walk forwards and lean backwards until you reach a high supine bridge position.
- The head and upper back should be supported on the ball and the shins should be vertical.
- Hold a dumbbell in one hand in a pronated grip with the arm extended straight up above the shoulder.
- Breathe in and brace the core.

Execution
- Slowly lower the dumbbell towards the side of the chest, taking 3–4 seconds to do so.
- Rotate the dumbbell to a semi-supinated grip.
- Pause briefly when the dumbbell reaches level with the sternum, without losing tension.
- Press the dumbbell upwards back to the start position.
- Focus on accelerating the dumbbell on the concentric phase.
- Repeat for the prescribed number of repetitions on both sides.

Technical considerations
- Keep the elbow close to the side and forearm vertical.
- Keep the core braced and hips level throughout.
- Variations include alternating dumbbell chest press on stability ball.

Exercise 4.16 Chest press throw

(a)

(b)

triceps) and integrating the core to improve pressing reactive strength.

Set-up
- Assume a split kneeling position.
- Hold the sandball with two hands on the chest.
- Have the elbow flared outwards.
- Lift the chest to ensure a good back position and brace the core.

Execution
- Throw the sandball slightly forwards and upwards.
- Use the chest, shoulders and arms to develop the force, keeping the rest of the body still.
- Have a partner catch the sandball and throw it back.
- Have the arms extended to catch the sandball.
- As soon as the sandball hits the hands, try to decelerate the load and send it back.
- Repeat for the prescribed number of repetitions.

Technical considerations
- Do not allow the sandball to hit the chest. If you cannot slow it down before it hits the chest, then the load is too heavy.
- Variations include sandbag one-hand split-kneel chest press throw or standing chest press throw.

Equipment
Sandball

Aim
This is a press pattern exercise to work the horizontal pressing muscles (pectorals, deltoids and

Exercise 4.17 Vintage supine press

(a)

(b)

Equipment
Dumbbell

Aim
This is a horizontal press pattern exercise to work the chest, shoulder and triceps muscles in a figure of four supine position on the floor. Utilising the figure of four position will allow for normal scapula motion and also greater core integration.

Set-up
- Lie on the floor in a supine position, with a single dumbbell next to one shoulder.
- Roll towards the dumbbell and lift it up with both hands.

- Extend the working arm and release the non-working hand – the palm should be facing the feet.
- Lift the working side leg straight up in the air and rotate the hips to place the foot on the floor on the opposite side.
- Have the non-working arm on the floor for balance and brace the core.

Execution
- Slowly lower the dumbbell towards the body by bending the elbow.
- Keep the elbow close to the body and allow it to brush against the latissimus dorsi.
- Lower until just before the elbow touches the floor or until full range of motion is reached.
- Pause briefly then press the dumbbell back to the start position rotating the hand back to a pronated position, keeping the elbow close to the body.
- Repeat for the prescribed number of repetitions on both sides.

Technical considerations
- The foot should be kept touching on the floor of the opposite side using the core muscles.
- Unlike a standard supine press, this position allows for normal scapula motion during pressing, ensuring optimal glenohumeral (shoulder joint) function and health.
- Keeping the elbow close to the body when pressing will increase shoulder stability benefits.
- Keep the repetitions at 12 or less and ensure a controlled tempo on the eccentric phase.

Exercise 4.18 Alternating chest press

(a)

(b)

Equipment
Cables

Aim
This is a press pattern exercise to work the horizontal pressing muscles (pectorals, deltoids and triceps) and integrating the core in a standing position.

Set-up
- Set up two cable handles just higher than shoulder height.
- Assume a standing position facing away from the dual cable columns.
- Adopt a split stance for stability.
- Take hold of the cable handle attachments.
- Press both handles forward with elbows wide.
- Lift the chest to ensure a good back position and brace the core.

Execution
- Allow the right arm to bend and slowly bring the handle back until it is level with the chest.
- Allow the shoulders to rotate to accommodate the motion, but keep the lower body and hips facing forwards.
- Pause briefly then contract the core and press the right hand forwards.
- As the right hand presses forwards, allow the left arm to bend and the hand to move towards the shoulder.
- Continue this alternating pressing action for the prescribed number of repetitions.
- Alternate the lead leg with each set.

Technical considerations
- Keep the hips facing forwards throughout.
- Variations include one arm cable chest press and downward cable chest press.

Exercise 4.19 Suspension system chest press

(a) (b)

Equipment

Suspension system (variation: weighted vest)

Aim

To work the press pattern muscles in the horizontal vector, specifically the sternal fibres of the pectorals, triceps, anterior deltoids, the shoulder stabilisers and the anterior and lateral core muscles for stability.

Set-up

*   Connect the two-strap suspension system to the anchor points, ideally at least 6ft high and shoulder width apart or slightly wider.
*   Stand facing away from the anchor points and hold one handle in each hand, with a pronated grip (palms facing downwards).
*   Brace the core and lean forward so that the arms are extended and the body is straight and rigid.
*   Move the feet forward or backwards to achieve the optimal level of intensity.

Execution

*   Move the hands apart and bend the elbows under control to slowly lower the body downwards.
*   Bring the elbows back until the hands are level with the shoulder, or before, and briefly hold.
*   Press the hands forward and together to lift the body back to the start position.
*   Focus on squeezing the pectorals for maximum benefit.
*   Maintain a rigid body position throughout the exercise, keeping the head in line with the spine and preventing chin poking.

Technical considerations

*   Press slightly upwards during the concentric phase to avoid the straps rubbing on the shoulders or arms.
*   Using a two-strap system will ensure an optimal tension throughout the full range of the exercise.
*   Allow the scapula to move together and do not fix their position.
*   Avoid the shoulders lifting up (scapula elevation) during any part of the exercise.
*   Avoid the hips sagging and the lower back overarching.
*   Move the feet further away from the anchor point to decrease the intensity.
*   Moving the feet closer or underneath and beyond the anchor point (if possible) or elevating the feet off the ground (against a wall or up on a bench), so that the body is horizontal or angled, will all increase the intensity.
*   Lifting one foot off the ground will increase the instability making the exercise more challenging from a balance perspective.
*   Variations include alternating chest press, alternating chest press-fly or chest press with a weighted vest.

DOWNWARDS PRESS EXERCISES

Exercise 4.20 Supine bridge press

(a)

(b)

Equipment
Barbell (variation: kettlebells)

Aim
This is a diagonal downward press pattern exercise to work the chest, shoulders and triceps muscles in a bridge position on the floor. Utilising the bridge position will allow for normal scapula motion and greater range of motion.

Set-up
- Lie on the floor in a supine position with the barbell on the floor above the head.

- Extend the hips off the floor into a bridge position.
- Brace the core and perform a pullover to lift the barbell from the floor
- Extend the arms and hold the barbell above the shoulders.

Execution
- Slowly lower the barbell towards the body by bending the elbows.
- Keep the elbows close to the body and allow them to brush against the latissimus dorsi.
- Lower the bar until just before the elbow touches the floor or until full range of motion is reached.
- Pause briefly then press the barbell back up to the start position keeping the elbows close to the body.
- Repeat for the prescribed number of repetitions.

Set-up
- This bridge press position allows for normal scapula motion during pressing, ensuring optimal glenohumeral function and health.
- This exercise was introduced by the strongmen before the bench press was popular.
- Keeping the elbow close to the body when pressing will increase shoulder stability benefits.
- Keep the repetitions at 12 or less and ensure a controlled tempo on the eccentric phase.
- Variations include alternating dumbbell bridge press or alternating wrestler's bridge press with kettlebells (a supine bridge position with the individual bridging on the head, rather than the upper back – used by wrestlers and mixed martial arts (MMA) fighters to improve neck strength for their sports).

Exercise 4.21 Dips

Execution
- Lower the body down until the biceps touch the forearms.
- Pause briefly without losing any tension.
- Press the body back up to just before full extension.
- Hold briefly again and repeat for the prescribed number of repetitions.

Technical considerations
- This version of the dip is *the* exercise to train the downward press pattern.
- The triceps dips version where you elevated your feet in front of you will put an excessive amount of stress on the anterior portions of the shoulder joints.
- If you do not have sufficient strength to be able to perform the concentric (pressing) phase of a dip, then this should be preceded with eccentric (lowering) only repetitions to develop a baseline level of strength.
- To progress this exercise use additional loads attached to a waist or vest attachment.

Equipment
Bars (variations: weighted waist or vest attachment)

Aim
This is a downward press pattern exercise to work the chest, shoulders and triceps muscles.

Set-up
- Adopt a position on the dip bars with hands shoulder width apart.
- The arms should be extended, the legs bent and the chest high.
- Brace the core.

OTHER PRESSING EXERCISES

Vintage two hand get-up

The vintage two hand get-up is not a pressing drill, but was used to assess that there was adequate mobility in the shoulders and thoracic spine to perform overhead pressing drills. It was also used to develop the required core strength and stability to press heavy loads above the head. As shown in figure 4.5, a bar was held above the shoulders with arms extended in a supine position. The torso and bar were then lifted to an upright seated position, by using the core and hip flexors. Moving into this position not only required good core strength, but also a good efficiency with the lower body to stabilise the hips and legs to provide a solid foundation. The upright, seated position also requires mobility at the hips (hamstrings) and upper torso to be able to hold the load above the shoulders and hips. Discomfort in this position will be an indicator of potential issues when performing overhead press exercises in a standing position.

Windmill

The windmill is not a pressing drill either but is a fantastic preparation exercise to develop lateral core and hip mobility and stability, required in single arm overhead press exercises, such as the vintage press, the side press or the bent press. Whereas the majority of modern weightlifting exercises are sagittal plane dominant, this drill will be very effective in making the body stronger in the frontal plane. This exercise is described in detail in chapter 10.

Barbell bench press – wide grip

The wide grip bench press is usually the preferred technique used by individuals performing the supine press in modern gyms. The wide grip

Figure 4.5 Vintage two-hand get-up

position is a powerlifting technique, used because it is easier to extend the arms to lockout when wide (a shorter height for the bar to travel).

As mentioned earlier in this chapter, if you are a powerlifter then you should practise the techniques required in your sport. However, if you are not a powerlifter then the potential issues of using a wide grip (i.e. possible shoulder damage) would outweigh the possible benefits of better pectoralis recruitment. A narrower grip will still help to develop upper body strength, but without the horizontal extension stress placed on the shoulder because of the scapula immobility.

Barbell inclined bench press

The inclined bench press will preferentially recruit the clavicular portions of the pectoralis major, while the horizontal and downwards pressing drills will recruit the sternal portions. For certain sports and occupations, the inclined bench press will have a better correlation with performance than the flat horizontal version. Examples of this would be a shot putter or SWAT member, because of the movements required in this sport or occupation. Keep the angle of the bench at about 30 degrees for pectoral recruitment, as above this it becomes more of a deltoid exercise.

PULL PATTERN

5

The pull pattern is an upper body movement pattern that is characterised by a movement of the hands towards the shoulders. It usually involves pulling an object towards the shoulders or chest (such as a row), or pulling the torso to an object (as in a chin-up). In everyday life it is used to climb a rope or tree, to saw wood in half, to lift a heavy object up using a pulley and to link with the lift muscles to pull an object onto the chest or shoulders. The pull pattern is antagonistic to the press pattern and thus should always be trained in balance with its opposite.

The pull pattern can be broken down into three primary groups:

1. Vertical upwards pull (lifting a weight up to the shoulders)
2. Vertical downwards pull (pull up)
3. Horizontal pull (sawing wood)

There are of course the diagonal downwards, diagonal upwards and the intermediary angles of pull as well, but we tend to usually limit the classification to one of the three primary groups.

It is important that all three of these movements are trained within the pull pattern, as different muscle groups and motor units will be activated depending on the vector. When a lat pull down is performed, a client may think they have a balanced programme because they are including a pull exercise to balance out the bench press action, but because of the different muscles worked with different pull vectors this is not the case. If we are pressing upwards, forwards and downwards, then the same must be repeated for the pull pattern. Training only one type of pull will be insufficient for optimal functional strength.

The pull pattern is important when climbing, particularly when the legs cannot provide any assistance, for example, when there are no

Figure 5.1 The pull pattern is used when sawing wood

Figure 5.2 Using the pull pattern to climb

foot holds on an overhang. This vertical downwards pull plays a very important part in exercise programming, since it is a movement that is very difficult to perform with freeweights. Many trainers will perform a variety of vertical upwards pull exercises, such as upright rows, high pulls, snatches, cleans, etc., but will not complement them with a downward pull action, such as a pull-up or lat pull down.

FUNCTIONS AND IMPORTANCE OF THE PULL PATTERN

All three types of the pull pattern (upwards, downwards and horizontal) have some link to performance. Pulling upwards and pulling downwards demonstrate a positive correlation to increased performance with increased strength, while horizontal pulling relates to improving stability and function at the shoulder and scapula. A variety of sports require strength in the pulling muscles such as judo, wrestling or the luge, or in occupations such as the fire service or the armed services (specifically soldiers).

Upwards pulling links with the lift pattern required to perform Olympic weightlifting movements, and has a high correlation (or carryover) with sports performance. One of the primary aspects of successful performance in many sports is the need to develop power (the product of force multiplied by velocity). In order to recruit the maximum number of motor units, complex multijoint exercises that allow maximal force generation in minimal time have formed the cornerstone of training exercises used by strength and conditioning specialists. The Olympic lifts (the snatch, clean and jerk), modified Olympic lifts (power clean and power snatch) and Olympic pulls (clean pulls and snatch pulls) are the major chosen resistance training exercises for developing power in many athletes from a plethora of different sports.

The potential benefits of including Olympic weightlifting within a resistance training programme include:

- Increased absolute strength
- Increased relative strength
- Increased power (explosive strength)
- Improved vertical jump
- Improved speed (acceleration between 0–5 metres, speed between 0–30 metres)
- Improved grip strength
- Improved body composition
- Low incidence of injuries in weightlifting
- Improved pulling, pressing, lifting and squatting ability and integration between these human movement patterns
- Strength and power carryover to sports performance

Below is a selection of articles and research that back up some of the potential benefits to including Olympic weightlifting in a resistance training programme:

- Weightlifting has been shown to improve vertical jump height and thus athletic performance (Hori, Newton & Nosaka, 2005; Waller, Townsend & Gattone, 2007).
- The kinematics (how the body moves) and kinetics of the Olympic lifts have been shown to be notably similar to vertical jumping (Canavan, Garrett and Armstrong, 1996).
- Vertical jump peak power (the highest power reached) has been shown to be strongly associated with weightlifting ability (Carlock et al, 2004).
- Ground reaction forces (forces exerted on the ground) were comparable between countermovement vertical jump and the snatch (Garhammer and Gregor, 1992).
- Kinematic similarities between the hang clean and vertical jump may account for the training transfer between the two (Burkhardt and Garhammer, 1988).
- When comparing the hang clean with sprint performance, jump performance, and change of direction, there was significant correlation between the hang power clean and sprinting and jumping (Hori, Newton and Andrews, 2008).

There is also a good correlation between performance and pull-ups (downward pulling). The pull-up requires a different recruitment pattern to the lat pull down (since the body moves in the first, but the remains still in the second), so don't think, as many trainers do, that the two exercises

Figure 5.3 The pull pattern within the Olympic lifts

are interchangeable. The pull-up is undoubtedly the superior exercise, since this is the pattern that more closely replicates real-world pulling motions and has the greatest carryover to athletic and functional performance.

To clarify, pull-ups are performed with a pronated grip and chin-ups are performed with a supinated grip. The primary purpose of the pull-up is to develop increased strength in the vertical downwards pull category. Based on research (Signorile, Zink & Szwed, 2002) on hand grip position and motor unit recruitment, the wide pronated grip position to the chest would seem to elicit the greatest recruitment (in the latissimus dorsi), more than any other grip position in the concentric or eccentric phase (wide pronated grip behind the head, narrow semi-supinated grip or the medium supinated grip). This wider pronated grip would also recruit the more superior and anterior fibres of the latissimus dorsi, and the brachialis, brachioradialis and pronator teres of the arm. The narrower, supinated grip would recruit more of the lower fibres (or illiacus portion) of the latissimus dorsi and also the posterior deltoids; the biceps brachii would also be placed in a more biomechanically effective position.

So which position is best? Well it depends which muscles you want to develop, and also which motor units of the lats are weakest and need strengthening. One client could be strong in the wide pronated grip, while another is stronger in the narrower supinated grip. Varying the grip regularly within the programme will allow you to develop the complete motor pool of the latissimus dorsi, as well as the different elbow flexors. Variations to the pull-up or chin-up could include:

- Pronated grip – wide width
- Pronated grip – medium width
- Semi-supinated grip – wide width
- Semi-supinated grip – medium width
- Semi-supinated grip – narrow width
- Supinated grip – medium width
- Supinated grip – narrow width
- Pronated grip – wide width, climber technique (pull up diagonally towards one hand and alternate between reps)
- Split grip – medium width, one hand pronated, one hand supinated

LIMITING FACTORS FOR THE PULL PATTERN

The following list highlights the five common limiting factors for the pull movement pattern:

1. Poor upper body strength balance
2. Poor connection with core (weak lifting muscles)
3. Poor exercise selection
4. Weak grip
5. Shoulder and scapula dysfunction
6. Weak elbow flexors

To improve the function of the pull pattern, these limiting factors should be addressed, in addition to improving the strength of the pull and the range of pulling ability. For this movement pattern, this would also include integrating the pull pattern with the lift and rotation patterns.

1. POOR UPPER BODY STRENGTH BALANCE

Poliquin (2006) believes that an optimal pull:press ratio can be calculated using the supinated grip chin-up (the pull portion) and the biacromial grip width barbell bench press (the press portion). He states that the chin-up should be 87 per cent of the load for the bench press (weight calculated as bodyweight plus external load). As long as the repetition max is the same these exercises can be compared whether it is 1RM:1RM or down to 6RM:6RM.

Boyle (2004) in comparison looks at the maximal number of bodyweight supinated grip chin-ups that can be performed. Males should be able to achieve 10–15 reps (high school level), with 15–20 a collegiate level, 20–25 being national calibre and 25+ scoring world class. For females a score of 3–5 minimum is ideal (high school level), with 5–10 a collegiate level, 10–15 being national calibre and 15+ scoring world class. This will be fine for the average athlete or person, but strength and power athletes (who are better trained for heavier loads, not necessarily higher rep ranges), may struggle with multiple reps but may be able to perform 2–3 reps with considerable weight attached to them.

According to Kinakin (2004) weaknesses in the upper back muscles will present as:

- An anterior head position (upper trapezius weakness)
- A rounded shoulder posture, scapula protraction and kyphosis (middle trapezius weakness)
- Elevated and protracted shoulders, with difficulty in depressing the scapula when the arm is overhead or pulling down (latissimus dorsi weakness)

2. POOR CONNECTION WITH CORE (WEAK LIFTING MUSCLES)

For many of the pulling exercises described later in this chapter, it is important that there is sufficient strength or strength-endurance in the lifting muscles to maintain an optimal posture or technique. For the horizontal cable rope row, these muscles must maintain a stable base so that the upper body can pull effectively. For the suspension system row, these same lifting muscles must maintain the hips in an extended position to keep the body in a straight line. Whether it is keeping the legs aligned in a pull-up, the back neutral for a single arm row or the connection between the core for an Olympic pull, the core (specifically the posterior core) must function well to allow the agonist pulling muscles to produce the force in a real world situation.

3. POOR EXERCISE SELECTION

There must be sufficient training on the back to balance out the pressing strength training undertaken. Many trainers and clients focus on an excessive amount of pressing exercises within their programme, which will cause the development of muscle imbalances over time. This may be due to focusing on 'mirror muscles', which are the muscles on the anterior of the body, while neglecting those muscles on the posterior side. It may also be due to the bodybuilding concept of training muscles and not movement patterns. Trainers are taught to include chest exercises, back exercise and shoulder exercises in programmes. A programme with three sets of chest press, three sets of lat pull down and three sets of shoulder press may seem balanced, but there is a ratio of six pressing to three pulling drills. Performing instead two sets of pulling upwards, two sets pulling downwards and two horizontal pulls would balance with presses in the same three vectors.

The other part of this limiting factor is the use of a common exercise to train the pulling muscles: the barbell bent over row. This is described by many as one of the best pulling exercises, but there are, in my opinion, some real issues with this drill. When performing the barbell bent over row the aim is to overload the lats, which usually requires quite a heavy load. However, the main limiting factor in this exercise is actually the ability of the core, in this case the spinal erectors, to hold a mid-deadlift position for the duration of the set. It is very common to see the back start to round or the torso become more upright, both indicating that the posterior core is fatiguing or that too heavy a load is being used. Most trainers would lower the weight in order to maintain a good technique, as we are normally taught.

However, this lighter load is probably not enough to reach an overload on the pulling muscles, and thus no adaptation will occur. So is the load the problem or the exercise itself? Functionally, when would you hold this mid-deadlift position for 40 seconds or longer? Even the Olympic lifts or their variations do not require you to hold this mid-lift position. Although the barbell bent over row is commonly grouped as one of the 'big' pulling exercises, it falls woefully short in functional carryover when compared to a pull-up, a barbell high pull or even the overload that can be achieved with a single arm (supported) dumbbell row.

4. WEAK GRIP

Just as with the lift pattern, the grip is probably one of the most commonly seen limiting factors for the pull pattern. Many individuals will find that it is their grip which fails when they are performing pull-ups. They are either unable to hold their weight (grip strength) or to hold on to the bar for the duration of the set (grip endurance). This is further worsened as the bar diameter increases, such as during fat grip pull-ups.

Performing grip-emphasised pulling exercises, such as fat grip dumbbell rows, fat grip pull-ups and supine pull-ups, and supplementary forearm and grip drills will help to correct this deficit.

5. SHOULDER AND SCAPULA DYSFUNCTION

To perform the pull pattern correctly, the shoulder and scapula stabilisers must be functioning optimally. This means that a client should have optimal shoulder mobility (in internal and external rotation) and thoracic mobility for flexion and extension. The muscles around the scapula must function well to allow the scapula to move (upwards, downwards or rotate) to accommodate the movement at the glenohumeral (shoulder) joint. Adhesions within the rotator cuff, or weakened trapezius or rhomboids, will limit ideal scapula movements and can lead to inflammation or impingement at the shoulder joint. Isolated strengthening work of any weak areas with supplementary exercises, as well as myofascial release work, using a foam roller or tennis ball, or through therapy, will help to limit these common issues.

6. WEAK ELBOW FLEXORS

The elbow flexors must be strong enough to assist in bringing the hands towards the shoulders, in whichever plane the pull is occurring. The biceps brachii, brachialis and brachioradialis will be preferentially recruited depending on the grip position adopted. For pull-ups, the biceps brachii will be in a position of biomechanical efficiency when the hand is supinated. The brachialis and brachioradialis will produce more force if the hand is semi-supinated (or neutral) or pronated. If the pronated or supinated pull-up variation is poor, it may be due to weakness in those specific elbow flexors. Supplementary exercises, such as EZ reverse curls, dumbbell Scott curls or seated inclined hammer curls, will allow a greater neural drive to these muscles, increasing the overload and subsequent strength adaptations. These strength increases can then be applied back into the 'more functional' pull pattern exercises.

PULL PATTERN EXERCISES
VERTICAL UPWARDS PULL

Exercise 5.1 Two arm upright row

Equipment
Dumbbells

Aim
This is a pull pattern exercise to work the upwards-pulling muscles (rhomboids, trapezius, deltoids and elbow flexors).

Set-up
- Assume a standing position, feet hip width apart.
- Hold the dumbbells in a pronated grip or semi-pronated position.
- Lift the chest to ensure a good back position and brace the core.

Execution
- Pull the dumbbells upwards, leading with the elbows.
- Bring the dumbbells up to about chest height, or lower if that feels uncomfortable.
- Briefly pause then slowly lower the dumbbells back to the start position, with the arms fully extended.
- Repeat for the prescribed number of repetitions.

Technical considerations
- Dumbbells are preferable to a barbell because they allow for a freer movement at the shoulder.
- Lifting the elbow above the shoulder, particularly in an internally rotated position, with limited freedom in movement (as would happen if using a barbell) may exacerbate shoulder impingement symptoms or may lead to shoulder issues.
- Variations include single arm dumbbell upright row, cable upright rows or the dumbbell high pull.

Exercise 5.2 Two arm diagonal upright row

(a)

(b)

Equipment
Cable rope

Aim
This is a pull pattern exercise to work the upwards-pulling muscles (rhomboids, trapezius, deltoids and elbow flexors).

Set-up
- Assume a standing position, feet hip width apart facing the cable column.
- Take hold of the cable rope with two hands and step back two paces.
- Hold the rope with the palms facing inwards and the thumbs on the top of the rope.
- Lift the chest to ensure a good back position and brace the core.

Execution
- Pull the rope diagonally upwards, leading with the elbows.
- Bring the rope up so that the hands are at chest height, or higher if possible.
- Limit the range of motion if that feels uncomfortable.
- Briefly pause then slowly lower the rope back to the start position, with the arms fully extended.
- Repeat for the prescribed number of repetitions.

Technical considerations
- The cable rope is preferable to a barbell because it allows for a freer movement at the shoulders.
- This exercise may exacerbate shoulder impingement symptoms. If so, avoid the exercise or modify to reduce the range of motion.
- Variations include single arm cable handle diagonal upright row, cable rope diagonal high pulls or the barbell high pull.

Exercise 5.3 Two arm cable diagonal high pulls

(a)

(b)

Equipment
Cable rope

Aim
This is a pull pattern exercise to work the upwards-pulling muscles (rhomboids, trapezius, deltoids and elbow flexors), and to link in with the lift pattern muscles (hip extensors and spinal erectors).

Set-up
- Assume a standing position, feet hip width apart facing the cable column.
- Take hold of the cable rope with two hands and step back two paces.
- Hold the rope with the palms facing inwards and the thumbs on the top of the rope.
- Lift the chest to ensure a good back position and brace the core.
- Flex forwards from the hips, keeping a neutral spine position.

Execution
- Extend the hips forcefully and pull the torso (shoulders) back.
- Pull the rope diagonally upwards, leading with the elbows, linking with the lift phase.
- Bring the rope up so that the hands are at chest height, or higher if possible.
- Limit the range of motion if it feels uncomfortable.
- Do not hold at the top, but extend the arms and control the load.
- Flex forward again and lower the rope back to the start position, with the arms fully extended.
- Reset the core and repeat for the prescribed number of repetitions.

Technical considerations

- This is a progression from the diagonal upright row, and is an easier version of the barbell high pull.
- Heavier loads can be used than for the upright row, due to the additional force provided by the lift muscles. Many people may find this variation better and more comfortable than the stricter upright row for shoulder impingement issues.
- Variations include single arm cable handle diagonal high pull or the barbell high pull.

Exercise 5.4 One arm high pulls

(a) (b)

Equipment

Sandbag (variations: kettlebell, dumbbell, cable handle, barbell)

Aim

This is a pull pattern exercise to work the upwards-pulling muscles (rhomboids, trapezius, deltoids and elbow flexors) and to link in with the lift pattern muscles (hip extensors and spinal erectors) with unilateral loading.

Set-up

- Assume a standing position, feet hip/shoulder width apart.
- Place the sandbag on the floor, just in front of the feet, and take hold with a single hand pronated grip.
- Adopt a deadlift position and limit knee bend to adequately load the posterior chain.
- Lift the chest to ensure a good back position and brace the core.

Execution

- Extend the hips and knees forcibly and aggressively.
- Pull the sandbag forcibly upwards, leading with the elbow and keeping the sandbag close to the body.
- Lift the sandbag up to about chest or head height, or lower if that feels uncomfortable.
- Do not hold at the top, but extend the arm and control the sandbag as it drops.
- Flex forward again and lower the sandbag back to the start position, with the arm fully extended.
- Reset the core and repeat for the prescribed number of repetitions.

Technical considerations

- This is a progression from the upright row, and allows the user to learn how to integrate the pull and lift patterns together. It is a good drill prior to teaching a dead snatch.
- The sandbag works well as an alternative because the load will shift as you move it.
- Variations include performing with a kettlebell, dumbbell, cable handle or barbell.

Exercise 5.5 One arm dead snatch

(a) (b)

Equipment

Sandball (variations: kettlebell, dumbbell, barbell)

Aim

This is a pull pattern exercise to work the upwards-pulling muscles (rhomboids, trapezius, deltoids and elbow flexors) and to link in with the lift pattern muscles (hip extensors and spinal erectors) with unilateral loading.

Set-up

- Assume a standing position, feet hip/shoulder width apart.
- Place the sandball on the floor and take hold with a single hand pronated grip.
- Adopt a deadlift position and limit knee bend to adequately load the posterior chain.
- Lift the chest to ensure a good back position and brace the core.

Execution

- Extend the hips and knees forcibly and aggressively.
- Pull the sandball forcibly upwards, leading with the elbow, and keeping the sandball close to the body.
- As the sandball accelerates upwards, punch upwards and forwards to flip the handle under the ball.
- In the finish catch position the ball should rest on the forearm with the arm extended above the head.
- Flex forward again and lower the sandball back to the start position, with the arm fully extended.
- Reset the core and repeat for the prescribed number of repetitions or time period.

Technical considerations

- This is a variation from the kettlebell version, which many people find uncomfortable when learning because of the banging on the forearm. The sandball is much easier on this area and is a good tool to progress into the kettlebell drill.
- The sandball also works well as an alternative because the load will shift as you move it.
- Variations include performing with a kettlebell, dumbbell or barbell (two hand or one hand).

Exercise 5.6 One arm (swing) high pulls

(a)

(b)

Equipment

Kettlebell

Aim

This is a pull pattern exercise to work the upwards-pulling muscles (rhomboids, trapezius, deltoids and elbow flexors) and to link in with the lift pattern muscles (hip extensors and spinal erectors) with unilateral loading.

Set-up

- Assume a standing position, feet about shoulder width apart, and the kettlebell facing forward on a position in line with the heels.
- Adopt a deadlift position and limit knee bend to adequately load the posterior chain.
- Lift the chest to ensure a good back position and brace the core.
- Extend the hips forcibly to lift the kettlebell.

Execution

- Allow the kettlebell to swing between the legs.
- Extend the hips and knees forcibly and aggressively.
- Pull the sandbag forcibly upwards, leading with the elbow and keeping the kettlebell close to the body.
- The bell should be projected upwards to about head height or above, with the arm bent at the elbow.
- As the bell becomes weightless, follow it downwards and guide it between the legs, just like the kettlebell one hand swing, and repeat.

Technical considerations

- This drill allows the user to learn how to integrate the pull and lift patterns together ballistically and continuously and is the prerequisite to teaching the kettlebell (swing) snatch.
- Variations include alternating arms after each repetition (use the hand-to-hand swing technique), adding a release at the top then catching on the way down, or progressing to the full (swing) snatch.

Exercise 5.7 One arm (swing) snatch

(a) (b)

Equipment

Kettlebell

Aim

This is a pull pattern exercise to work the upwards-pulling muscles (rhomboids, trapezius, deltoids and elbow flexors) and to link in with the lift pattern muscles (hip extensors and spinal erectors) in a continuous, ballistic method.

Set-up

- Assume a standing position, feet about shoulder width apart, and the kettlebell facing forward on a position in line with the heels.
- Adopt a deadlift position and limit knee bend to adequately load the posterior chain.
- Lift the chest to ensure a good back position and brace the core, and hold with one hand.
- Extend the hips forcibly to lift the kettlebell.

Execution

- Perform 1–2 one arm swings to initiate the snatch, rather than trying to lift it above the head straight from the floor.
- As the kettlebell falls from the peak of the swing, push the hips backwards so that the kettlebell swings between the legs.
- As the kettlebell become weightless, forcefully extend the hips and knees to create the force to elevate the kettlebell.
- The effort for the snatch should be twice as aggressive as for the one arm swing.
- As the kettlebell moves forward of the hips as part of the swing, pull upwards and backwards on the kettlebell as if starting a lawnmower.
- As the kettlebell accelerates upwards, punch upwards and forwards to flip the handle under the kettlebell.
- In the finish catch position, the kettlebell should rest on the forearm with the arm extended above the head.
- Drop the elbow and rotate the forearm so that the thumb rotates outwards, and the kettlebell rolls off of the forearm and into the standard one arm swing grip.
- Guide the kettlebell through the legs, to load the hips for the next snatch repetition and repeat.

Technical considerations

- This exercise is one of the events in kettlebell competitions. It is performed for 10 minutes (5 minutes each hand) to see how many repetitions the competitor can perform in this time, with the kettlebell held off the floor throughout.
- Develop good posterior chain strength and endurance prior to using the one arm snatch.
- Treat each snatch as a separate lift or repetition. Make sure you pause between each rep – release the grip and hold the arm extended for a second or two before undertaking the next rep.
- When first learning the one arm snatch, it may be easier to start off with a half snatch. The half snatch is essentially the same technique as the (swing) snatch described previously, but instead of performing the full eccentric phase, the kettlebell is lowered to the rack position on the chest then cast off into a swing between the legs.
- Variations include alternating arms after each repetition (use the hand-to-hand swing technique).

Exercise 5.8 One arm dead clean

(a)   (b)

Equipment
Kettlebell (variations: dumbbell, barbell)

Aim
This is a pull pattern exercise to work the upwards-pulling muscles (rhomboids, trapezius, deltoids and elbow flexors) and to link in with the lift pattern muscles (hip extensors and spinal erectors) with unilateral loading.

Set-up
- Assume a standing position, feet hip/shoulder width apart.
- Place the kettlebell on the floor, between the heels, and take hold with a single hand pronated grip.
- Adopt a deadlift position and limit knee bend to adequately load the posterior chain.
- Lift the chest to ensure a good back position and brace the core.

Execution
- Extend the hips and knees forcibly and aggressively.
- Pull the kettlebell forcibly upwards, leading with the elbow, and keeping the kettlebell close to the body.
- As the kettlebell gets to just over hip height, punch the handle upwards and inwards as if trying to uppercut your own chin.
- This should cause the kettlebell to 'roll' over the forearm into the finishing rack position. The elbow should be close to the body and just above the front of the hip.
- Hold briefly, then with either one or two hands (easier) lower the kettlebell to the start position between the feet and hold the dead position for 1–3 seconds before starting the next repetition.
- Reset the core and repeat for the prescribed number of repetitions or time period.

Technical considerations
- The dead clean means that there is no pre-loading eccentric phase, where elastic energy can be generated to help lift the kettlebell. As a result it will overload the pulling muscles more than the swing clean.
- The two kettlebell dead clean involves lifting two kettlebells, one in each hand, from the floor to the rack position. It is good for improving strength and co-ordination with kettlebells.
- Other variations include the two kettlebell alternating dead clean or the one hand dumbbell/barbell dead clean.

Exercise 5.9 (Swing) clean bottoms-up grip

(a)

(b)

Equipment
Kettlebell

Aim
This is a pull pattern exercise to work the upwards-pulling muscles (rhomboids, trapezius, deltoids and elbow flexors) and to link in with the lift pattern muscles (hip extensors and spinal erectors) in a continuous, ballistic method, with a heavy grip emphasis.

Set-up
- Assume a standing position, feet about shoulder width apart, and the kettlebell facing forward on a position in line with the heels.
- Adopt a deadlift position and limit knee bend to adequately load the posterior chain.
- Lift the chest to ensure a good back position and brace the core and hold with one hand.

Execution
- Swing the kettlebell between the legs then extend the hips and catch the kettlebell with the elbow bent and the forearm vertical.
- The handle should be about shoulder height in an upside down position (bottoms-up grip or pistol grip).
- The hand should be in a semi-supinated position.
- Squeeze the handle tightly to ensure the kettlebell does not flip over.
- Briefly hold then swing between the legs again, to load the hips for the next repetition and repeat.

Technical considerations
- This exercise is really good for improving grip strength when training with kettlebells. The thicker the handle, the harder it is.
- Add a squat or press after the clean with the kettlebell still in the bottoms-up position to add a further grip challenge.

Exercise 5.10 Vintage dead clean

(a)   (b)

Equipment
Dumbbell (variations: barbell, kettlebells)

Aim
This is a pull pattern exercise to work the upwards-pulling muscles (rhomboids, trapezius, deltoids and elbow flexors) and to link in with the lift pattern muscles (hip extensors and spinal erectors) with unilateral loading.

Set-up
- Assume a standing position, feet hip/shoulder width apart.
- Place the dumbbell on the floor at an angle to the outside of one foot, and take hold with a single hand pronated grip.
- Adopt a deadlift position and limit knee bend to adequately load the posterior chain.
- Lift the chest to ensure a good back position and brace the core.

Execution
- Extend the hips and knees forcibly and aggressively.
- Pull the dumbbell forcibly upwards, leading with the elbow, and keeping the dumbbell close to the body.
- Curl the dumbbell up on the last phase, keeping the elbow close to the body, until it finishes at shoulder height with the forearm vertical.
- Hold briefly, then lower the dumbbell to the start position.
- Reset the core and repeat for the prescribed number of repetitions or time period.

Technical considerations
- The dead clean means that there is no pre-loading eccentric phase, where elastic energy can be generated to help lift the dumbbell. As a result it will overload the pulling muscles more than the swing clean.
- Variations include the two dumbbell dead clean, the kettlebell dead clean or the barbell one hand dead clean.

Exercise 5.11 Two hand high pulls with chains from floor

(a)

(b)

Equipment

Barbell, chains

Aims

To work the pull and lift muscles in an explosive movement with progressive resistance; to teach the integration between the first pull and transition phases of the two hand barbell snatch.

Set-up

- Set up an Olympic bar with chains attached to the ends, outside of any plates used.
- Stand with feet about hip width apart.
- Adopt a deadlift position and grip the bar with a wide hook grip.
- Have the shoulders positioned over the bar.
- Keep the chest up, look forward and brace the core.

Execution

- Lift the bar up off the floor by pushing the ground away from you.
- The knees should move backwards and the shoulders should stay over the bar.
- As the bar passes the kneecaps, scoop the knees under the bar by pushing the hips forward and pulling the shoulders back.
- The bar should continue to move upwards through this transition phase.
- From this power position, jump upwards using the hips and legs, coming up onto the toes, and powerfully shrug.
- As the bar is moving up, allow the arms to bend.
- Allow the bar to reach about chest height then 'catch' the bar on the way down.
- Return to the start position and repeat.

Technical considerations

- High pulls allow you to develop speed-strength in the lift and pull patterns, without having to catch the bar in an overhead squat position.
- Chains added to the sides of the bar increase tension on the concentric phase with progressive resistance.
- Variations include one hand barbell high pulls with chains.

Exercise 5.12 Power clean with chains

(a)

(b)

(c)

(d)

Equipment
Barbell, chains

Aims
To work the pull, lift and squat muscles in a heavy, stable and explosive movement, with the addition of progressive resistance.

Set-up
- Stand with the feet about hip width apart.
- Adopt a deadlift position and grip with the bar with a hook grip, just wider than shoulder width apart.
- Have the shoulders positioned over the bar.
- Keep the chest up, look forward and brace the core.

Execution
- Lift the bar up off the floor by pushing the ground away from you.
- The knees should move backwards and the shoulders should stay over the bar.
- As the bar passes the kneecaps, scoop the knees under the bar by pushing the hips forward and pulling the shoulders back.
- The bar should continue to move upwards through this transition phase.
- From this power position jump upwards using the hips and legs, coming up onto the toes and powerfully shrug.
- As the bar is moving up, allow the arms to bend.
- Quickly pull yourself underneath the bar, as it moves upwards towards its peak.
- Drop into a shallow front squat position, catching the bar in the rack position and actively push up against the bar to slow its descent.
- Push up to a standing position, then return the bar to the start position and repeat.

Technical considerations

- The power clean is a total body strength and power combination exercise that focuses on the strength end of the power continuum.
- Keep the number of repetitions per set very low (maximum of 6) to ensure optimal acquisition of motor skills and to limit fatigue in the scapula stabilisers.
- Chains added to the sides of the bar increase tension on the concentric phase with progressive resistance.
- Variations include power clean from a hang position, split power clean or squat clean.

Exercise 5.13 Two hand power snatch parallel stance, high hang position

(a)

(b)

(c)

(d)

Equipment

Barbell

Aims

To work the pull, lift and squat muscles in a heavy, stable and explosive movement; to teach the second pull phase of the two hand barbell snatch from a high hang position, and the pull under and catch phases.

Set-up

- Stand with feet hip/shoulder width apart with the bar held with a wide hook grip.
- The barbell should be on the mid-upper thighs.
- Have the shoulders positioned over the bar at the start.
- Keep the chest up, look forward and brace the core.

Execution

- Jump upwards using the hips and legs, coming up onto the toes, and powerfully shrug.
- As the bar is moving up, allow the arms to bend.
- Quickly pull yourself underneath the bar as it moves upwards towards its peak.
- Drop into a shallow overhead squat position and actively push up against the bar to slow its descent.
- Push up to a standing position then return the bar to the start position and repeat.

Technical considerations

- The power snatch is a total body strength and power combination exercise that focuses on the speed end of the power continuum.
- Keep the number of repetitions per set very low (1–3) to ensure optimal acquisition of motor skills. Performing sets with high number of reps, such as 10–12 will mean that the technique will change as you fatigue.
- Variations include power snatch from the knees, low hang position or the floor.

Exercise 5.14 One hand high pulls parallel stance, from floor

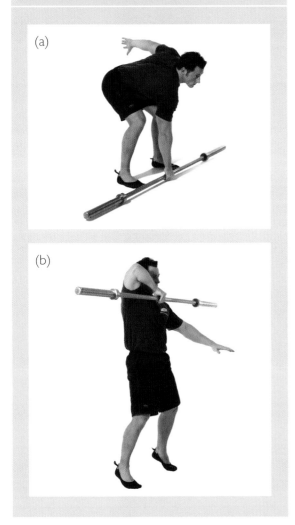

(a)

(b)

Equipment
Barbell (variations: dumbbell, kettlebell)

Aims
To work the pull and lift pattern muscles; to challenge the grip muscles, wrist and shoulder stabilisers.

Set-up
- Stand with the feet about hip width apart.
- Adopt a deadlift position and take hold of the centre of the bar with a single hand pronated grip.
- Have the shoulders positioned over the bar.
- Keep the chest up, look forward and brace the core.

Execution
- Lift the bar up off the floor by pushing the ground away from you.
- The knees should move backwards and the shoulders should stay over the bar.
- As the bar passes the kneecaps, scoop the knees under the bar by pushing the hips forward and pulling the shoulders back.
- Jump upwards using the hips and legs, coming up onto the toes, and powerfully shrug.
- Pull explosively upwards, keeping the elbow high.
- Allow the bar to reach about chest height then 'catch' it on the way down.
- Return to the start position and repeat.

Technical considerations
- This exercise is fantastic for improving both the grip strength on the lift and pull phases.
- Alternate hands with each repetition, or perform the whole set on one side to overload the grip endurance.
- Variations include dumbbell one hand high pulls, kettlebell (swing) high pulls, one hand barbell power snatch, or one hand high pulls with a fat grip.

Exercise 5.15 One hand power snatch parallel stance, from floor

(a)

(b)

Equipment

Barbell (variations: dumbbell, kettlebell)

Aims

To work the pull and lift pattern muscles; to challenge the grip muscles, wrist and shoulder stabilisers.

Set-up

- Stand with the feet about hip width apart (adopt the same start position as the high pull, p.162).
- Adopt a deadlift position and take hold of the centre of the bar with a single hand pronated grip (see figure (b) from the high pull, p.162).

- Have the shoulders positioned over the bar.
- Keep the chest up, look forward and brace the core.

Execution

- Lift the bar up off the floor by pushing the ground away from you.
- The knees should move backwards and the shoulders should stay over the bar.
- As the bar passes the kneecaps, scoop the knees under the bar by pushing the hips forward and pulling the shoulders back.
- The bar should continue to move upwards through this transition phase.
- From this power position, jump upwards using the hips and legs, coming up onto the toes, and powerfully shrug.
- As the bar is moving up allow the arm to bend.
- Quickly pull yourself underneath the bar as it moves upwards towards its peak.
- Drop into a shallow overhead squat position and actively push up against the bar to slow its descent.
- Push up to a standing position then return the bar to the start position and repeat.

Technical considerations

- This exercise is fantastic for improving both the grip strength on the lift and pull phases, but also for improving wrist stability for the catch.
- Alternate hands with each repetition, or perform the whole set on one side to overload the grip endurance.
- Keep the number of repetitions on the low side.
- Variations include dumbbell one hand dead snatch, dumbbell vintage swing, kettlebell dead snatch or one hand barbell snatch to windmill.

HORIZONTAL PULL EXERCISES

Exercise 5.16 Two hand bent over row

(a)

(b)

Equipment
Barbell

Aims
To work the pull pattern muscles in the horizontal plane; to challenge the lift pattern muscles to stabilise isometrically.

Set-up
- Stand with the feet about hip width apart.
- Adopt a deadlift position and take hold of the bar with pronated grip about shoulder width apart.
- Brace the core and lift the bar off the floor.

- Bend the knees slightly and bend forward from the hips so that the torso is between 45 degrees and horizontal.

Execution
- Pull the bar towards the upper abdomen/lower chest.
- Keep the elbows low and close to the body to maximally recruit the latissimus dorsi.
- As the bar touches the torso, briefly hold and squeeze the shoulder blades down and together.
- Lower the bar back to the start position slowly without fixing the scapula and repeat.
- Do not allow the legs or torso to move at all during the exercise.

Technical considerations
- The limiting factor for this exercise is the ability to hold a mid-deadlift position for the duration of the set. Commonly the legs will perform a mini squat to transmit momentum to the bar to help lift it, or the torso will round over as the spinal erectors fatigue.
- Keep the reps on the lower side (6–12) to keep the total time under tension down.
- Pulling the bar to the chest, with a wide grip and the elbows out, will recruit the retractors rather than the latissimus dorsi. The load will need to be lighter and the lever arm will be greater as the bar is further from the hips, further stressing the core stabilisers.
- The bar can be taken from a rack rather than lifting from the floor.
- This exercise is best performed one arm at a time, so that the other arm can support the torso, helping to allow a greater load to be lifted without the limiting factor of holding the mid-deadlift position.

Exercise 5.17 High rows to face

Equipment
Sled (variation: tyre)

Aims
To work the pull pattern muscles in the horizontal plane; to integrate with the lift pattern muscles of the lower body to provide a stable base.

Set-up
- Stand with the feet about hip/shoulder width apart facing the weighted sled.
- Ensure the straps are long enough and the weight appropriate so that the sled will not hit the shins.
- Grip the straps with the hands and step back until there is tension on them.
- Lean forward slightly from the hips, bend the knees and brace the body in preparation for the pull.

Execution
- Pull explosively backwards and upwards with the straps.
- Lift the elbows back high and pull the hands towards either side of the face.
- After the completion of the pull, step back until there's sufficient tension on the straps.
- Repeat for a prescribed number of repetitions, a set distance or duration.

Technical considerations
- This exercise allows a full concentric horizontal pull to be performed without having to slow down at the end of the concentric phase.
- It is a concentric-only exercise without the normal eccentric loading.
- Grip the ends of the straps, rather than having the loop round the wrist or use a SAQ® Milokit instead of the straps if preferred.
- Variations include one hand sled high rows, two hand sled high pulls, two hand sled rows.

Exercise 5.18 Low rows

Equipment
Sled (variation: tyre)

Aims
To work the pull pattern muscles in the horizontal plane; to integrate with the lift pattern muscles of the lower body to provide a stable base.

Set-up
- Stand with the feet about hip/shoulder width apart facing the weighted sled.
- Ensure the straps are long enough and the weight appropriate so that the sled will not hit the shins.
- Grip the straps with the hands and step back until there is tension on them.
- Lean forward slightly from the hips, bend the knees and brace the body in preparation for the pull.

Execution
- Pull explosively backwards with the straps, keeping the elbows close to the latissimus dorsi.
- Have the hands in a semi-supinated position during the pull, and keep the shoulders down.
- After the completion of the pull, step back until there's sufficient tension on the straps.
- Repeat for a prescribed number of repetitions, a set distance or duration.

Technical considerations
- This exercise allows a full concentric horizontal pull to be performed without having to slow down at the end of the concentric phase.
- It is a concentric-only exercise without the normal eccentric loading.
- Grip the ends of the straps, rather than having the loop round the wrist, or use a SAQ® Milokit instead of the straps if preferred.
- Variations include one hand sled low rows – place the other hand on the hips during the pull.

Exercise 5.19 Standing horizontal rows

(a)

(b)

Equipment

Cable rope (variation: sat on a step or bench)

Aims

To work the pull pattern muscles in the horizontal plane; to integrate with the lift pattern muscles of the lower body to provide a stable base.

Set-up

- Position the cable rope attachment at about mid-abdomen height with a heavy load.
- Stand with the feet about hip/shoulder width apart facing the cable column.
- Grip the cable rope with both hands and step back about two to three paces.
- Bend the knees and hips to adopt a slight squat and sit back to counterbalance the weight on the stack.
- Brace the body in preparation for the pull.

Execution

- Pull the hands backwards, keeping the elbows close to the body and the shoulders pulled down.
- At the completion of the pull, briefly hold and squeeze the shoulder blades down and together.
- Extend the arms back to the start position slowly without fixing the scapula and repeat.
- Do not allow the legs or torso to move at all during the exercise.
- Repeat for a prescribed number of repetitions.

Technical considerations

- Reach fully forwards during the eccentric phase and allow the scapula to move apart. This will ensure optimal recruitment of the latissimus dorsi.
- This exercise can be performed with one arm at a time, with the other hand placed on the side of the hips.
- This exercise can also be performed in a seated position with the feet on the floor or on a step to brace and resist the natural pull forward of the weight.

Exercise 5.20 Renegade row

(a)

(b)

Equipment
Dumbbells (variation: step, Powerbag™)

Aims
To work the pull pattern muscles in the horizontal plane; to challenge the anterior and lateral core, hips and shoulders to provide a stable base.

Set-up
- Adopt a prone plank position with the hand on the two dumbbells and the palms facing inwards (semi-supinated).
- Have the dumbbells directly under the shoulders, keeping the shoulders pulled down, away from the ears.
- Ensure the ankles, knees, hips and shoulders are in a straight line and the spine is neutral.
- Squeeze the elbows in to help activate the scapula stabilisers and brace the body in preparation for the pull.

Execution
- Row one arm into the body as you push strongly into the resting dumbbell.
- Strongly contract the glutes and abdominals to prevent a shifting through the hips. Briefly hold then lower the dumbbell back down to the floor, reset and repeat on the other side.
- Keep the hips level so that the weight is even into both knees, and press down strongly into the dumbbell on the floor.
- Repeat for a prescribed number of repetitions.

Technical considerations
- The renegade row is a great exercise that not only works the muscles of the back, the latissimus dorsi, erector spinae and rhomboids, but will also demand stability and control of the glutes, obliques and anterior core muscles.
- Support the lower body on the balls of the feet, having feet wider than the hips to make it easier to balance.
- This exercise can be performed with one arm at a time, with the other hand placed on an elevated surface, such as a step or Powerbag™.
- Rotation through the torso will create an excessive strain on the lower wrist and demonstrates a weak core. The challenge is to maintain a neutral alignment and counteract the rotational forces of lifting one dumbbell up.
- Shifting in the hips will commonly expose a weakness with the core and hip stabilisers, and will create a faulty loading pattern.
- Rounding through the back or hunching in the shoulders will present in those with weak lower trapezius or rhomboids. As these muscles fatigue, the upper trapezius will start to compensate causing this deviation in the upper back.

Exercise 5.21 Single arm high elbow pull

(a)

(b)

Equipment
Cable handle

Aims
To work the pull pattern muscles in the horizontal plane, specifically the retractors and posterior deltoid muscles.

Set-up
* Position the cable handle attachment at about chest height with a moderate load.
* Adopt a split stance facing the cable column, with the opposite leg forward.
* Grip the cable handle with one hand and step back to ensure sufficient space for the complete range of motion (ROM).
* Have the arm extended and brace the body in preparation for the pull.

Execution
* Pull the hand backwards along a horizontal line, with the elbow high and out to the side.
* Ensure the shoulder is kept down (no hitching up) and the elbow is slightly lower than the shoulder.
* Keep the chest up and squeeze the shoulder blade back to ensure maximal retraction.
* At the completion of the pull, briefly hold then slowly extend the arm back to the start position.
* Repeat for a prescribed number of repetitions.

Technical considerations
* Reach fully forwards during the eccentric phase and allow the scapula to move apart.
* The load for this exercise will be significantly lower than close grip pulls, because the lats will only be slightly used, and the focus is more on

the upper back muscles between the shoulder blades.

- Because these are postural muscles with a greater proportion of slow twitch fibres, perform with a strength endurance rep range of 12–20.
- Variations include: one arm pull with ipsilateral split stance (same leg forward); one arm pull with parallel stance; two arm high elbow pull with parallel or split stance; two arm alternating high elbow pull and slight diagonal downwards or upwards pull.

Exercise 5.22 Single arm row

(a)

(b)

Equipment
Dumbbell

Aims
To work the pull pattern muscles in the horizontal plane, in a stable, supported position with increased neural drive to one side.

Set-up

- Lift a single dumbbell up and adopt a split stance.
- Bend over so that the torso is near horizontal and support the torso by placing the lead forearm on the lead thigh.
- The dumbbell should be off the floor with the palm facing inwards.
- Brace the core in preparation for the pull.

Execution

- Pull the dumbbell towards the side of the ribcage.
- Keep the elbow low and close to the body to maximally recruit the latissimus dorsi.
- As the dumbbell touches the torso, briefly hold and squeeze the shoulder blades down and together.
- Lower the dumbbell back to the start position slowly without fixing the scapula, and repeat.
- Do not allow the legs or torso to move at all during the exercise.

Technical considerations

- For more of a grip emphasis, either use some Fat Gripz™, a barbell or using a dumbbell, or kettlebell you can drop from the top and catch them in midflight before the weight hits the floor.
- Keep the reps on the lower side (6–12) to keep the total time under tension low.
- Pulling the dumbbell to the chest, with a wide grip and the elbows out, will recruit the retractors rather than the latissimus dorsi. The load will need to be lighter and the lever arm will be greater as the dumbbell is further from the hips, further stressing the core stabilisers.
- This exercise is best performed one arm at a time, so that the other arm can support the torso, helping to allow a greater load to be lifted without the limiting factor of holding the mid-deadlift position.
- Variations include: parallel stance with hand/arm support on thigh; parallel stance with hand/arm support on bench and single arm row with knee and arm on bench. This is the most stable position, which will usually allow the heaviest load to be lifted and requires the least stability through the hips and core.

Exercise 5.23 Suspension system row with close grip

(a) (b)

Equipment
Two-strap suspension system, bodyweight

Aims
To work the pull pattern muscles in the horizontal vector, specifically the latissimus dorsi, biceps, the scapular stabilisers (rhomboids and trapezius), the grip muscles and the posterior chain muscles for stability (glutes, hamstrings and erector spinae).

Set-up
- Connect the two-strap suspension system to the anchor points, ideally at least 6ft high and about shoulder width apart.
- Stand facing the anchor points and hold one handle in each hand, with a semi-supinated grip (palms facing inwards).
- Brace the core and lean back so that the arms are extended and the body is straight and rigid.
- Move the feet forward or backwards to achieve the optimal level of intensity.

- Place an object against the feet, if required, to prevent sliding.

Execution
- Pull the chest towards the hands by flexing the arm and keeping the elbows close to the body, and maintaining the semi-supinated grip throughout.
- Hold briefly at the completion of the pull, and then slowly lower back to the start position.
- Maintain a rigid body position throughout the exercise, keeping the head in line with the spine and preventing chin-poking.
- It may help technique acquisition to breath in during the concentric phase.

Technical considerations
- Avoid fixing the scapula or executing the pull with a retraction, and allow the retraction to occur naturally as part of the pull.
- Avoid the shoulders lifting up during the pull (scapula elevation).
- Avoid the hips sagging (flexing) at the end of the eccentric phase.
- Move the feet further away from the anchor point to decrease the intensity.
- Move the feet closer to the anchor point, or underneath and beyond the anchor point (if possible) or elevate the feet off the ground (against a wall or up on a bench), so that the body is horizontal or angled, all of which will increase the intensity.
- Lifting one foot off the ground will increase the instability making the exercise more challenging from a balance perspective.
- Variations include supinated grip, pronated grip, split grip, and pronated-to-semi-supinated grip.

DOWNWARD PULL EXERCISES

Exercise 5.24 Pull-ups with fat grips, wide pronated grip

(a)

(b)

Equipment
Bars, Fat Gripz™ (variations: weighted belt or vest)

Aims
To work the pull pattern muscles in the vertical downward vector (latissimus dorsi, biceps) with one of the primary pull exercises, and with the additional overload of a fat grip to improve hand and forearm strength.

Set-up
- Place the Fat Gripz™ over a pull-up bar, wider than shoulder width apart.
- Have the opening of the Fat Gripz™ facing you, so they can be held in the palms.
- Take hold of the grips with a pronated grip (hands facing away).
- Hang from the bar with the arms extended and allow the scapula to elevate.
- The torso should be in line with the upper arms.
- Inhale and brace the core.

Execution
- Draw the elbows back and down, lifting the chest to the bar.
- Ensure the torso and legs remain in line and avoid any 'kicking up' of the knees.
- Continue to pull the body up until the chin clears the bar.
- The torso will naturally lean back slightly as you pull up.
- Focus on accelerating on the ascent.
- Hold briefly at the top, and then slowly lower the body by extending the arms.
- Exhale during the descent, and fully extend the arms until the torso is upright again and the scapula are elevated.

- Repeat for the prescribed number of repetitions.

Technical considerations

- The number of repetitions that can be performed (bodyweight or loaded) is always significantly decreased when using a fat grip. This may mean less overload for the pulling muscles in the short term, but will provide a greater overload on the hand and forearm muscles responsible for grip strength and endurance. These will improve with this overload, helping to optimise any agonist-synergist strength imbalances.
- Using wrist straps on this exercise would defeat the point of using a fat grip.
- Add additional weight when appropriate using a belt or vest.

Exercise 5.25 Chin-ups with semi-supinated grip

(a)

(b)

Equipment

Cable rope (variations: vest or waist attachment)

Aims

To work the pull pattern muscles in the vertical downward vector (latissimus dorsi, biceps) with one of the primary pull exercises, and with the additional overload of weight using cable resistance and a vest attachment.

Set-up

- Put on a vest or waist attachment and connect to two low cable attachments with a low-moderate load.
- Take hold of the grips with a semi-supinated grip (palms facing inwards).
- Hang from the bar with the arms extended and allow the scapula to elevate.
- The torso should be in line with the upper arms.
- Inhale and brace the core.

Execution

- Draw the elbows back and down, lifting the chest to the bar.
- Ensure the torso and legs remain in line, and avoid any 'kicking up' of the knees.
- Keep the head in line with the spine and avoid chin-poking.
- Continue to pull the body up until the chin clears the bar. The torso will naturally lean back slightly as you pull up.
- Focus on accelerating on the ascent.
- Hold briefly at the top, and then slowly lower the body by extending the arms.
- Exhale during the descent, and fully extend the arms until the torso is upright again and the scapula are elevated.

- Repeat for the prescribed number of repetitions.

Technical considerations

- The vest or waist attachment allows a load to be progressively applied to the chin-up as strength increases. This method is more comfortable than using a dumbbell between the feet and also prevents the increased lordosis and anterior pelvic tilt that occurs if weight plates are attached to a weights belt.
- Wrist straps can be used by individuals with very weak grip/forearm strength in order to allow overload of the agonist muscles, which would otherwise be limited by this muscle imbalance. However, continued use of the straps will not help this muscle strength balance to be optimised, and would in fact probably only make matters worse.
- Variations include supinated grip, medium pronated grip or split grip.

Exercise 5.26 Single arm pull in plank

(a)

(b)

Equipment
Cable handle

Aims
To work the pull pattern muscles in the vertical downward vector; to challenge the anterior and lateral core, hips and shoulders to provide a stable base.

Set-up
- Adopt a prone plank position with the head facing the cable column, and sufficient space to allow the arm to extend forwards (upwards) to the weight stack.

- Attach a cable handle to a low point on the column and apply a moderate load.
- Lift one hand off the ground and take hold of the cable handle.
- Ensure the ankles, knees hips and shoulders are in straight line and the spine is neutral.
- Squeeze the elbows in to help activate the scapula stabilisers and brace the body in preparation for the pull.

Execution
- Row one arm down into the body as if performing a one arm lat pull down.
- Strongly contract the glutes and abdominals to prevent a shifting through the hips. Briefly hold then extend the arm back to the start position.
- Keep the hips level so that the weight is even into both knees and press down strongly into the hand on the floor.
- Repeat for a prescribed number of repetitions.

Technical considerations
- This will challenge the anterior core, shoulder and hip stabilisers, and thus will mean that less load will be lifted than with a more stable one arm lat pull down.
- This exercise can also be performed lying on the back, which allows a much heavier load to be used. The other arm should brace against a solid object to stop you getting pulled along the floor.
- Variations also include performing the one arm pull in a kneeling position. This is a great exercise and will also provide a great overload for the lateral core muscles if applied with a slight oblique crunch at the same time.

OTHER PULL EXERCISES

Vintage one hand barbell clean

This exercise allows the user to move the barbell from the floor to a position by the shoulder. When strongmen performed this exercise the barbell would have been moved above the head using the side press, bent press or jerk methods. Once above the head it could then be used for a windmill or a one hand overhead squat. However, this wasn't a worldwide method, with many tilting the barbell onto one end and then rolling it onto the shoulder.

To perform the vintage one hand barbell clean, adopt a dead clean lifting position with a supinated grip on the barbell with the hand facing forwards. Perform a combination lift and bicep curl to bring the bar to the shoulder. From there the bar can be rotated round so that the palm is facing forwards again and is in the correct position for the bent press or side press.

Lat pull down

Position the seat directly beneath the pulley, so that you can pull the bar straight down towards the top of the sternum. Lean back slightly as you pull and keep the forearms vertical throughout the exercise. Rotating the forearms will excessively stress the medial rotators of the shoulder, potentially leading to rotator cuff adhesions, inflammation or dysfunction. Allow the scapula to move freely, both on the eccentric and concentric phases and avoid 'fixing' the scapula in place. Keep the chest up and avoid flexing at the spine to get the bar down. This usually indicates that the spinal flexors at the core are trying to compensate for comparably weaker latissimus dorsi or elbow flexor muscles.

Perform the lat pull down only to build strength in the latissimus dorsi muscles so that this strength can then be applied in a more functional bodyweight pull up or weighted pull-up exercise.

Supine pull-up

The supine pull-up, also known as inverted rows, is a bodyweight pull-up performed in the horizontal plane. The individual lies underneath the bar, suspended at about hip height on a squat rack or Smith machine. The hips are lifted off the ground so that the body is straight and rigid, and the chest is pulled up to the bar, commonly using a wide pronated grip.

Because this wide grip horizontal pull will work the antagonistic muscles to the bench press, it is often used as a postural correction exercise. It is preferable to train these muscles, and this exercise, for strength endurance (12+ reps) rather than pure strength because of their fibre make-up and function. Boyle (2004) uses the inverted row as a method of assessing for potential issues relating to the rotator cuff (as a result of a weak upper back), particularly for swimmers, tennis players and other throwing athletes. Using his target scores, female clients should aim for a minimum of 5RM (10–15 being national standard and 15+ being world class), while males should aim for a minimum of 15RM (20–25 being national standard and 25+ being world class).

ROTATION PATTERN

6

The rotation pattern is a core dominant movement pattern that is characterised by a movement of the torso in the transverse plane. It is one of the four basic functions of the torso musculature (Boyle, 2004) alongside stabilisation, lateral flexion and flexion. Boyle (2004) suggests that the majority of programmes should commence with stabilisation work in all three positions (quadruped, kneeling and standing), and that programmes should focus less on flexion and extension work and more on rotational and lateral flexion drills, since these are less trained by most individuals.

The rotation pattern is hugely important for numerous sports including golf, baseball, tennis, squash and cricket, and for everyday tasks like throwing an object over a wall, throwing a ball and chopping down a tree.

The pattern consists of three movements:

1. Horizontal rotation
2. Diagonal downwards rotation
3. Diagonal upwards rotation

The diagonal rotation movements are actually antagonistic, while the horizontal rotation movement towards the left or right are also antagonistic. Over recent years it has become clear to many trainers that the rotation pattern, and therefore the transverse plane, is one of the most neglected movement patterns performed by gym users. Many of the traditional fixed path and freeweight exercises are sagittal-plane dominant, so people can neglect this plane and its associated movements. Just as with the other movement patterns, such as the pull and press, it is important that all three of these movements are trained, as different muscle groups and motor units will be activated depending on the vector.

In addition to these movement patterns, the ability to control undesirable movement (to stabilise) against rotation – known as counter rotation – is also highly important. Lifting one hand off the ground when performing a supine plank, for example, is a counter rotation exercise, which will work selected rotational muscles despite the fact that no rotation is seen.

This movement pattern can be performed with freeweights, but one of the best functional tools to train this pattern is the cable column, since the angle of pull is more horizontal, and thus is not affected by gravity like other tools are.

The rotation pattern links with the lift and smash patterns to form a complete spectrum of movement.

- The lift pattern is a pure sagittal extension from flexion.
- The diagonal upwards rotation is effectively a combined lift and rotation.
- This then leads to pure horizontal rotation.
- The diagonal downwards rotation is effectively a combined rotation and smash.
- This then leads to pure sagittal flexion, which is the smash pattern.

Some trainers believe that a woodchop (diagonal downwards rotation) and reverse woodchop (diagonal upwards rotation) are interchangeable, but this is obviously not the case, considering that different muscles are responsible for these movements.

LIMITING FACTORS FOR THE ROTATION PATTERN

There are two common limiting factors for the rotation movement pattern:

1. Poor hip mobility
2. Poor thoracic mobility

To improve the function of the rotation pattern, these limiting factors should be addressed, in addition to improving the strength of the rotation and the range of rotational ability. Such improvement can only occur through integration of the rotation pattern with the lift, smash, pull and press patterns.

1. POOR HIP MOBILITY

Many trainers will teach rotation drills, such as the cable horizontal rotation (or Russian twist), with a fixed pelvis so that rotation occurs in the

Figure 6.1 Diagonal upwards rotation.

spine only. However, when performing a rotation in the real world, such as swinging a baseball bat or golf club, the rotators of the spine must link with the hip rotators to generate significant levels of force.

The hips must be able to rotate freely and without restriction through internal and external rotation, otherwise it will compromise the subsequent torso rotation. How this limitation presents will be influenced by whether it is the medial or lateral external rotators that are tight and in which direction the person is rotating. Performing self-myofascial release (SMFR) techniques with a foam roller and/or tennis ball on the muscles around the hips will help to ensure optimal range of motion.

2. POOR THORACIC MOBILITY

When performing any of the three rotational patterns, the load is almost always held with the hands. Therefore, when performing a rotation the range of motion that is achieved will be influenced by the mobility of the thoracic spine. A simple test to present this involves sitting up straight and rotating maximally in each direction. If the upper back rounds over (such as we see in clients with poor posture), and the test is repeated, the range of motion will be reduced. Clients with an excessive kyphotic curve will usually demonstrate limitations in rotation for this reason. Thoracic mobilisation techniques, including SMFR, will

Figure 6.2 Swinging a golf club relies on rotation in both the hips and the spine.

help to gain mobility in this region, which will translate to a more efficient and greater rotational range of motion.

ROTATION PATTERN EXERCISES
DIAGONAL UPWARDS ROTATION EXERCISES

Exercise 6.1 Reverse woodchop with cable bar

(a)

(b)

Equipment
Cable bar and handle (variation: cable rope)

Aim
This is a rotation pattern exercise to work the diagonal-upwards muscles (glutes, latissimus dorsi, internal and external obliques), as well as the associated hip and upper body muscles.

Set-up
*   Attach a long cable bar to a cable column, at a low point.
*   Assume a standing position, feet hip width apart, sideways on to the cable column.
*   Hold the cable bar with both hands in a wide pronated grip.
*   Lift the chest to ensure a good back position and brace the core.

Execution
*   Squat down and rotate towards the bottom of the cable column.
*   Drive upwards and across with the near hand.
*   Keep the far foot flat on the ground, but lift the near heel and pivot on the ball of the foot.
*   Rotate fully around; without pausing, slowly rotate back to the start position.
*   Repeat for the prescribed number of repetitions and then change sides.

Technical considerations
*   The cable bar attached only at one end is probably the most effective cable attachment for this exercise.
*   Ensure adequate thoracic and hip mobility by preceding this drill with SMFR techniques.
*   Variations include one arm cable handle reverse woodchop or cable rope reverse woodchop.

Exercise 6.2 Reverse woodchop with suspension system

(a)

(b)

Equipment
Two-strap suspension system

Aim
To work the rotation pattern muscles in a diagonal upwards vector in a parallel stance position.

Set-up
*   Connect the two-strap suspension system to the anchor points, ideally at least 6ft high and about shoulder width apart.
*   Stand facing anchor points; hold one handle with both hands, with a semi-supinated grip.
*   Brace the core and lean back so that the arms are extended and the body is straight and rigid.
*   Move the feet forward or backwards to achieve the optimal level of intensity.
*   Squat downwards, keeping arms extended forward.

Execution
*   Pull both hands up and over one shoulder, keeping the arms extended throughout.
*   Keep the elbows soft and use the core to drive the rotation.
*   Pause briefly then return back to start position and repeat on the other side.
*   Link the upwards phase of the squat and the rotation together in a smooth action.
*   Allow the heel of the foot on the opposite side to which you are rotating to lift during rotation.

Technical considerations
*   Adjust the feet closer to or further from the anchor point to achieve optimal tension throughout the entire range of motion.
*   Variations include single arm rotation or removing the squat phase.

Exercise 6.3 Reverse woodchop with plate

(a)

(b)

Equipment

Weight plate (variation: sandbag)

Aim

This is a rotation pattern exercise to work the diagonal-upwards muscles (glutes, latissimus dorsi, internal and external obliques), as well as the associated hip and upper body muscles.

Set-up

- Assume a standing position, feet hip width apart.
- Hold the weight plate with two hands.
- Lift the chest to ensure a good back position and brace the core.

Execution

- Squat down and rotate downwards, lowering the plate towards the outside of the calf on one side.
- Drive the plate upwards and across in the opposite direction, i.e. in a diagonal pattern.
- Keep the far foot flat on the ground, but lift the near heel and pivot on the balls of the foot.
- Rotate fully around.
- Without pausing slowly rotate back to the start position.
- Repeat for the prescribed number of repetitions and then change sides.

Technical considerations

- The weight plate works well since it is easy to grip and available in most training facilities.
- Ensure adequate thoracic and hip mobility by preceding this drill with SMFR techniques on these areas.
- Variations include a split stance, kneeling split stance or kneeling.

Exercise 6.4 Diagonal lift to shoulder

(a)

(b)

Aim

This is a rotation pattern exercise to work the diagonal-upwards muscles (glutes, latissimus dorsi, internal and external obliques), as well as the associated hip and upper body muscles.

Set-up

* Assume a standing position, feet hip width apart.
* Place the sandbag to the outside of one foot.
* Squat down and hold the sandbag with two hands.
* Lift the chest to ensure a good back position and brace the core.

Execution

* Drive upwards and across with the sandbag in a diagonal pattern.
* Lift the sandbag diagonally up and onto the opposite shoulder.
* Shrug the sandbag off the shoulder and rotate back to the start position.
* Repeat for the prescribed number of repetitions or duration and then change sides.

Technical considerations

* The sandbag will challenge both the grip and the core muscles because of the instability involved in the exercise.
* Ensure adequate thoracic and hip mobility by preceding this drill with SMFR techniques on these areas.
* This drill can be used as a rotation or lift pattern exercise, since it is a combination of the two.
* Variations include using a Powerbag™ or performing in a kneeling split stance.

Equipment

Sandbag (variation: Powerbag™)

Exercise 6.5 Thigh to thigh rotations

(a)

(b)

(c)

Equipment
Sandbag (variations: Powerbag™, medicine ball)

Aim
This is a rotation pattern exercise to work the diagonal-upwards muscles (glutes, latissimus dorsi, internal and external obliques), as well as the associated hip and upper body muscles.

Set-up
- Assume a standing position, feet hip width apart and squat down slightly.
- Hold the sandbag with two hands and rotate so that it rests on one thigh.
- Lift the chest to ensure a good back position and brace the core.

Execution
- Drive upwards and rotate to the middle, lifting the sandbag overhead.
- Rotate to the opposite side, lowering the sandbag until it reaches the opposite thigh.
- Repeat the process, lifting the sandbag over the head each time and rotating as you do so.
- Keep the feet flat on the ground and repeat for the prescribed number of repetitions or duration.

Technical considerations
- The sandbag will challenge both the grip and the core muscles because of the instability involved in the exercise.
- Ensure adequate thoracic and hip mobility by preceding this drill with SMFR techniques on these areas.
- Variations include using a Powerbag™ or medicine ball.

HORIZONTAL ROTATION EXERCISES

Exercise 6.6 Plank with leg sweep

(a)

(b)

Set-up
- Adopt a prone plank position with the arms extended and hands positioned beneath the shoulders.
- Lift the chest to ensure a good back position and brace the core.

Execution
- Lift one foot off the ground and sweep it underneath the other leg.
- Reach as far as possible with the foot, rotating the hips to do so.
- Bring the foot back to the full plank position and sweep the other leg.
- Repeat for the prescribed number of repetitions or duration.

Technical considerations
- Ensure adequate thoracic and hip mobility, by preceding this drill with SMFR techniques on these areas.
- Variations include using a hand raise.

Equipment
Bodyweight

Aim
This is a rotation pattern exercise to work the horizontal rotation muscles (internal and external obliques) as well as the associated hip and upper body muscles.

Exercise 6.7 Cable rotations

(a)

(b)

Equipment
Cable handle

Aim
This is a rotation pattern exercise to work the horizontal rotation muscles (internal and external obliques) as well as the associated hip and upper body muscles.

Set-up
- Attach a cable handle to a cable column, at about upper abdomen height.
- Assume a standing position, feet hip width apart, sideways on to the cable column.
- Hold the cable handle with both hands.
- Lift the chest to ensure a good back position and brace the core.

Execution
- Rotate towards the cable column, moving both the torso and hips.
- Drive the handle across the body with both hands.
- Keep the arms extended forwards and do not allow the elbows to bend.
- Rotate fully around.
- Briefly pause then slowly rotate back to the start position.
- Repeat for the prescribed number of repetitions and then change sides.

Technical considerations
- Imagine the arms form a triangle in front of the body, so that the torso initiates the movement rather than the arms.
- Ensure adequate thoracic and hip mobility by preceding this drill with SMFR techniques on these areas.
- Variations include single arm cable handle rotations, split stance rotations or split kneeling rotations.

Exercise 6.8 Standing rotations

(a)

(b)

Equipment

Powerbag™ (variations: sandbag, medicine ball)

Aim

This is a rotation pattern exercise to work the horizontal rotation muscles (internal and external obliques), as well as the associated hip and upper body muscles.

Set-up

- Assume a standing position, feet hip width apart.
- Hold the Powerbag™ in two hands in front of the body.
- Lift the chest to ensure a good back position and brace the core.

Execution

- Rotate towards one side, moving both the torso and hips.
- Drive the Powerbag™ across the body with both hands.
- Keep the arms extended forwards and do not allow the elbows to bend.
- Rotate fully around.
- Without pausing, rotate back to the start position.
- Repeat for the prescribed number of repetitions or duration and then change sides.

Technical considerations

- Imagine the arms form a triangle in front of the body, so that the torso initiates the movement rather than the arms.
- Ensure adequate thoracic and hip mobility by preceding this drill with SMFR techniques on these areas.
- Variations include split stance rotations, split kneeling rotations, single leg rotations and kneeling rotations. This exercise can also be performed with a sandbag or medicine ball.

Exercise 6.9 Rotation throw

(a)

(b)

Equipment
Sandball (variations: medicine ball, rebounder (mini trampoline))

Aim
This is a rotation pattern exercise to work the horizontal rotation muscles (internal and external obliques) to improve reactive strength as well as the associated hip and upper body muscles.

Set-up
- Assume a standing position, feet hip width apart, and squat down slightly.
- Stand facing a partner.
- Hold the sandball in two hands at about abdomen height.
- Lift the chest to ensure a good back position and brace the core.

Execution
- Rotate towards one side, moving both the torso and hips.
- Use this rotation to load the core muscles.
- Drive the sandball across the body and release to throw it forwards.
- Have your partner catch the sandball and throw it back.
- Catch the sandball, rotating as you do so, to load the core muscles again and repeat the process.
- Continue for the prescribed number of repetitions or duration, training both sides.

Technical considerations
- Perform alternating rotations or perform a set all on one side and then swap.
- Ensure adequate thoracic and hip mobility by preceding this drill with SMFR techniques on these areas.
- Variations include using a medicine ball against a wall or with a rebounder (mini trampoline).

Exercise 6.10 Seated rotations

(a)

(b)

Equipment
Kettlebell (variations: Powerbag™, medicine ball)

Aim
This is a rotation pattern exercise to work the horizontal rotation muscles (internal and external obliques) as well as the associated hip and upper body muscles. It will also recruit the stabilisers of the lower back and the hip flexors.

Set-up
- Assume a seated position with the legs slightly bent in front.
- Lift the chest to ensure a good back position and brace the core.
- Lean back, keeping the feet planted on the floor.
- Hold the kettlebell in both hands by the handle or by crushing the bell (a).

Execution
- Rotate towards one side, moving the torso and shoulders.
- Keep the kettlebell close to the body and rotate fully around.
- Without pausing, rotate back to the start position.
- Repeat for the prescribed number of repetitions or duration.

Technical considerations
- It is suitable for a range of individuals, but not those with a lower back weakness.
- Ensure adequate thoracic and hip mobility by preceding this drill with SMFR techniques on these areas.
- Variations include using a Powerbag™ or medicine ball.

Exercise 6.11 High bridge rotations

(a)

(b)

Equipment
Stability ball and dumbbell (variations: Powerbag™, medicine ball)

Aim
This is a rotation pattern exercise to work the horizontal rotation muscles (internal and external obliques) as well as the associated hip and upper body muscles.

Set-up
- Sit on top of a stability ball.
- Walk forwards and lean backwards until you reach a high supine bridge position. The head and upper back should be supported by the ball and the shins should be vertical.
- Hold a dumbbell in both hands with the arms extended straight up above the shoulders.
- Take a breath in and brace the core.

Execution
- Keeping the arms locked and forming a triangle, rotate the torso to one side.
- Rotate until the dumbbell is level with the chest.
- Briefly hold then rotate back to the start position.
- Repeat on both sides for the prescribed number of repetitions or duration.

Technical considerations
- Ensure adequate thoracic and hip mobility by preceding this drill with SMFR techniques on these areas.
- Keep the core braced and hips level throughout.
- Variations include using a Powerbag™ or medicine ball.

DOWNWARD ROTATION EXERCISES

Exercise 6.12 Judo throw

(a)

(b)

Equipment

Cable rope

Aim

This is a rotation pattern exercise to work the diagonal-downwards muscles (internal and external obliques), as well as the associated hip and upper body muscles.

Set-up

- Attach a cable rope to a cable column, at about shoulder height.
- Assume a standing position, feet hip width apart, sideways on to the cable column.
- Hold the cable rope with both hands.
- Lift the chest to ensure a good back position and brace the core.
- Rotate towards the cable column, moving both the torso and hips, and hold.

Execution

- Quickly rotate away from the cable column, pulling the rope towards the shoulder.
- Once the hands are on the chest, rotate fully around, pivoting on the foot.
- Push through with the shoulder and bend the back leg as if throwing a person.
- Crunch downwards as you rotate to the end position.
- Briefly pause then slowly rotate back to the start position.
- Repeat for the prescribed number of repetitions and then change sides.

Technical considerations

- Break the movement down into a pull, rotate and drop (the same technique for throwing a person over the leg in Judo for the bodydrop throw).
- Ensure adequate thoracic and hip mobility by preceding this drill with SMFR techniques on these areas.
- Variations include cable rope woodchop.

Exercise 6.13 Jackknife with rotation

(a)

(b)

Equipment
Suspension system

Aim
This is a rotation-flexion pattern exercise to work the diagonal-downwards muscles (internal and external obliques), the anterior core and hip flexors, as well as the shoulder stabiliser muscles.

Set-up
- Connect the two-strap suspension system to the anchor points, at about hip width apart, so that the straps are about 12–18in off the ground.
- Kneel on the floor facing away from the straps and place both feet into each of the straps.
- Lie on the chest, hips and knees on the floor.
- Move the body closer or further from the anchor points to achieve the optimal level of intensity.
- Brace the core and lift the hips and knees off the ground, keeping the body straight and rigid, into a prone plank position with the weight on the hands.

Execution
- Pull the knees diagonally forward towards one of the forearms.
- Try to achieve maximal hip and spinal flexion with rotation and briefly hold.
- Extend the legs back to the start position and then repeat, coming up and across to the opposite side.
- The hips should maintain their position in space without significantly rising or dropping.
- Repeat for the prescribed number of repetitions.
- Focus on keeping the chest up and the core braced, particularly at the start/finish position.

Technical considerations
- Keep the arms locked during the exercise.
- Avoid overarching the lower back, particularly at the start/finish position.
- Move the feet closer to the anchor points, or beyond the anchor point to decrease the intensity.
- Move the feet further away from the anchor points to increase the intensity.
- Variations include jackknife, jackknife with crunch or press-up to jackknife with rotation.

Exercise 6.14 Counter rotation

(a)

(b)

Equipment
Tornado ball

Aim
This is a counter rotation pattern exercise to work the stabilising muscles against rotation forces.

Set-up
- Assume a kneeling position and hold a tornado ball with both hands.
- Lift the chest to ensure a good back position and brace the core.

Execution
- Swing the tornado ball in a figure of eight pattern across the body and to each side.
- Maintain tension of the rope of the tornado ball throughout the drill.
- Repeat for the prescribed number of repetitions or duration.

Technical considerations
- Ensure adequate thoracic and hip mobility by preceding this drill with SMFR techniques on these areas.
- Variations include performing the exercise standing or seated.

SMASH PATTERN

7

The smash pattern is a core dominant movement pattern that is characterised by a flexion movement of the torso in the sagittal plane. It is one of the four basic functions of the torso musculature (Boyle, 2004) alongside stabilisation, lateral flexion and rotation. It has been used since primal times to smash objects downwards, such as a coconut onto a rock or a club onto an animal. In sports, it is seen in football during a throw in (figure 7.1).

The smash pattern is antagonistic to the lift pattern and is used to balance out the extensor strength of the posterior chain muscles. It is also important to control undesirable movement (to stabilise) against extension. When lifting a heavy load above the head it is crucial that the smash pattern muscles of the anterior core can stabilise and protect the spine.

The smash pattern is not as important as the lift or rotation patterns, but correct function in the smash is required when generating force downwards or forwards from above the head. This could be throwing an object forward or accelerating a hammer downwards. In comparison with associated movement patterns, such as the lift, you should dedicate a lower volume of exercise to this movement pattern. As a rough guide the lift pattern exercises should be approximately three to six times the volume of the smash pattern exercises, despite being antagonistic movements. This would have been the case in primal times, as it is today, as a caveman would have performed a considerable amount more lifting each day than smashing. This is also the reason why the posterior chain muscles responsible for lifting (the hamstrings, glutes and latissimus dorsi) are considerably larger than the smaller flexors (rectus abdominis and iliopsoas) responsible for the smash pattern.

Figure 7.1 The smash pattern is used during a throw-in in a football game

LIMITING FACTORS FOR THE SMASH PATTERN

The following list highlights the two common limiting factors for the smash movement pattern:

1. Poor hip flexor mobility
2. Poor thoracic mobility

To improve the function of the smash pattern, these limiting factors should be addressed, in addition to improving the strength of the flexor muscles and the functional range of smash pattern ability.

1. POOR HIP FLEXOR MOBILITY

In order for the smash pattern to develop force, the hip flexors must be mobile enough to allow for spinal extension to occur in order for the muscle spindles to be stimulated. When the arms are lifted above the head to throw a medicine ball forward or to slam a hammer downwards, the force generated will be dependant on this eccentric loading phase. If the hip flexors are tight then they will not allow the normal degree of extension to occur, effectively switching off the potential muscle activation. They may also cause the pelvis to be held in a constant anterior tilt, which will limit the extension available. This postural deviation is very common in a range of individuals nowadays – whether this is due to the prolonged seating position that people are predisposed to when driving or seated at a desk all day, or other reasons, is always up for debate. However, what is true is that when it comes to improving core flexion activation, mobilising the hip flexors seems to be of huge benefit to most people. This can be achieved with self-myofascial release (SMFR) or stretching, such as shown in the supplementary chapter.

2. POOR THORACIC MOBILITY

In addition to the hip flexors, the thoracic spine must also be able to flatten to allow for spinal extension to take place. If individuals present with an excessive kyphotic curvature, then their ability to reach above their heads is greatly reduced. Just as it will limit their ability to press overhead or rotate their arms back for squatting, it will also limit the potential for the extension to load the spinal flexors to generate force.

Thoracic mobilisation, like hip mobilisation, is of great benefit to most individuals who participate in training. Again the reasons for a fixed, or immobile, upper back can be quite varied, but most trainers will agree that it is a very common dysfunction. SMFR in particular, whether with a foam roller or a tennis ball, seems to be of huge benefit when trying to correct this fault. In addition, assessing the press:pull strength balance and treatments to work on adhesions within the rotator cuff muscles will also greatly help to improve the thoracic extension in most people.

SMASH PATTERN EXERCISES

Exercise 7.1 Slam onto tyre

Equipment
Tyre, hammer

Aims
This is a smash pattern exercise to work the rectus abdominis, hip flexors and upper body muscles with an unconventional training tool.

Set-up
- Assume a standing position, feet hip width apart, facing a tyre.
- Take hold of a hammer with both hands.
- Lift the chest to ensure a good back position and brace the core.

Execution
- Lift the hammer straight above the head and extend the core to load the smash pattern muscles.

- Without pausing, slam the hammer downwards towards the tyre. Hit the tyre with the side of the hammer.
- Control the hammer as it rebounds and use the momentum to help lift it up for the next repetition.
- Repeat for the prescribed number of repetitions.

Technical considerations
- When hitting a tyre, hold the hammer sideways on so that the flat side makes contact with the tyre, to limit the subsequent bounce.
- Ensure adequate thoracic and hip mobility by preceding this drill with SMFR techniques on these areas.
- Variations include alternating the hand position with each slam.

Exercise 7.2 Slam

(a) (b)

Execution

- Lift the sandball straight above the head and extend the core to load the smash pattern muscles.
- Without pausing, slam the sandball downwards towards the floor.
- Release the sandball at the appropriate point so that it lands just in front of the feet.
- Pick the sandball up and lift it up for the next repetition.
- Repeat for the prescribed number of repetitions.

Technical considerations

- A sandball is preferable to a medicine ball because of the potential of a medicine ball to bounce up and hit the face.
- Ensure adequate thoracic and hip mobility by preceding this drill with SMFR techniques on these areas.

Equipment

Sandball

Aims

This is a smash pattern exercise to work the rectus abdominis, hip flexors and upper body muscles with an unconventional training tool.

Set-up

- Assume a standing position, feet hip width apart.
- Take hold of a sandball with both hands.
- Lift the chest to ensure a good back position and brace the core.

Exercise 7.3 Crunch over stability ball

(a)

(b)

Equipment

Stability ball, weight plate (variations: sandball, medicine ball, dumbbell)

Aims

This is a smash pattern exercise to work the rectus abdominis, hip flexors and upper body muscles on an unstable surface.

Set-up

- Assume a seated position on top of a stability ball.
- Walk forward and lean back until the lower back is supported by the ball.
- Take hold of a weight plate with both hands.
- Arch the body over the ball and brace the core.

Execution

- Curl up on the ball as if throwing the weight plate forward.
- Keep hold of the plate and briefly hold the fully flexed position at the top.
- Extend the body back over the ball and repeat for the prescribed number of repetitions.

Technical considerations

- A sandball, medicine ball or dumbbell can be used instead of a weight plate.
- For a more effective variation, use a medicine ball or sandball and throw the weight at the peak of the curl to a partner. Have them throw it back, loading the flexors by extending the back over the ball, and repeat.
- Ensure adequate thoracic and hip mobility by preceding this drill with SMFR techniques on these areas.

Exercise 7.4 Kneeling crunch

(a)

(b)

Equipment
Cable rope (variation: cable handle)

Aims
This is a smash pattern exercise to work the rectus abdominis, hip flexors and upper body muscles with an unconventional training tool.

Set-up
* Attach a cable rope to a high point on a cable column.
* Assume a kneeling position in front of the cable column.
* Take hold of the cable rope with both hands.
* Lift the chest to ensure a good back position and brace the core.

Execution
* Allow the load of the weights stack to extend the core to load the smash pattern muscles.
* Without pausing, flex the core and curl downwards towards the floor.
* Keep the arms flexed and rigid so that the smash muscles of the core initiate the movement and not the arms.
* Briefly hold the fully flexed position, then sit up and extend the cable rope back towards the top of the column and repeat for the prescribed number of repetitions.

Technical considerations
* This can be performed as a single arm with a cable handle exercise.
* Ensure adequate thoracic and hip mobility by preceding this drill with SMFR techniques on these areas.

Exercise 7.5 Kneeling overhead throw

(a)

(b)

Equipment
Sandball (variations: medicine ball, rebounder (mini trampoline))

Aims
This is a smash pattern exercise to work the rectus abdominis, hip flexors and upper body muscles with an unconventional training tool.

Set-up
- Assume a kneeling position, facing a partner.
- Take hold of a sandball with both hands.
- Lift the chest to ensure a good back position and brace the core.

Set-up
- Lift the sandball above and behind the head and extend the core to load the smash pattern muscles.
- Without pausing, throw the sandball forwards towards the partner.
- Release the sandball at the appropriate point so that the partner can catch it.
- Have the partner throw the sandball back so that it can be caught above the head.
- Allow the sandbag to go above and behind the head again, to load and extend the core, and repeat for the prescribed number of repetitions.

Technical considerations
- Correctly using the momentum of the partner's throw will allow for greater activation of the smash pattern muscles.
- A medicine ball against a wall or rebounder can be used as an alternative to a partner.
- Ensure adequate thoracic and hip mobility by preceding this drill with SMFR techniques on these areas.

MOVING AND CARRYING LOAD PATTERN

//

8

The moving and carrying load pattern is some-what of a mixture of the outstanding methods of movement, kind of like the 'irregular bone' in bone categorisation. It is difficult to describe as an actual movement pattern, since the category is made of a number of different movements. The moving and carrying load pattern is simply a method of moving a load from one place to another – such as dragging or pushing – or carrying a load – such as in the hands, across the back, on the shoulders or above the head. It may be moving the load a set distance, or it may be moving the body with load from a supine position to a standing position.

In my opinion, it is the moving and carrying load pattern that is probably the least trained movement pattern in modern resistance training programmes, but it is a pattern that has a huge carryover to many functional tasks and sports including:

Figure 8.1 Moving a load to a standing position

- Carrying heavy shopping to the car
- Dragging a casualty out of a burning building (fireman) or out of a firefight (soldier)
- Carrying a casualty on the shoulders away from danger (as above)
- Pushing a car to get it jump-started
- Carrying a sofa – walking with and lifting it over a fence or banister.
- Getting up from a position on your back to a standing position while being held down (rugby, fighting or mixed martial arts (MMA)).

The moving and carrying load pattern is inherently linked with the gait and locomotion pattern (since most of the movements within this category are actually loaded locomotion) and the lift

Figure 8.2 Locomotion with a load on one shoulder

pattern (since many of the movements require the load to first be lifted from the floor). Just as with the other movement patterns, it is important that all of these individual movements are trained, as different muscle groups and motor units will be activated depending on which is used.

The emergence of unconventional training exercise and equipment and the use of modified strongmen training techniques inherently use a multitude of moving and carrying load exercises.

So if this movement pattern has such a good carryover to many facets of daily life, sports performance or injury resilience, why is it not trained more frequently in the gym? The main reason is the lack of space in many training facilities, which are packed with lots of cardiovascular and fixed path machines. This leaves very little space for the average gym user to pick up a couple of barbells and carry them across the gym in a farmer's walk, for example. However, there is a move towards creating space which can be used for rope training, sled work, plyometrics, sprinting, dragging or carrying weights. Both performance centres and health clubs are embracing these functional training areas as a key trend and important criteria in their clients' and members' functional training.

LIMITING FACTORS FOR THE MOVING AND CARRYING LOAD PATTERN

The following list highlights the three common limiting factors for the moving and carrying load movement pattern:

- Poor grip
- Poor lifting strength and endurance
- Weak core

To improve the function of the moving and carrying pattern these limiting factors should be addressed, in addition to training the range of these movements.

1. POOR GRIP

Just as with the lift and pull patterns, the grip is probably one of the most commonly seen limiting factors for the move and carrying load pattern. Many individuals will find that it is their grip which fails when they are performing farmer's walks, for example. They are either unable to hold the load (grip strength) or to hold on to the load for the duration of the set (grip endurance). This is further worsened as the bar diameter increases, such as when using fat grip bars. Performing grip-emphasised pulling and lifting exercises (see chapters 5 and 3) and supplementary forearm and grip drills will help to correct this deficit.

2. POOR LIFTING STRENGTH AND ENDURANCE

Walking deadlifts, farmer's walks, overhead barbell walks with chains, zercher carry and super

Improvements gained through moving-carrying drills
- Ankle stability
- Hip stability
- Shoulder stability
- Core strength and stability
- Lateral speed
- Grip strength and endurance
- Anaerobic fitness
- Body composition

yoke walks all have one thing in common: the individual must first lift the load up off the ground to the required position before they can move it any distance. If the lifting pattern is weak in either functional applied strength or functional range, it is likely to have a strong correlation with poor moving-carrying load ability. Train the properties and limiting factors of the lift pattern so this carryover does not occur.

3. WEAK CORE

All muscles of the core can be trained with moving-carrying load exercises, and as such weak core muscles will translate to poor performance in certain exercises:

- The core flexors will be required when lifting the torso from a supine position (such as in a Turkish get-up or get-up anyhow) to prevent spinal extension when stabilising a load overhead (such as an overhead barbell walk with chains) or when pushing an object (car push).
- The core lateral flexors will be required when performing any unilateral loaded exercise to prevent the body from leaning to one side (such as in a one hand farmer's walk, one hand kettlebell overhead walks, Turkish get-up or walks with Powerbag™ on one shoulder).
- The core rotators will also be required for counter rotation control in the same unilateral loaded exercises as well as any drills that require rotation (such as when turning around in the farmer's walk or overhead walks).
- The core extensors will be required to lift any loads with the other lift pattern muscles, and will also be required to resist being pulled into a hunched over, flexed spine posture when the load is heavy (farmer's walk) or held in front (barbell walking deadlift, backwards sled drags).

MOVING AND CARRYING LOAD EXERCISES

Exercise 8.1 Farmer's walk

(a)

(b)

Equipment
Barbell (variations: Powerbag™, sandbag, kettlebells, weight plate, Fat Gripz, chain)

Aims
This is a carrying load exercise to improve grip strength and endurance, lateral core strength and back stability strength-endurance.

Set-up
- Set up a single barbell with an equal load at each end.
- Adopt a parallel stance with the barbell directly to one side.
- Take hold of the barbell with one hand in the centre of the bar.
- Lift the bar up with a pronated grip, so that it is alongside the body.

Execution
- Lift the chest, brace the core and squeeze the bar.
- Walk forwards keeping the bar in a horizontal position.
- Control any compensatory lean of the bar using a strong grip.
- Walk for a set distance or time. If there is limited space, walk in a figure of eight pattern over 8–10m.
- Repeat for the prescribed number of sets with each hand.

Technical considerations
- Keep the shoulders pulled back and the chest up throughout the set.
- The two hand farmer's walk is one of the best exercises for improving grip strength and endurance as well as upper back endurance and even hip, core and ankle stability.
- Variations include heavy Powerbag™/sandbag, heavy kettlebell or two kettlebells in one hand, farmer's walk bar, pinch grip on flat weight plate, barbell farmer's walk with Fat Gripz™, farmer's walk with chain drag.

Exercise 8.2 Overhead walk

Equipment
Barbell with chains (variations: Powerbag™, sandbag, kettlebells, chain)

Aims
This is a carrying load exercise to improve shoulder and upper back strength and endurance and anterior core activation.

Set-up
- Set up a single barbell with chains attached to each end, outside of any plates used.

- Adopt a parallel stance with the barbell directly in front and take hold with a pronated grip wider, shoulder width apart.
- Lift the bar up and above the head using a clean and press, clean and jerk or snatch technique.
- The chains will either be off the ground and swing, or will touch the ground and drag.

Execution
- Lift the chest, brace the core and tighten the muscles around the scapula.
- Walk forwards keeping the bar in a horizontal position above the head with arms locked.
- Control any compensatory movement of the bar using the core.
- Walk for a set distance or time. If there is limited space, walk in a figure of eight pattern over 8–10m.
- Repeat for the prescribed number of sets.

Technical considerations
- Maintain optimal back position, with chains swinging or dragging on floor throughout the set.
- Chains dragging will challenge the anterior core. Chains swinging will challenge the lateral core
- Keep the duration or distance on the sets low because of shoulder fatigue.
- Variations include: Heavy Powerbag™/sandbag in each hand, heavy kettlebells in each hand, backwards-overhead barbell walk with chains and sideways overhead barbell walk with chains attached on one end.

Exercise 8.3 Turkish get-up

(a)

(b)

(c)

(d)

Equipment
Dumbbell

Aims
This is a moving load exercise from a supine to a standing position, to improve shoulder stability and mobility and anterior and lateral core stability.

Set-up
- Lie in a supine position (facing the ceiling) with the dumbbell sideways on next to one shoulder.
- Roll towards the dumbbell and grip the handle with both hands.
- Pull the dumbbell onto the nearest side of the chest/shoulder and roll back into the supine position.
- Have the contralateral (opposite side) arm extended on the floor at about 45 degrees from the body.
- Bend the knee of the ipsilateral (same side) leg and place the foot flat on the ground.
- Inhale and brace the core.
- Press the dumbbell from the chest into a locked arm position pointing straight upwards.

Execution
- Push the dumbbell upwards by lifting the torso from the floor and pushing up onto the contralateral elbow.
- Then push the body up onto the hand so that the arm is straight and the torso is in a fully upright, seated position.
- Push down with the supporting hand and foot to lift the hips off the floor.
- Bring the knee back to the chest and underneath the body until into a supported kneeling lunge position.

- Lift the supporting hand off the floor using the lateral core, until you reach an unsupported kneeling lunge position.
- Stand upright so that the feet are parallel, shoulder width apart, with the 'working' arm extended upwards in a locked position.
- To return to the start position, step backwards with the opposite leg, place the hand on the floor, sweep the leg through the hips and extended leg on the floor, lower onto the elbow then lower the shoulders.

Technical considerations

- Watch the dumbbell at all times throughout both the concentric and eccentric phases. Not looking at the dumbbell will usually allow the arm to bend or move from an upright position, causing it to fall or balance to be lost.
- Undertake each phase slowly.
- Focus on keeping the arm in a straight vertical position throughout all phases.
- Not having sufficient space between the hips and the supporting hand will make it very difficult to 'sweep' the leg through when the hips are lifted up.
- There are no specific prerequisite exercises to perform the Turkish get-up, apart from ensuring optimal thoracic, shoulder and hip mobility with stretches and self-myofascial release (SMFR).
- Keep the reps low as the time under tension for each rep is quite long.
- Variations include using a kettlebell, barbell, fit bar or Powerbag™ for different benefits.

When learning the exercise it can be split into different phases, which can be taught separately and then integrated together:

- Phase 1 – Supine to upright seated position
- Phase 2 – Hip and leg lift
- Phase 3 – Leg sweep underneath
- Phase 4 – Split kneeling position
- Phase 5 – Split kneeling to standing

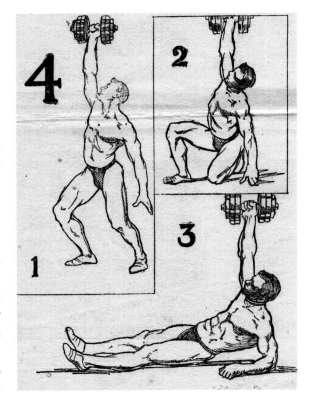

Figure 8.3 This is a classic preparation exercise to develop core, hip and shoulder stability and strength and proprioception.

Exercise 8.4 Turkish get-up, squat variation

(a)

(b)

(c)

(d)

Equipment
Kettlebell (variations: dumbbell, barbell, fit bar)

Aims
This is a moving load exercise from a supine to a standing position, to improve shoulder stability and mobility and anterior and lateral core stability.

Set-up
- Lie in a supine position (facing the ceiling) with the kettlebell sideways on next to one shoulder.
- Roll towards the kettlebell and grip the handle with both hands.
- Pull the kettlebell onto the nearest side of the chest/shoulder and roll back into the supine position.
- Have the contralateral (opposite side) arm extended on the floor at about 45 degrees from the body.
- Bend the knee of the ipsilateral (same side) leg and place the foot flat on the ground.
- Inhale and brace the core.
- Press the kettlebell from the chest into a locked arm position pointing straight upwards.

Execution
- Push the kettlebell upwards by lifting the torso from the floor and pushing up on to the contralateral elbow.
- Then push the body up onto the hand so that the arm is straight and the torso is in a fully upright seated position.
- Push down with the supporting hand and foot to lift the hips off the floor.
- Bring the knee back to the chest and place the foot in line with the other in a supported squat position.

- Lift the supporting hand off the floor and stand upright.
- To return to the start position, squat down, place the hand on the floor, extend one leg on the floor, lower down on to the elbow then lower the shoulders on to the floor.

Technical considerations

- Watch the kettlebell at all times throughout both the concentric and eccentric phases. Undertake each phase slowly.
- Focus on keeping the arm in a straight vertical position throughout the different phases.
- Ensure the heels do not lift off of the ground during the ascent or descent of the overhead squat phase.
- Variations include using a dumbbell, barbell or fit bar.

Exercise 8.5 Two hand get-up sit-up

Equipment

Fit bar

Aims

This is a moving load exercise from a supine to a seated position, to improve shoulder mobility and anterior core stability.

Set-up

- Lie in a supine position with the fit bar held above the shoulders with both arms extended.
- The legs should be straight on the floor with the feet apart and the toes pulled towards the shins.
- Inhale and brace the core.

Execution

- Push the fit bar upwards by contracting the core muscles and lifting the torso from the floor.
- Come up until the torso is in a fully upright seated position.
- The arms should be locked and extended upwards in a position above the shoulders.
- To return to the start position, slowly lean backwards and lower the torso back down to the floor.

Technical considerations

- Focus on keeping the arms straight throughout the different phases.
- In the upright-seated position the bar should be above the shoulders and the back should in a neutral spine position.
- This is a preparation drill for any standing overhead pressing exercise, to ensure adequate hip and thoracic mobility and core stability.

Exercise 8.6 Get-up anyhow

(a)

(b)

(c)

Equipment
Sandbag (variation: kettlebells)

Aims
This is a moving load exercise from a seated to a standing position, to improve core stability.

Set-up
- Adopt a seated position with the legs extended or crossed.
- The sandbag should be held across the chest with the arms crossed.
- Inhale and brace the core.

Execution
- Move from a seated position into a kneeling position and then to standing.
- Keep an upright torso position throughout and avoid leaning forward.
- Use any technique to move between positions.
- To return to the start position, move down into a kneeling and then seated position.

Technical considerations
- Keep hold of the sandbag with both hands throughout the drill.
- Alternate which legs come up first so that lower body muscular balance is maintained.
- This type of drill is great for mixed martial arts (MMA) fighters who must get off the floor while holding an opponent away with their arms.
- Variations include starting from a supine position instead of a seated position, using two kettlebells in a rack position or two sandbags (one on each shoulder).

Exercise 8.7 Walk with Powerbag™ on one shoulder

Execution
- Lift the chest, brace the core and tighten the muscles around the scapula.
- Walk forwards, keeping the Powerbag™ in a horizontal position on the shoulder.
- Control any compensatory leaning to one side using the core muscles.
- Walk for a set distance or time. If there is limited space, walk in a figure of eight pattern over 8–10m.
- Repeat for the prescribed number of sets on both shoulders

Technical considerations
- Maintain an optimal back position throughout the set.
- Variations include using a sandbag or performing a get-up at the beginning or within each set.

Equipment
Powerbag™ (variation: sandbag)

Aims
This is a carrying load exercise to improve loaded gait strength and endurance and activation of the lateral core muscles.

Set-up
- Adopt a parallel stance with the Powerbag™ directly in front of the body.
- Take hold of the Powerbag™ and lift up onto one shoulder
- Hold in place with one hand.

Exercise 8.8 Zercher walk

Equipment
Sandbag

Aims
This is a carrying load exercise to improve back, shoulder and arm strength and endurance and core activation.

Set-up
- Adopt a parallel stance position with the sandbag in front on the feet.
- Lift the sandbag up so it is held across the chest with the arms crossed.
- One hand can be placed over the other

Execution
- Lift the chest, brace the core and tighten the muscles around the scapula.
- Walk forwards, keeping the sandbag in a horizontal position
- Walk for a set distance or time. If there is limited space, walk in a figure of eight pattern over 8–10m.
- Repeat for the prescribed number of sets.

Technical considerations
- Maintain an optimal back position throughout the set by keeping the chest high.
- Variations include sideways Zercher walk or backwards Zercher walk, or adding a Zercher get-up anyhow to the exercise.

Exercise 8.9 Forwards drag with load held in arms

Equipment
Sled, weight plates (variation: sled straps)

Aims
This is a moving load exercise to improve leg strength and endurance, anterior core strength and stability.

Set-up
- Load a sled with an appropriate amount of weight plates.
- Adopt a parallel stance, facing away from the sled.
- Take hold of the straps with both arms.
- Lift the chest, brace the core and tighten the muscles around the scapula.

Execution
- Lean forwards slightly and walk forwards.
- Walk forwards for a set distance or time.
- Repeat for the prescribed number of sets.

Technical considerations
- Maintain an optimal back position throughout the set by keeping the chest high.
- Sled strap loops can either be held passively around the wrists or in the grip.
- The sled can provide indications of bilateral strength differences – does the sled deviate off a straight line when being pulled or dragged?
- Can be used during lower body injury rehabilitation, prior to full squatting.
- Variations include attaching sled straps to waist or shoulders.

Exercise 8.10 Lateral drag with load held in arms

Equipment

Sled, weight plates (variation: sled straps)

Aims

This is a moving load exercise to improve lateral leg strength and lateral core stability.

Set-up

- Load a sled with an appropriate amount of weight plates.
- Adopt a parallel stance sideways on to the sled.
- Take hold of the straps with both arms, one in each hand.
- Keep the lead arm (the one furthest from the sled) bent at a 90 degree angle – the trailing arm should be fully extended.
- Lift the chest, brace the core and tighten the muscles around the scapula.

Execution

- Step outwards with the furthest leg.
- Step with the nearest leg to bring the feet back to a hip width distance apart.
- Walk sideways for a set distance or time.
- Repeat for the prescribed number of sets on both sides.

Technical considerations

- Maintain an optimal back position throughout the set by keeping the chest high.
- Sled work is one of the fastest ways to improve lateral speed. Lateral speed is almost always expressed in a situation where inertia has to be overcome; hence the need for load.
- Variations include attaching sled straps to waist or shoulders, or single arm lateral sled drag and carioca lateral sled drag (with alternating leg crossovers).

Exercise 8.11 Backwards drag with load attached to hips

Equipment

Sled, weight plates and attached vest (variation: sled straps)

Aims

This is a moving load exercise to improve leg strength and endurance, posterior core strength and back stability.

Set-up

- Load a sled with an appropriate amount of weight plates.
- Adopt a parallel stance facing the sled.
- Connect the straps to the attachment vest at the hips.
- Lift the chest and brace the core.

Execution

- Squat down slightly and lean backwards fractionally.
- Drive back forcefully with one foot, then the other in an alternating pattern.
- Keep the upper body still and avoid pulling the torso back from a flexed position to gain momentum on the sled.
- Move the feet as rapidly as possible. Keep the toes pointing forwards throughout.
- Walk backwards for a set distance or time.
- Repeat for the prescribed number of sets.

Technical considerations

- Maintain an optimal back position throughout the set by keeping the chest high.
- Sled strap loops can also be held passively around the wrists or in the grip.
- The sled can provide indications of bilateral strength differences – does the sled deviate off a straight line when being dragged?
- The feet rotating outwards indicates tight lateral hamstrings or tight piriformis.
- Can be used during lower body injury rehabilitation, prior to full squatting.

- This exercise is fantastic for lactic acid training. Always place at the end of the end of the workout.
- Use less weight with a waist attachment, as the upper body mass cannot be used to counter the weight on the sled.
- When attaching a strap to one side of the body, the other hand should be placed on the hip. This helps to avoid any movement of the free arm, which would potentially help to counterbalance the uneven loading pattern of this exercise. This technique forces asymmetrical compensation of the torso muscles, which will mimic the forces involved with many sports, such as football, ice hockey, throwing a ball, or punching. The stress will be felt on the contralateral side (the side not holding the strap) which includes the obliques, quadratus lumborum and gluteus medius.
- Variations include sled attached to waist (see photos), sled attached to shoulders, nose-to-sky backwards drag (head tilted back, looking straight upwards) and single arm backwards drag (hold strap with one arm and place the other on the hip).

Exercise 8.12 Peterson backwards drag with load held in arms

Equipment
Sled, weight plates (variation: sled straps)

Aims
This is a moving load exercise to improve leg strength and endurance, particularly the vastus medialis obliquus (VMO), posterior core strength and back stability.

Set-up
- Load a sled with an appropriate amount of weight plates (less than the backwards drag).
- Adopt a parallel stance facing the sled.
- Take hold of the straps with both arms.
- Lift the chest, brace the core and tighten the muscles around the scapula.

Execution
- Place the ball of the right foot just behind the left heel and turn out the foot by about 20 degrees.
- There should be a slight bend in the knee and the heel should be lifted up over the toes as much as possible.
- Press the heel downwards to the floor as quickly as possible to extend the leg.
- Allow the left leg to lift off the ground passively.
- Place the ball of the left foot behind the right heel and repeat the process.
- Drive back with one foot, then the other in an alternating pattern.
- Keep the torso upright throughout.
- Each step should have to overcome the inertia of the sled. Ensure it is perfectly still before pushing back with each step.

- Walk backwards for a set distance or time.
- Repeat for the prescribed number of sets.

Technical considerations

- There will be a greater quadriceps recruitment with the waist attachment.
- If the load is too high, the torso will be forced to lean forward.
- Keep the upper body still and avoid pulling the torso back from a flexed position to gain momentum through the sled.
- Maintain optimal back position throughout the set by keeping the chest high.

Exercise 8.13 Forwards push

Equipment

Sled, weight plates (variation: car push)

Aim

This is a moving load exercise to improve leg strength and endurance, anterior core strength and stability.

Set-up

- Load a sled with an appropriate amount of weight plates.
- Adopt a split stance facing from the sled from behind.
- Take hold of the rear bar with both arms and lean forward.

- Lift the chest, brace the core and tighten the muscles around the scapula.

Set-up

- Keeping the arms extended, drive downwards and backwards with the lead leg to push the sled forwards.
- Bring the rear leg forwards, plant on the floor and drive downwards and backwards.
- Continue this alternating pattern, moving the feet as rapidly as possible.
- Move the sled forwards for a set distance or time.
- Repeat for the prescribed number of sets.

Technical considerations

- Maintain optimal back position throughout the set by keeping the chest high.
- Do not allow the arms to bend or the force from the lower body will not be efficiently transferred through the core and upper body to the sled.
- This exercise is fantastic for lactic acid training. Always place at the end of the workout.

OTHER MOVE AND CARRYING LOAD EXERCISES

Car push

This is the same drill as the forwards sled push, but instead performed by pushing a car. This is a very popular drill with MMA fighters and rugby players for metabolic conditioning. This exercise is performed on a flat, quiet road or car park – if there is any incline or decline it will make it too hard or too easy to perform correctly. Adopt a position behind the car, with a colleague in the driving seat, the hand brake off, the engine off and the car in neutral. Take hold with both arms and lean forward, and keeping the arms extended, drive downwards and backwards with the lead leg to push the car forwards. Bring the rear leg forwards, plant on the floor and drive downwards and backwards. Continue this alternating pattern, moving the feet as rapidly as possible. Move the car forwards for a set time, usually 30–60 seconds.

Lift barbell into back squat position

This is a great drill to train the core muscles and assistant muscles that move the barbell into the back squat position with the bar resting on the upper back, behind the head. Before there were squat racks, this was the preferred technique for weightlifters to move the barbell into this starting position for the squat. Start with an appropriate amount of weight on the barbell, and lift one end of the bar up off the ground. Pull the bar up until it is vertical, then adopt a parallel stance sideways on to the bar. Grip the bar with two hands, one at each end, squat and lean towards the bar to place the upper back on the bar, behind the head. Shift the weight of the bar onto the back and lift the lower end off the floor. Lean the body back to an upright, deep squat position and stand up.

Figure 8.4 The supine shuffle with one kettlebell held above head

Perform this exercise alternating sides with each rep or set.

This exercise will develop the accessory and stabiliser muscle strength, not just the strength of the squat muscles that would be developed if the bar was lifted off the racks.

Lift barbell into single arm press position

This is a similar drill to the one just described and involves moving the barbell into a position so that it rests on one side of the upper back, diagonally behind the head. Before there were racks this was the preferred technique for weightlifters to move the barbell into the starting position for a one hand side press or bent press. Start with an appropriate amount of weight on the barbell and lift one end of the bar up off the ground. Pull the bar up with until it is vertical, and adopt a parallel stance diagonally on to the bar. Grip the bar with one hand in the middle. Squat and roll the bar onto one side of the upper back, pushing up with the hand lifting the other end off the floor. Lean the body back and stand to an upright position. Perform this exercise alternating sides with each rep or set.

Supine shuffle with one kettlebell held above head

The supine shuffle involves holding a single kettlebell above the body, while the core and legs are used to move the body along the floor. Avoid using the other arm, which can also hold another kettlebell for an additional challenge. Make sure that the kettlebell is always watched and kept under control and perform for a set distance or time. Repeat on both sides.

Tyre push over – partner wrestle

This is a combination moving load and pressing drill performed with a large heavy tyre and a partner. Lift the tyre up so that is resting on one side and adopt a split stance on one side. Have your partner adopt a similar stance on the other side of the tyre. Place both arms near the top of the tyre and lean forward, keeping the arms extended. With your partner replicating the action, drive downwards and backwards to push the tyre over. Continue to 'wrestle' the tyre forwards until one person succeeds. Repeat for a prescribed number of sets or time.

Bent over hamstrings drag

This variation of the forwards sled drag is a fantastic hamstring builder, integrating the entire posterior chain. Adopt a stance facing away from the sled and hold the straps by the hips. Bend forwards from the waist so that the arms are extended backwards with the forearms by the sides of the hips. Ensure that the torso is horizontal and the spine neutral. Walk forwards, keeping the legs straight, with a slight knee bend. Walk in a straight line in a rapid heel-to-toe action, not allowing the legs to swing out to the side and keeping the shoulders still. Repeat for a prescribed number of sets or time.

Sled pull-through

The sled pull-through is one of the most effective exercises to improve explosive posterior chain strength, and is a hip extension drill like the kettlebell swing, barbell Romanian deadlift or razor curl. Adopt a stance facing away from the sled, and hold the straps with two hands between the legs. Bend forwards from the waist so that the arms are extended backwards between the legs with the straps taut and the elbows at a point even with the knees. Forcefully stand upright by pulling the hips forwards to full extension. Keep the core and upper body rigid and use the hips and not the arms or shoulders to pull the sled towards you. The force generated by the hips will be transferred through the core and upper body to the sled. Move forwards to take the slack off of the straps, bend forwards to the start position and repeat for the prescribed number of repetitions, time or distance. Ensure an adequate load on the sled so that it doesn't hit the back of the ankles.

Blast starts

This exercise is fantastic for lactic acid training and is a variation of the forwards facing sled drag. Attach the straps to the waist and assume a three-point stance (sprint start with one hand on the floor) or a four-point stance (two hands on the floor). Sprint from a dead start for 5–10m, rest for 10–15 seconds and repeat four to five times. Poliquin & McDermott (2010) advise that this drill is not performed with athletes from sports with refined sprinting skills, such as track/field sprinters, as it will negatively affect their running biomechanics.

Variations include a more upright position for throwers or MMA fighters (to replicate the position from which they must accelerate) or adding a pop-up from a prone position on the floor, great for rugby, football and MMA fighters, to improve their ability to move from the floor and accelerate.

Figure 8.5 Performing blast starts

GAIT AND LOCOMOTION PATTERN

9

The gait and locomotion movement pattern is focused on improving the individual's ability to move from one place to another as efficiently and easily as possible. Locomotion is described as the act of self-propulsion by an animal, which (depending on the animal) can include crawling, walking, running, swimming and flying, in order to find food, a suitable place to live, to evade predators or to find a mate. For humans, locomotion would include:

- Gait (walking, jogging, running)
- Crawling
- Swimming

GAIT

Gait is described as the way in which locomotion is achieved in humans using the lower limbs. Gait could then be described as the method by which an individual walks, runs or sprints, and would vary depending on surface, velocity and individual biomechanics. Gait analysis is a common technique used to assess any biomechanical dysfunctions when running or walking, which may eventually cause pain, inflammation or injury.

A gait cycle is defined as the time period between successive ipsilateral heel strikes, with each foot striking the ground between 10 to 15,000 times per day (Michaud, 1997). It is an important functional movement in relation to moving and carrying load, and especially important for optimal performance in many sports. If the gait pattern is dysfunctional, it will illicit a much greater energy expenditure and will eventually lead to excessive stress on the joints and structures on the foot, ankle, knee, hip and spine. In walking there will be a heel strike, with the heel landing first then pronating onto the ball of the foot. In jogging there is usually a mid-foot strike with the heel and ball landing simultaneously. In sprinting there will be a forefoot strike with the ball of the foot landing first and the heel of the foot commonly not contacting the floor at all. The gait and locomotion movement pattern would also include a variety of the speed, agility and quickness (SAQ®) drills used in sports conditioning, such as the cut or crossover step, which will help develop optimal lateral acceleration. The development of speed of locomotion is critical in the pursuit of improved performance for athletes. Acceleration, linear and lateral speed are critical components of many sports including football, rugby, hockey, basketball and athletics.

CRAWLING

Crawling is the method of human locomotion while on the back, on the belly or on all four limbs (also known as a quadruped position). In evolutionary terms, these constitute normal human development from a baby to a child, and the ability to move on two legs – babies will first move on their bellies, then on all four limbs and eventually on two legs.

Crawling has also been an important method of locomotion, when stealth is important. When hunting or approaching an enemy, an individual could approach their target while keeping in a low position to avoid being seen. Although many individuals no longer hunt, it is still an important quality for modern soldiers to be able to effectively and efficiently crawl, particularly when holding weapons.

The use of quadruped exercises, such as the bear and tiger walk, has increased in popularity recently as a type of unconventional bodyweight training.

SWIMMING

Swimming can be described as human locomotion from one place to another through the medium of water. This movement pattern has evolved over the generations to allow humans to cross bodies of water, such as rivers and lakes, as well as for diving in the pursuit of food, such as fish, mussels or oysters. Whereas cycling is a relatively recent form of cardiovascular training, swimming has been undertaken by humans for many thousands of years. Cycling may also be considered a type of fixed-path machine, whereas swimming, crawling, walking, jogging and running are all unrestricted, free-forms of cardiovascular training, and should thus have a greater functional carryover.

This movement pattern is covered within a number of current methodologies of training, including:

- Plyometrics – bounding
- Speed, agility and quickness – ladders, hurdles, cones, resistance bands and bodyweight running drills
- Unconventional training – bodyweight crawling and quadruped drills
- Cardiovascular training – walking, jogging, running (including sprint and hill interval training).

As with any movement pattern, care should be taken that the individual has acquired optimal movement skills before progressing their training programme with increased intensity or volume. For example, if a client is unable to move at a low speed (walking) effectively, what would happen if they were asked to run? This poor movement technique would translate to increased stress on the joints because of poor biomechanics and may eventually lead to pain and possible injury.

GAIT AND LOCOMOTION EXERCISES

Exercise 9.1 Tiger walk

(a)

(b)

Equipment
Bodyweight (variations: sled, band)

Aim
This is a locomotion exercise performed in a quadruped position to develop dynamic core strength and to challenge the hip and shoulder muscles.

Set-up
- Ensure there is sufficient space in front to move forwards.
- Adopt a prone plank position on the feet and hands with the arms extended.

- Lift the chest up to maintain an optimal spinal position.
- Look forward and brace the core.

Execution
- Lift the left hand up and place it on the floor in front of you.
- Lift the right foot off the ground, bring the knee towards the chest and place the toes on the ground.
- Push off the right foot and reach forwards with the right hand.
- At the same time as the right leg is straightening, lift the left leg forwards and place the toes on the ground.
- Repeat this action, alternating sides for a set number of repetitions, distance or time.

Technical considerations
- Keep the chest up and spine neutral throughout.
- Look forwards.
- Keep the hips low.
- A variation is the tiger walk pulling sled or band (see photos).

Exercise 9.2 Spiderman crawl

(a)

(b)

Equipment
Bodyweight (variations: sled, band)

Aim
This is a locomotion exercise performed in a quadruped position, with an increased emphasis on pressing muscles.

Set-up
- Ensure there is sufficient space in front to move forwards.
- Adopt a prone plank position on the feet and hands, with the arms extended.
- Lift the chest up to maintain an optimal spine position.
- Look forward and brace the core.

Execution
- Lift the left hand up and place it on the floor in front of you.
- Lift the right foot off the ground, then bring the knee upwards and outwards.
- Place the toes on the ground with the knee pointing out to the side.
- Place the left ear near the floor and look to the left.
- Push off the right foot and reach forwards with the right hand.
- At the same time as the right leg is straightening, lift the left leg upwards and outwards and place the toes on the ground.
- Place the right ear near the floor and look to the left.
- Repeat this action, alternating sides for a set number of repetitions, distance or time.

Technical considerations
- Keep the entire body as low as possible.
- Variations include Spiderman crawl pulling sled or band (see photos).

Exercise 9.3 Bear walk

Equipment
Bodyweight (variations: sled, band)

Aim
This is a locomotion exercise performed in a quadruped position to develop dynamic core strength and to challenge the hip and shoulder muscles.

Set-up
- Ensure there is sufficient space in front to move forwards.
- Adopt a prone position on the feet and hands with the arms extended and the hips raised up in the air.
- Lift the chest up to try and maintain an optimal spine position.
- Look forward and brace the core.

Execution
- Walk forwards, moving one arm and the opposite leg in an alternating pattern.
- Keep the legs relatively straight and move on the toes.
- Keep the arms relatively straight as well.
- Repeat this action, alternating sides for a set distance or time.

Technical considerations
- Keep the chest up and spine neutral throughout.
- Look forwards.
- Keep the hips high.
- Variations include bear walk pulling sled or bear walk attached to band.

Exercise 9.4 Plyometric bounds

Equipment
Bodyweight (variations: sled, band)

Aim
This is a locomotion exercise to work the lower body muscles in an explosive, dynamic manner to develop reactive strength and to challenge the lower body stabilisers.

Set-up
- Ensure there is sufficient space in front to move forwards.
- The chest should be high with the spine in a neutral position.
- Stand on one leg.
- Brace the core to stabilise and protect the back.

Execution
- Push the free leg backwards and drop into a semi-squat position on the stance leg.
- Without pausing, immediately drive the free leg forwards and upwards.
- Land on the opposite leg, flexing at the ankle, knee and hips back.
- Continue to perform this exaggerated running action, trying to cover maximum distance with each stride.
- Repeat this action, alternating sides for a set distance or time.

Technical considerations
- The bound makes use of the elastic energy generated in the stretch shortening cycle and is used to improve reactive strength.
- Focus on landing in a balanced position.
- Keep the chest up and spine neutral throughout.
- Look forwards.
- Variations include forward bounds with lateral emphasis.

Exercise 9.5 Resisted sprint

Execution
- Accelerate forwards, keeping the body angled and driving with the legs and arms.
- Try to accelerate through as the band becomes taut.
- Allow the tension of the band to pull you back to the start position and repeat.
- Alternate the side you start on and repeat for a set number of repetitions or time.

Technical considerations
- Try to cover maximum distance with each attempt.
- Focus on acceleration and driving down through the floor with each foot strike.
- Keep the chest up and spine neutral throughout.
- Look forwards.
- Variations include resisted lateral acceleration.

Equipment
Viper belt and band

Aim
This is a locomotion exercise to work the lower body muscles in a dynamic manner to develop acceleration.

Set-up
- Ensure there is sufficient space in front to move forwards.
- Attach a viper belt round the waist and a resistance band to an anchor and face away.
- The chest should be high with the spine in a neutral position.
- Adopt a two-point or three-point start stance.
- Brace the core to stabilise and protect the back.

Exercise 9.6 Ladder single leg run-through

Equipment
Ladder

Aim
This is a locomotion exercise to enhance stride frequency, while strengthening the hip flexors.

Set-up
- Set up a ladder with the sticks about 18in or 46cm apart.
- Adopt a position facing ladder, but just to one side so that one leg will move over the ladder but the other leg will not.
- The chest should be high with the spine in a neutral position.

Execution
- Run with one leg outside of the ladder and the other leg moving over the ladder.
- With the inside leg focus on pulling the knee high, while keeping the ankle close to the glutes and dorsiflexed.
- Complete this running action over the ladder, with a high knee drive on the inside leg.
- Alternate sides with each set and repeat.

Technical considerations
- Focus on acceleration and driving down through the floor with each foot strike of the near leg.
- Keep the chest up and spine neutral throughout.
- Look forwards.
- Variations include run-through (both legs perform the high knee drive, taking one or two foot strikes between sticks of the ladder).

Exercise 9.7 Single leg run-through

Equipment
Hurdles

Aims
This is a locomotion exercise to enhance stride frequency while strengthening hip flexors and improving lower body co-ordination.

Set-up
- Ensure there is sufficient space in front to move forwards.
- Set up 8–10 hurdles (15–32cm height) in a single line, about 3ft apart.
- Adopt a position facing the hurdles, but just to one side so that one leg will move over the hurdles but the other leg will not.
- The chest should be high with the spine in a neutral position.

Execution
- Run with one leg outside of the hurdles and the other leg moving over the hurdles.
- With the outside leg emphasise a straight leg position, focusing on fast ground contact with the ball of the foot and pulling through with the hips.
- With the inside leg focus on pulling the knee high, while keeping the ankle close to the glutes and dorsiflexed.
- Complete this running action over the hurdles, with one leg straight and the other with a high knee drive.
- Alternate sides with each set and repeat.

Technical considerations
- Keep the foot of the outside leg dorsiflexed.
- Focus on acceleration and driving down through the floor with each foot strike of the near leg.
- Keep the chest up and spine neutral throughout.
- Look forwards.
- Variations include run through (both legs perform the high knee drive, taking one or two foot strikes between hurdles).

Exercise 9.8 Icky shuffle

(a)

(b)

Equipment
Ladder

Aims
This is a locomotion exercise to enhance lower body co-ordination for first step acceleration from a start position.

Set-up
- Set up a ladder with the sticks about 18in or 46cm apart.
- Adopt a position on the left of the ladder.
- The chest should be high with the spine in a neutral position.

Execution
- Step laterally with the right foot and place it in the first square, then place the left foot in the same square.
- Step laterally with the right foot to the right side of the ladder and step forwards with the left foot to the next square.
- Step inwards with the right foot so that it is in the same square.
- Step outwards with the left foot so that is on the left side of the ladder and step forwards with the right foot.
- Continue this pattern for the length of the ladder and repeat for the prescribed number of sets.

Technical considerations
- Focus on quick and efficient foot movements.
- Keep the torso in an athletic position over the feet at all times.
- Look forwards.
- There are many variations of ladder drills to improve lower body co-ordination – some coaches are huge fans of this type of conditioning for athletic performance with certain sports, while others believe that it only improves your ability to perform ladder tasks.

231

OTHER GAIT AND LOCOMOTION EXERCISES

Crawl on elbows

This drill is an upper body dominant exercise to practise crawling in a low position. Adopt a prone lying position on the floor, with space in front to move. Pull the body forward using the upper body and keeping the lower body still. This can be performed in an alternating arm action, or a two arm pulling action.

Power skip

This power skip is an exaggerated running action, similar to the bounds, but with a vertical emphasis. To perform adopt a standing position with space in front of you. Take a couple of steps forward, increasing in speed, and on the third step, drive off the single leg into the air. Use the arms for added propulsion. Land on two feet and immediately commence the next three steps, driving off the opposite leg for the following skip. Continue for a set distance, time or number of repetitions.

SUPPLEMENTARY EXERCISES

10

Supplementary exercises are used to support the primary exercises listed previously in the individual human movement pattern chapters. As discussed in chapter 1, performance in a movement pattern can be increased by improving functional strength or functional range by isolating and training the agonist muscles, by isolating and training synergists or assistant muscles, or by training the antagonist muscles to that movement pattern, to improve the agonist-antagonist strength balance.

These primary exercises can be complemented by supplementary exercises, which would commonly be classified under 'stretching', or similar, and include self-myofascial release (SMFR) using foam rollers, tennis balls or other similar tools. This will help to release tight muscles, which will negatively affect an individual's ability to contract and produce force, as well as affecting the function of any joints that they attach to. Releasing and relaxing a tight hamstring will not only help with hamstring development during lift pattern sessions, it would also be of benefit for quad-dominant squat pattern sessions as well because a tight hamstring would also affect the body's ability to generate force within the antagonistic quad-

riceps. The ideal programme would then consist of any required 'release work' to optimise the ability of the muscles to contract, followed by strengthening work of the weaker muscles in the kinetic chain of the movement pattern, and eventually to apply this strengthening work into full movement pattern exercises.

For most of these exercises, training one side at a time is usually preferable, as it increases the neural drive to that area. What that means is, for example, performing a standing dumbbell biceps curl with two dumbbells at the same time means that the energy available to each elbow flexor is slightly less than if you were to perform the same exercise with one dumbbell at a time. To explain this further, you may use a 16kg dumbbell, as opposed to two 14kg dumbbells, for the same number of repetitions. Performing the exercise one arm at a time will allow a greater overload on the biceps (16kg vs 14kg), and with a greater overload comes increased adaptations. This can also be achieved by alternating the arms, which is a commonly seen alteration. Two dumbbells are held in the hands, one complete repetition is performed on the first side, then when the arm is back at the start position, the second rep involves the opposite arm. This allows heavier loads to be utilised, while training both arms within the same set, and gives each elbow flexor a number of seconds rest between repetitions to help facilitate recruitment of the faster twitch fibres; in essence it is a type of cluster training.

Although the biceps are given as an example, this principle is the same for most muscles and exercises – legs curls, dumbbell lateral raise, or kettlebell shoulder press – the exceptions to this being the leg extension, or any drill where the balance is compromised because of the unilateral loading, such as a dumbbell chest press or squats.

The other way to increase the neural drive is to make the exercise more stable, for example, by adopting a seated or supported position. Using our same example, a standing biceps curl will require neural energy to the core and hip stabilisers, which is not required when performing the exercise seated. Some trainers will say that this makes the exercise non-functional because it is not performed standing, and it is not integrated with the rest of the body.

The idea of the inclusion of supplementary exercises is to develop strength, which can then be incorporated with the full human movement pattern exercises. Using our example, the biceps curl is used to develop elbow flexor strength, which is then applied in the pull up, row or high pull.

The supplementary exercises detailed in this chapter are listed under the primary movement patterns they benefit, although some will provide a benefit across multiple patterns. For example, the hamstring supplementary exercises are listed under the lift pattern, but improving the hamstring strength to help balance the quadriceps: hamstrings strength ratio would also improve the squat pattern.

The exercises that are listed are those that provide some of the greatest carryover to functional performance. There are obviously a plethora of other exercise variations, but as long as the principles discussed previously are applied logically, then the trainer can utilise these where they feel appropriate.

LIFT PATTERN SUPPLEMENTARY EXERCISES

Exercise 10.1 Kneeling hip extension

(a)

(b)

Equipment
Bodyweight, Powerbag™

Aims
This is a supplementary exercise to work the hamstrings, glutes, posterior core muscles (erector spinae) and the upper back muscles (rhomboids, trapezius and posterior deltoid).

Set-up
- Assume a kneeling position on top of a Powerbag™.
- Extend hips so that you are upright, with the knees, hips and shoulders aligned.
- Have your partner take hold of your heels and apply downward pressure.
- Place hands behind your head, pull your elbows back and hold.

Execution
- Take a breath in and brace your core.
- Bend (flex) forward from the hips, keeping your chest up and spine neutral.
- Keep the thighs vertical and avoid pushing the hips back or moving forward.
- Lower torso to a horizontal position and briefly hold, then extend the hips quickly to lift the torso back up to the start position.
- Repeat for the prescribed number of repetitions.

Technical considerations
- Focus on keeping the hips in the same place. Moving them backwards makes the exercise easier, while moving them forwards makes it harder. Have the partner use their shoulder as a guide to ensure you keep it in the same place.
- Keep the chest high, the head up and elbows pulled back throughout the exercise.
- Have the hips held a few inches back to regress the exercise or held a few inches forward of vertical to progress the exercise.
- Have the arms by the sides to regress the exercise.
- Variations include the razor curl (moving the torso forward when it reaches horizontal) or the full Russian curl (lowering the torso to the floor, pivoting at the knees not the hips).

Exercise 10.2 Kneeling razor curl

(a)

(b)

Equipment
Bodyweight, Powerbag™.

Aims
This is a supplementary exercise to work the hamstrings, glutes, posterior core muscles (erector spinae) and the upper back muscles (rhomboids, trapezius and posterior deltoid).

Set-up
- Assume a kneeling position on top of a Powerbag™.
- Extend hips so that you are upright, with the knees, hips and shoulders aligned.
- Have your partner take hold of your heels and apply downward pressure.

- Place hands behind your head, pull your elbows back and hold.

Execution
- Take a breath in and brace your core.
- Bend (flex) forward from the hips, keeping your chest up and spine neutral.
- Keep the thighs vertical and avoid pushing the hips back or moving forward.
- Lower torso to a horizontal position and briefly hold.
- Push torso forward, along the horizontal, as if reaching forward with the head.
- Pull back and then extend the hips quickly to lift the torso back up to the start position.
- Repeat for the prescribed number of repetitions.

Technical considerations
- Focus on keeping the hips in the same place when lowering to the horizontal. Have the partner use their shoulder as a guide to ensure you keep it in the same place.
- Keep the chest high, the head up and elbows pulled back throughout the exercise.
- Have the arms by the sides to regress the exercise.
- Try to reach further forward to progress the exercise.
- Variations include the kneeling hip extension or the full Russian curl (lowering the torso to the floor, pivoting at the knees not the hips).

Exercise 10.3 Kneeling Russian curl

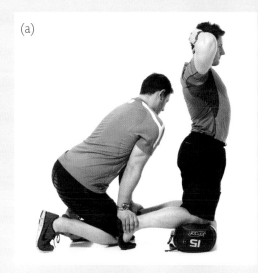

(a)

(b)

Equipment
Bodyweight, Powerbag™

Aims
This is supplementary exercise to work the hamstrings predominantly as well as the glutes and posterior core muscles (erector spinae).

Set-up
- Assume a kneeling position on top of a Powerbag™.
- Extend hips so that you are upright, with the knees, hips and shoulders aligned.
- Have your partner take hold of your heels and apply downward pressure.
- Place hands behind your head, pull your elbows back and hold.

Execution
- Take a breath in and brace your core.
- Lower the thighs and body forwards, towards the floor, pivoting from the knees.
- Keep your chest up and spine neutral, with the knees, hips and shoulders aligned.
- Avoid pushing the hips back or forwards.
- Try to slowly lower the torso to a horizontal position on the floor.
- Have the hands ready to place on the floor to control the 'fall'.
- Then reassume the start position (don't try to 'pull' yourself back up) and repeat for the prescribed number of repetitions.

Technical considerations
- Focus on keeping the hips and thighs aligned with the torso.
- Keep the chest high and the head up throughout the exercise.
- Variations include the kneeling hip extension or the razor curl.

Exercise 10.4 Leg curl machine

Equipment
Leg curl machine

Aim
This is a supplementary exercise to isolate the hamstrings.

Set-up
- Assume the correct position on the machine – be it seated (see photo), prone, kneeling or standing.

Execution
- Take a breath in and brace your core.
- Curl one or both heels (depending on the machine) to the glutes.

Technical considerations
- As the hamstrings both flex the knee and extend the hips, it is important to include both types of exercise within your training programme for optimal hamstring development.
- Train one leg at a time for optimal strength development and to correct any bilateral strength differences.
- Point the toes (plantarflexion at the ankle) to activate the gastrocnemius and hamstrings, or pull the toes towards the shin (ankle dorsi-flexion) to isolate the hamstrings and limit gastrocnemius activation (Kinakin, 2004).
- Turn the feet inwards to increase the stress on the lateral hamstrings and turn them outwards to increase the stress on the medial hamstrings (Kinakin, 2004). Be cautious if you have a knee issue, as these positions can put the knee under stress when flexed.
- Keep the rep range on the leg curl on the lower side (10 reps or less at an appropriate load). Doing 20 reps will have little impact on improving strength.

Exercise 10.5 Leg curl stability ball

(a)

(b)

Equipment

Stability ball

Aims

This is a supplementary exercise to work the knee flexor and hip extensor muscles (hamstrings and gluteals), as well as the posterior core muscles for stability.

Set-up

- Assume a lying position on the floor facing upwards (supine).
- Have the stability ball between the feet.
- Place the heels on top of the stability ball, on the near side of the apex.
- Brace the core and lift the hips off floor into a low supine bridge position, so that the ankles, knees, hips and shoulders are in a straight line.
- The arms can be positioned on the floor for more stability, or across the chest to make it more unstable.

Execution

- Roll the ball towards you by bending the knees and contracting the hamstrings.
- Keep the hips in line with the knees and shoulders throughout.
- Flex the knees as much as possible to bring the ball as close to the hips as you can.
- Keep the feet pointing upwards and dorsiflex at the ankle throughout (pull toes to shins) to ensure maximum recruitment of hamstrings and to limit involvement of calves.
- Pause briefly then extend the legs slowly, and lower the hips at the same speed, to return to the ball to the start position.
- Repeat for the prescribed number of repetitions.

Technical considerations

- If your client is suffering from a cervical disc injury, use a smaller stability ball or avoid the exercise altogether.
- Keeping the hips low and allowing flexion to occur at the hips when the knee is bending will make the exercise easier as the hip flexors can be recruited to pull the ball towards you. This will have the impact of decreasing the involvement of the hamstrings, as they shorten at the knee and are also being lengthened at the hip.
- Pointing the toes (ankle plantarflexion) will allow recruitment of the gastrocnemius as a knee flexor and should be avoided.
- One or both feet turning out during the exercise can mean either an overactive piriformis

(hip rotator) and/or stronger medial hamstrings (compared to lateral hamstrings).

- Variations include single leg stability ball leg curl or eccentric only single leg stability ball leg curl. The eccentric only progression allows you to build up the strength to perform the single leg variation, which for many is too much of a jump from the two-leg version. To perform, pull the stability ball towards you as normal with two feet, then lift one leg off and extend back to the start position with the one remaining leg. Because muscles are stronger eccentrically, you can build up strength performing this phase initially, and then build up to performing the concentric and eccentric phases with just one leg.

Exercise 10.6 Hamstring curl

(a)

(b)

Equipment
Two-strap suspension system

Aims
This is a supplementary exercise to work the knee flexor and hip extensor muscles (hamstrings and gluteals), as well as the posterior core muscles for stability.

Set-up
- Connect the two-strap suspension system to the anchor points, at about hip width apart so that the straps are about 12–18in off of the ground.
- Sit on the floor facing the straps and place both heels into the suspension system.

- Lie back on the floor, facing upwards, with the arms by the sides for support.
- Move the body forwards or backwards to achieve the optimal level of intensity.
- Brace the core and lift the hips off the ground, keeping the body straight and rigid.

Execution
- Flex the knees and draw the heels towards the hips.
- Lift the hips up while the heels are being drawn to the body.
- Keep the knees and feet pointing upwards to avoid any rotation at the hips.
- Hold briefly when the knees are flexed maximally then slowly extend the legs back to the start position.
- Focus on keeping the toes pulled back throughout the exercise.

Technical considerations
- Avoid the feet or hips rotating outwards during the exercise.
- Avoid the lower back overarching during the concentric phase.
- Move the feet closer to the anchor points, or beyond the anchor point to decrease the intensity.
- Move the feet further away from the anchor points to increase the intensity.
- Variations include hamstring curl without hip lift, alternating hamstring curl or single leg hamstring curl.

Exercise 10.7 Superman

(a)

(b)

Equipment
Stability ball

Aim
This is a supplementary exercise to work the spinal erectors in a low intensity position.

Set-up
- Assume a kneeling position on the floor with the stability ball in front of you.
- Lean onto the ball so that the umbilicus is over the apex.
- The hands should be on the floor in front of the ball and the feet on the floor behind the ball (legs extended).

Execution

- Lift one arm up and forwards, while balancing on the ball.
- At the same time lift the opposite leg upwards, so that the hand and foot are at the same height as the shoulder and hip respectively.
- Hold the position briefly then lower back to the start position and repeat using the opposing limbs.
- Repeat for the prescribed number of repetitions.

Technical considerations

- Keep the chest up and spine neutral throughout the exercise, limiting any movement of the torso.
- Squeeze the scapula downwards when lifting the arm up to recruit the lower trapezius muscle fibres.
- One variation is the reverse hip extension (where you place the stability ball on a step, hold the step with the arms and brace the upper torso, then lift the extended legs from a hip-flexed position on the floor to level with the torso).
- Another variation is the wheelbarrow (where a partner holds the feet and pushes you back and forward or tilts sideways and you have to stabilise yourself on the ball while keeping your torso up).

Exercise 10.8 Quad and hip flexor stretch

(a)

(b)

Equipment

Stability ball

Aims

This is a supplementary drill to stretch the quadriceps, hip flexors and spinal flexors. Achieving optimal range of motion and decreasing tension in these muscles will facilitate optimal hamstrings and posterior chain muscle activation.

Set-up

- Assume a four-point kneeling position on the floor with the stability ball behind you and pressed up against a wall or in a corner.
- Move back and place the knee as close as possible to the base of the ball, with the shin against the side of the ball.

Execution

- Bring the foot of the other leg forwards and into a kneeling lunge stance.
- Push up with the hands on this thigh until tension is felt on the other thigh and the front of the hip.
- The heel of the stretched leg should be against the glute and the knee maximally flexed.
- Reach up and behind with the hands to stretch the anterior core as well.
- Hold the position for 10–15 seconds or until the tension drops off then increase the stretch by reaching up or leaning back more.
- Change position and repeat on the opposite side.

Technical considerations

- Rotate the pelvis backwards into a posterior tilt to stretch the hip flexor.
- Breathe out and relax during the stretch.
- Rotate the torso by pulling the ipsilateral (same side) shoulder backwards.
- Perform with a partner to add resistance as a Proprioceptive Neuromuscular Facilitation (PNF) stretch for improved results.
- Perform between lift pattern and lift supplementary exercises for maximum benefit as well as part of a regular stretch routine.

SQUAT PATTERN SUPPLEMENTARY EXERCISES

Exercise 10.9 Seated leg extension

Equipment

Leg extension machine

Aims

This is a supplementary exercise to isolate the quadriceps for increased neural drive to assist with developing strength or size in this muscle.

Set-up

- Assume a seat on the machine with the back supported and the knees in line with the pivot point on the machine.
- The angle of the seat should be at 90 degrees for optimal quadriceps recruitment.

- Place the shin pad on the lower shins, above the ankle joint to allow free movement of the foot.
- Adjust the start position to a point of comfortable maximal knee flexion.

Execution

- Take a breath in and brace your core.
- Pull the toes towards the shins into dorsiflexion.
- Slowly extend one or both legs until the knees are locked.
- Keep the head in a neutral position and avoid gripping the handles too tightly.
- Pause briefly then slowly lower the feet back to the start position and repeat.

Technical considerations

- It is critical to execute the leg extension at a slow concentric tempo, unlike many exercises. The knee is under shear stress anyway with this exercise (the tibia being 'sheared' off the femur at the end of the concentric phase), and accelerating the pad upwards off the shin will greatly increase the shear force upon landing.
- Because of the shear forces inherent with this exercise, it is better utilised as a post-exhaustion supplementary exercise, to be trained when the quads are fatigued after squats or similar exercises. Because of the fatigue from the previous exercises, less weight will be required to overload the muscles, meaning less shear force.
- Again to keep the load (and shear force) lower, use either an 8–12 or 12+ rep range.
- Some authors, such as Poliquin (2006), suggest that it is preferable to train both legs at the same time in this exercise: 'Research has shown that leg extensions are an oddity. Most exercises show enhanced motor unit recruitment if

done unilaterally. Leg extensions do not. They show greatest activation when done bilaterally.'
- Kinakin (2004) reports that you can preferentially recruit either the vastus lateralis or vastus medialis by turning the hips in or out respectively. For most people, working on the toes out (vastus medialis) version will be preferable for improving knee stability. Be cautious if you have a knee issue, as these positions can put the knee under stress when flexed.

Exercise 10.10 Calf raise

(a)

(b)

Equipment
Calf raise machine

Aims
This is a supplementary exercise to isolate the plantarflexors of the ankle. The standing variation is used to isolate the gastrocnemius and the seated variation is used to isolate the soleus.

Set-up
- Set up and adjust the machine as indicated by each manufacturer.
- Place the toes on the end of the step.

Execution
- Load the calf muscle by slowly lowering the heels into a dorsiflexed position.
- Press down through the toes to come up into a plantarflexed position, focusing on rising up onto the big toes at the top of the movement.
- Repeat for the prescribed number of repetitions.

Technical considerations
- Standing calf raise variations will preferentially recruit the gastrocnemius muscle, as it is a biarticular muscle (goes over two joints), and it is in a biomechanical advantage when the knee is extended. When the knee is bent, as in the seated calf raise variations, then the gastrocnemius cannot produce the same degree of force and so this favours overload on the soleus muscle instead. This is the same principle when stretching the calf muscles.
- Push up through the big toe with both exercise variations. This favours recruitment of the plantarflexor that is being targeted, and also helps recruit the flexor hallucis longus and brevis muscles (Kinakin, 2004).
- For the seated exercise use a rep range of 12–20, as the soleus has a greater proportion of slow twitch fibres and will respond better to this time under tension.
- For the standing exercise vary the type of session more, as the gastrocnemius has a greater proportion of fast twitch fibres and will respond better to a more varied stimulus. Perform some sessions at a higher intensity (more weight, fewer reps) and other sessions with a higher volume (lower weight, more repetitions/sets).
- Freeweights can be used, but these are generally more difficult to apply the load as effectively as the machines, and can be limited by such factors as grip strength or endurance. Imagine the load you use on a standing calf raise machine – could you hold the equivalent load as a dumbbell in one hand? Probably not. If you hold two dumbbells or a barbell across the back, then balance is usually the limiting factor.

PRESS PATTERN
SUPPLEMENTARY EXERCISES

Exercise 10.11 Chest fly

(a)

(b)

Equipment
Dumbbells

Aim
This is a press pattern supplementary exercise to work the chest and shoulder muscles in the horizontal vector.

Set-up
- Lift the dumbbells up and adopt a supine position on a bench or equivalent.
- Extend the arms so that the dumbbells are positioned directly above the shoulders.
- Position the hands in a semi-supinated grip with the palms facing each other.
- Brace the core.

Execution
- Keeping a slight bend at the elbows, allow the arms to slowly lower outwards, controlling the descent of the dumbbells.
- Allow the dumbbells to descend until the arms are horizontal, and a stretch is felt in the pecs.
- Pause briefly then squeeze the pecs to pull the dumbbells back up to the start position.
- Repeat for the prescribed number of repetitions.

Technical considerations
- The exercise is most effective at the end of the range, when the arms are horizontal, and the lever arm is greatest and against gravity. There is very little resistance pulling the arms apart at the beginning of the range when the arms are above the shoulders. A cable fly, although a little more of a pain to set up, will allow for a more constant resistance throughout the range.
- Variations include declined flies, inclined flies or cable flies.

Exercise 10.12 Chest fly with suspension system

(a)

(b)

Equipment
Suspension system

Aims
This is a press pattern supplementary exercise to work the chest and shoulder muscles in the horizontal vector, and the anterior and lateral core muscles for stability.

Set-up
- Connect the two-strap suspension system to the anchor points, ideally at least 6ft high and wider than shoulder width apart.
- Stand facing away from the anchor points and hold one handle in each hand, with a semi-supinated grip (palms facing inwards).
- Brace the core and lean forward so that the arms are extended and the body is straight and rigid.
- Move the feet forward or backwards to achieve the optimal level of intensity.

Execution
- Move the arms apart under control to slowly lower the body downwards.
- Hold briefly when the hands are level with the shoulder, or before.
- Maintain a rigid body position throughout the exercise, keeping the head in line with the spine and preventing chin-poking.
- Push down with the hands and bring them together to lift the body back to the start position.
- Focus on squeezing the pectorals for maximum benefit.

Technical considerations

- Avoid fixing the scapula or executing the pull with a retraction, and allow the retraction to occur naturally as part of the pull.
- Avoid the shoulders lifting up during the pull (scapula elevation).
- Avoid overarching the hips and the lower back.
- Move the feet further away from the anchor point to decrease the intensity.
- Move the feet closer to the anchor point, or underneath and beyond the anchor point (if possible) or elevate the feet off the ground (against a wall or up on a bench), so that the body is horizontal or angled. These variations will all increase the intensity.
- Lifting one foot off the ground will increase the instability making the exercise more challenging from a balance perspective.
- Variations include supinated grip, pronated grip, split grip and pronated-to-semi-supinated grip.

Exercise 10.13 Standing external shoulder rotation, teres minor position

(a)

(b)

Equipment

Cable handle

Aims

This is a press pattern supplementary exercise to work the external rotators of the shoulder, specifically the teres minor muscle of the rotator cuff.

Set-up

- Connect the cable handle to the column at a position about navel height.
- Stand sideways on to the cable column, about 2–3ft away.
- Take hold of the handle with the furthest hand and hold with the arm bent at 90 degrees, the elbow tucked in close to the body and the forearm across the abdomen.
- The back of the hand should be facing forwards.

Execution

- Pull the handle outwards, using the back of the shoulder and keeping the elbow close to the body.
- Keep the rest of the body still to avoid bringing any other muscles into play.
- Rotate the shoulder out as far as possible, usually between 90–135 degrees.
- Briefly hold then slowly return the handle to the start position.
- Repeat for the prescribed number of repetitions.

Technical considerations

- Focus on keeping the elbow close to the body throughout the exercise to ensure that shoulder rotation is emphasised.
- Keep the rest of the body still throughout the exercise.
- Perform with a slow tempo, such as 4.1.2.1, to limit momentum.
- Variations include shoulder external rotation at different positions of shoulder abduction to emphasis the different muscles of the rotator cuff.

Exercise 10.14 Seated external shoulder rotation, mid-abduction position

(a)

(b)

Equipment
Dumbbell

Aims
This is a supplementary exercise to work the external rotators of the shoulder (teres minor and infraspinatus muscles of the rotator cuff).

Set-up
- Sit on a bench and place one foot on the bench next to you.
- Place the elbow of the arm on the same side as the elevated foot on the knee.
- The elbow should be about 4in lower than the shoulder.
- Hold the dumbbell in the hand, with the forearm vertical.

Execution
- Lower the dumbbell slowly towards the bench by rotating the shoulder inwards.
- Allow the shoulder to rotate maximally without altering the position of the torso.
- Keep the rest of the body still to avoid bringing any other muscles into play.
- Pause at the bottom position then pull the dumbbell back upwards to the start position.
- Repeat for the prescribed number of repetitions.

Technical considerations
- Keep the elbow on the knee throughout and maintain an upright chest position.
- Perform with a slow tempo, such as 4.1.1.1, to limit momentum.
- Variations include shoulder external rotation at different positions of shoulder abduction to emphasis the different muscles of the rotator cuff.

Exercise 10.15 Standing overhead triceps extension

(a)

(b)

Equipment
Cable rope

Aims
This is a supplementary exercise to work the elbow extensors (triceps brachii) and the anterior core muscles as stabilisers.

Set-up
- Connect the cable rope to the column at a high point position.
- Take hold of the cable rope with two hands and turn away from the cable column.
- Brace the core and assume a split stance leaning away from the column, with the torso and rear leg aligned.
- Have the arms extended above and in front of the head, with the hands in a semi-supinated grip.

Execution
- Bend the elbows and allow the hands to slowly move towards the cable column.
- Keep the elbows up and the upper arms still as the arms bend.
- Pause briefly as the arms reach full flexion.
- Straighten the arms quickly back to full extension, focusing on squeezing the triceps as you do so.
- Hold briefly and then repeat for the prescribed number of repetitions.

Technical considerations
- Focus on keeping the core braced and the spine neutral throughout the exercise.
- Keep the elbows tucked in and the upper arms still.
- Variations include triceps cable pushdown, triceps kickback and supine triceps extension.

Exercise 10.16 Kneeling triceps extension

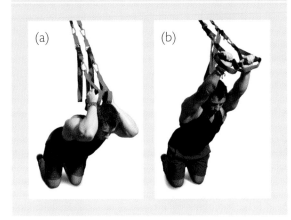

(a) (b)

Equipment

Two-strap suspension system

Aims

This is a supplementary exercise to work the elbow extensors muscles (triceps brachii), as well as the anterior and lateral core muscles for stability.

Set-up

- Connect the two-strap suspension system to the anchor points, ideally at least 6ft high and wider than shoulder width apart.
- Kneel on the floor facing away from the anchor points and hold one handle in each hand, with a pronated grip (palms facing downwards).
- Brace the core and lean forward so that the arms are extended and the body is straight and rigid.
- Move the knees forward or backwards to achieve the optimal level of intensity.

Execution

- Flex the elbows under control to slowly lower the body downwards.
- Hold briefly when the elbows are flexed maximally.
- Maintain a rigid body position throughout the exercise, keeping the head in line with the spine and preventing chin-poking.
- Push down with the hands to extend the arms and lift the body back to the start position.
- Focus on squeezing the triceps for maximum benefit.

Technical considerations

- Avoid the shoulders lifting up (scapula elevation) during the exercise.
- Avoid the hips sagging and the lower back overarching.
- Move the knees further away from the anchor point to decrease the intensity.
- Move the knees closer to the anchor point to increase the intensity.
- Variations include supinated grip, semi-supinated grip with a cable rope attachment or standing triceps extension.

Exercise 10.17 Standing triceps push-down

(a)

(b)

Equipment
Cable bar

Aim
This is a supplementary exercise to work the elbow extensors (triceps brachii).

Set-up
* Connect the cable bar to the column at a high point position.
* Take hold of the bar with two hands in a pronated grip facing the cable column.
* Brace the core and allow the arms to flex.

Execution
* Extend the arms to 99 per cent of full extension.
* Keep the upper arm still and pivot around the elbow.
* Pause briefly as the arms reach full flexion and repeat for the prescribed number of repetitions.

Technical considerations
* Keeping the bar closer to the body, allowing the elbows to move out to the side, a technique required when lifting heavier loads, will activate the long head of the triceps.
* Variations include triceps cable overhead extension, triceps kickback and supine triceps extension.

Exercise 10.18 Supine triceps extension to forehead

(a)

(b)

Equipment

EZ bar (variation: chains)

Aim

This is a supplementary exercise to work the elbow extensors (triceps brachii).

Set-up

- Lift the EZ bar up and adopt a supine position on the floor, a bench or similar.
- Extend the arms so that the bar is positioned directly above the shoulders.
- Position the hands in a semi-pronated grip with the palms angled downwards to the feet.
- Brace the core.

Execution

- Allow the arms to slowly bend at the elbows and control the descent of the bar.
- Allow the arms to fully flex so that the bar is just above the forehead.
- Keep the upper arms still and pivot around the elbows.
- Pause briefly as the arms reach full flexion then extend back up to the start position.
- Repeat for the prescribed number of repetitions.

Technical considerations

- The EZ bar is preferable to a straight bar because it decreases the stress on the wrist.
- Variations include bringing the EZ bar down to the bridge of the nose, the chin or the neck.
- Add chains to the bar to provide a means of progressive resistance, where the load increases as more weight is lifted off the floor.

PULL PATTERN
SUPPLEMENTARY EXERCISES
UPPER BACK EXERCISES

Exercise 10.19 Standing Shrugs

(a) (b)

Equipment

Dumbbell with Fat Gripz™ (variations: barbell, cable)

Aims

This is a supplementary exercise to work the upper trapezius and to overload the forearm musculature with Fat Gripz™.

Set-up

- Place the Fat Gripz™ over a pair of dumbbells.
- Assume a standing position with feet hip width apart.
- Take hold of the dumbbells with a semi-supinated grip (palms facing inwards).
- Position the arms in an extended position by the sides of the body.

Execution

- Brace the core and lift the shoulders upwards towards the ears.
- Keep the body upright and stiff and ensure no movement occurs at the torso.
- Ensure the movement is purely vertical and do not roll the shoulders during the shrug.
- Briefly pause at the top position and then slowly lower the dumbbells back to the start.
- Repeat for the prescribed number of repetitions.

Technical considerations

- Focus on lifting the shoulders straight upwards to the ears.
- Keep the dumbbells in a semi-supinated grip position to ensure optimal biomechanics.
- Rolling during the shrug will potentially stress the acromial-clavicular joint.
- Variations include single arm dumbbell shrug, cable shrugs or barbell overhead shrugs.

Exercise 10.20 Reverse fly

(a)

(b)

Equipment

Cable handle (variations: dumbbell, suspension system)

Aims

This is a supplementary exercise to work the middle trapezius and rhomboids.

Set-up

*   Set up a cable handle attachment at about sternum height.
*   Stand with feet hip width apart, facing at an angle to the column.
*   Take hold of the handle in one hand and take a step away.

Execution

*   Brace the core and pull the handle back.
*   Keep the arm almost straight with just a slight bend in the elbow.
*   Pull the cable handle back in an arc until level with shoulder.
*   Keep the elbow facing out.
*   Pause, then slowly control back to the start position.
*   Repeat for the prescribed number of repetitions.

Technical considerations

*   Keep shoulder down during the pull.
*   Focus on squeezing the shoulder blades together.
*   Variations include double cable reverse flies, bent over dumbbell reverse fly or suspension system reverse flies.

BICEPS EXERCISES

Exercise 10.21 Kneeling Scott Curl (preacher curl), one hand supinated grip

(a)

(b)

Equipment
Stability ball, dumbbell

Aims
This is a supplementary exercise to work the biceps brachii and other elbow flexors, as a Scott curl exercise when a Scott curl bench is not available.

Set-up
- Assume a kneeling position on the floor with the stability ball in front of you.
- Rest the torso on the near side of the stability ball.
- Reach over the stability ball with one arm and take hold of the dumbbell.
- Grip the dumbbell with a supinated grip (palm facing upwards).

Execution
- Brace the core and lift the dumbbell upwards towards the shoulder.
- Keep your weight positioned behind the stability ball to ensure you don't get pulled forward.
- Flex (bend) the elbow maximally or until the forearm is vertical.
- Briefly pause and then slowly lower the dumbbell back to the start position just off the floor.
- Repeat for the prescribed number of repetitions.

Technical considerations
- Focus on keeping your weight back behind the stability ball.
- Do not allow the dumbbell to touch the floor between repetitions.
- The supinated grip will preferentially recruit the biceps brachii.
- This exercise will particularly emphasise the elbow flexors in the initial range of elbow flexion.
- Variations include Scott curl with semi-supinated grip, Scott curl with pronated grip or Scott curl with supinated grip and an extended (cocked) wrist.

Exercise 10.22 Standing concentration curl, supinated grip

(a)

(b)

Equipment
Dumbbell with Fat Gripz™

Aims

This is a supplementary exercise to work the biceps brachii and other elbow flexors, and to overload the forearm musculature with the Fat Gripz™.

Set-up
- Place the Fat Gripz™ over a dumbbell and place between the feet.
- Assume a standing position with feet shoulder width apart.
- Bend down and take hold of the dumbbell with the palm facing inwards.
- Position the upper arm or elbow against the inside part of the distal part of the thigh.

Execution
- Brace the core and lift the dumbbell upwards towards the shoulder.
- Pivot against the thigh to keep the upper arm still.
- Flex (bend) the elbow maximally or until the forearm is vertical.
- Briefly pause and then slowly lower the dumbbell back to the start position.
- Repeat for the prescribed number of repetitions.

Technical considerations
- Focus on contracting the biceps maximally during the curl.
- There should be no movement of the upper arm.
- The supinated grip will preferentially recruit the biceps brachii.
- This exercise will particularly work the elbow flexors in the end-range.
- Variations include concentration curl with semi-supinated grip, seated concentration curl or concentration curl with supinated grip and an extended (cocked) wrist.

Exercise 10.23 Standing curl, supinated grip

(a) (b)

Equipment
Dumbbell with Fat Gripz™

Aims
This is a supplementary exercise to work the biceps brachii and other elbow flexors, and to overload the forearm musculature with Fat Gripz™.

Set-up
- Place the Fat Gripz™ over a pair of dumbbells.
- Assume a standing position with feet hip width apart.
- Take hold of the dumbbells with a supinated grip (palms facing forwards).
- Position the arms in an extended position by the sides of the body.

Execution
- Brace the core and lift the dumbbells upwards towards the shoulders.
- Keep the body upright and stiff and ensure no movement occurs at the torso.
- Flex (bend) the elbows maximally or until the forearms are vertical.
- Briefly pause and then slowly lower the dumbbells back to the start position.
- Repeat for the prescribed number of repetitions.

Technical considerations
- Focus on contracting the biceps maximally during the curl.
- Limit movement of the upper arm.
- The supinated grip will preferentially recruit the biceps brachii.
- This exercise will particularly work the elbow flexors in the mid-range.
- Variations include curl with semi-supinated grip, curl with pronated grip or curl with supinated grip and an extended (cocked) wrist.

Exercise 10.24 Biceps curl

(a)

(b)

Equipment
EZ bar with chains

Aims
This is a supplementary exercise to work the biceps brachii and other elbow flexors with progressive resistance.

Set-up
- Attach the chain to an EZ bar, outside the plates if being used.
- Assume a standing position, with feet hip width apart.
- Take hold of the EZ bar with a supinated grip (palms facing upwards).
- Position the arms in an extended position by the sides of the body.

Execution
- Brace the core and lift the bar upwards towards the shoulders.
- Keep the body upright and stiff and ensure no movement occurs at the torso.
- Flex (bend) the elbows maximally or until the forearms are vertical.
- Briefly pause and then slowly lower and rotate the bar back to the start position.
- Repeat for the prescribed number of repetitions.

Technical considerations
- Focus on contracting the biceps maximally during the curl.
- Limit movement of the upper arm.
- The supinated grip will preferentially recruit the biceps brachii.
- Chains added to the bar will increase the tension on the concentric phase.
- Variations include reverse curl with chains.

Exercise 10.25 Reverse curl

(a)

(b)

Equipment
EZ bar with chains

Aim
This is a supplementary exercise to work the brachialis and brachioradialis, with progressive resistance.

Set-up
- Attach the chain to an EZ bar, outside the plates if being used.
- Assume a standing position, with feet hip width apart.
- Take hold of the EZ bar with a pronated grip (palms facing downwards).
- Position the arms in an extended position by the sides of the body.

Execution
- Brace the core and lift the bar upwards towards the shoulders.
- Keep the body upright and stiff and ensure no movement occurs at the torso.
- Flex (bend) the elbows maximally or until the forearms are vertical.
- Briefly pause and then slowly lower and rotate the bar back to the start position.
- Repeat for the prescribed number of repetitions.

Technical considerations
- Focus on contracting the biceps maximally during the curl.
- Limit movement of the upper arm.
- The pronated grip with rotation will preferentially recruit the brachialis and brachioradialis.
- Chains added to the bar will increase the tension on the concentric phase.
- Variations include Scott reverse curl with chains.

Exercise 10.26 Scott biceps curl

(a)   (b)

Equipment

Suspension system (variation: cable rope)

Aim

This is a supplementary exercise to work the elbow flexor muscles (specifically the biceps brachii), the grip muscles and the posterior chain muscles for stability.

Set-up

- Connect the two-strap suspension system to the anchor points, ideally at least 6ft high and about shoulder width apart.
- Stand facing the anchor points and hold one handle in each hand, with a supinated grip (palms facing upwards).
- Brace the core and lean back so that the arms are extended and the body is straight and rigid.
- Move the feet forward or backwards to achieve the optimal level of intensity.

Execution

- Pull the handles towards the ears by flexing the arms and keeping the upper arms elevated and high, maintaining the supinated grip throughout.
- Hold briefly when the elbows are flexed maximally, and then slowly lower back to the start position.
- Maintain a rigid body position throughout the exercise, keeping the head in line with the spine and preventing chin-poking.

Technical considerations

- Focus on bringing the handles to the ears to maintain correct positioning of the upper arms – bringing the handles to the shoulders usually causes the elbows to drop.
- Avoid the hips sagging (flexing) at the end of the eccentric phase.
- Move the feet further away from the anchor point to decrease the intensity.
- Move the feet closer to the anchor point to increase the intensity.
- Extending the wrists on the eccentric phase or on both phases will increase the extension on the elbow flexors.
- Variations include supinated grip with extended wrists, pronated grip and semi-supinated grip with cable rope attachment.

CORE SUPPLEMENTARY EXERCISES

Exercise 10.27 Reverse crossover step and lateral overhead reach

(a) (b)

Equipment
Cable handle

Aims
This is a supplementary exercise to work the lateral core (obliques) and lateral hip muscles (glute medius, minimus and the tensor fascia latae), as well as promoting frontal plane mobility, at the hips, core and shoulders.

Set-up
- Connect the cable handle to the column at high point position.
- Stand sideways on to the cable column, about 2–3ft away.
- Take hold of the handle with the furthest hand and hold behind the head, with the arm bent.

- The palm should be facing the back of the head with the elbow high.

Execution
- Lift the far foot and take a step backwards and towards the cable column.
- At the same time, reach upwards and towards the cable column with the handle, and allow the torso to bend to the side (laterally flex) to increase the range.
- This will stretch and stimulate the lateral core muscles and the lateral hip muscles.
- Allow the stance leg to bend as required, keeping the foot flat on the ground.
- Without holding this position, drive the elbow downwards, as if performing a one-arm lat pull down, and step back to the start position.
- Repeat for the prescribed number of repetitions.

Technical considerations
- Focus on keeping the hips and shoulders aligned in the frontal plane throughout the exercise.
- Keep the chest up and the palm facing forwards throughout.
- To stimulate the muscle spindles effectively, this exercise should be performed dynamically and without holding the end position.
- Variations include performing off of a raised step, crossover step with lateral overhead reach or lateral overhead reach without the step.

Exercise 10.28 Windmill

(a)

(b)

Equipment
Barbell (high position)

Aims
This is a supplementary exercise to work the lateral core (obliques) and lateral hip muscles (glute medius, minimus and the tensor fascia latae), as well as improving shoulder stability and promoting frontal plane mobility at the hips and core.

Set-up
- Lift the barbell up to the overhead press position, using the clean and press or snatch technique.
- Position the feet about hip to shoulder width apart.
- Turn both feet out about thirty degrees with the heels on the same line, keeping the opposite knee stiff.
- Inhale and brace the core.

Execution
- Look up at the bar and place the other hand on the lead thigh.
- Push the rear hip (the one beneath the bar) over the rear foot.
- Slide the back of hand down the inner thigh and lower leg.
- Pause briefly at the bottom, then focus on pulling the hips forwards back to the middle position to lift the torso back to vertical.
- Return to the start position and repeat for the prescribed number of repetitions.
- Watch the bar throughout the drill when held above the head.
- Undertake each rep slowly, taking 3–4 seconds on the way down with a 1–2 second hold at the bottom.

- Keep the arm extended vertically upwards throughout the drill.

Technical considerations

- The windmill is used to develop standing frontal plane stability, working the lateral core, hip stability and shoulder mobility, and stability is essential when pressing a load above the head in one hand or when lifting a weight from the floor with one hand.
- It is a key preparation exercise for exercises such as the side press and bent press, as well as the single hand snatch and jerk. Commonly used with kettlebells, the barbell windmill and dumbbell windmill (see figure 10.1) are both excellent variations.
- One of the main errors with the windmill is not keeping the rear hip pushed back. When the hips move towards the lead leg, they take the tension off the hip stabilisers and puts more stress on the lateral core. These muscles should work together to stabilise the hips and core during this drill. To correct this, have the individual perform the exercise with the rear hip touching a wall so that they can feel when it moves off.

Progressions for the windmill exercise are:

1. One hand windmill – bar held in lower hand
2. One hand windmill – bar held in upper hand
3. One hand windmill – bar held in upper hand with lower hand held behind the back
4. Two hand windmill – two bars, one high and one low.

Figure 10.1 Dumbbell windmill

Exercise 10.29 Side plank

(a)

(b)

(c)

Execution
- Lift the hips off the ground and adopt the lateral bridge or side plank position.
- The hips and shoulders should be level and the body should be in a straight line.
- Hold the position for the prescribed period of time.

Technical considerations
- Variations include side plank with feet elevated lateral line emphasis (b) or side plank with feet elevated medial line emphasis (c).
- Athletes should be able to hold each position for 20–40 seconds with minimal difference bilaterally. All athletes at elite level will have the strength to easily hold the position for 40 seconds, but, since the function of the fascia is being tested, any sensation of burning, cramping, pain or strain in the muscle indicates diminished mobility of fascia on that line (de Witt and Venter, 2009). Inability to adopt the position is noted as 0 seconds.

Equipment
Bodyweight

Aims
This is a supplementary exercise to work the lateral core (obliques) and lateral hip muscles (glute medius, minimus and the tensor fascia latae), as well as improving shoulder stability.

Set-up
- Adopt a side lying position on the floor.
- Rest the forearm of the lower arm on the floor beneath the shoulder.
- Inhale and brace the core.

Exercise 10.30 Side plank with hip drop

(a)

(b)

Equipment

Two-strap suspension system

Aims

This is a supplementary exercise to work the lateral core (obliques) and lateral hip muscles (glute medius, minimus and the tensor fascia latae), as well as the shoulder stabiliser muscles.

Set-up

- Connect the two-strap suspension system to the anchor points, at about hip width apart or less, so that the straps are about 12–18in off of the ground.
- Sit on the floor facing the straps and place both feet into each of the straps.

- Lie back on the floor, and roll onto one side, into a side plank position, with the hips on the ground.
- Move the body closer or further from the anchor points to achieve the optimal level of intensity.
- Brace the core and lift the hips off the ground, keeping the body straight and rigid, into a side plank position, with the weight on the forearm.

Execution

- Slowly lower the hips towards the floor, without rotating the torso at all.
- Pause just before the hips touch the floor, or when maximal range of motion in the frontal plane.
- Contact the lateral core to lift the hips back up to the start position and hold for a few seconds.
- Repeat for the prescribed number of repetitions or hold for a set period of time.
- Focus on keeping the hips and shoulders aligned in the frontal plane throughout the exercise.

Technical considerations

- Avoid the shoulders or hips rotating during the exercise.
- Avoid the lower back overarching.
- Move the feet closer to the anchor points, or beyond the anchor point to decrease the intensity.
- Move the feet further away from the anchor points to increase the intensity.
- Support the body on the hand to increase the stability requirements at the shoulder and to make the exercise harder.
- Variations include side plank only, single leg side plank (lower or upper leg) or side plank with hip flexion.

Exercise 10.31 Roll out

(a)

(b)

(c)

Equipment
Stability ball (variation: Lifeline power wheel)

Aims
This is a supplementary exercise to work the anterior core, as well as improving shoulder stability.

Set-up
- Adopt a kneeling position on the floor with the stability ball in front of you.
- Rest the forearms on the near edge of the stability ball.
- Inhale and brace the core.

Execution
- Push the forearms forward rolling the stability ball away from you.
- Push the hips forward at the same speed as the forearms.
- Briefly hold this end position, then pull the elbows back and return to the start position.
- Repeat for the prescribed number of repetitions.

Technical considerations
- Maintain a normal lumbar curvature throughout.
- Keep the chest up and the head in line.
- Variations include performing with a Lifeline power wheel (c).

Exercise 10.32 Jackknife

(a)

(b)

(c)

Set-up
- Adopt a kneeling position on the floor with the stability ball in front of you.
- Put the chest on the stability ball and roll forward into a press-up position.
- The stability ball should be positioned under the shins.
- Inhale and brace the core.

Execution
- Bring the knees up towards the chest.
- Maintain a neutral spine and keep the hips in the same position.
- Briefly hold this end position, then push the stability ball back and return to the start position.
- Repeat for the prescribed number of repetitions.

Technical considerations
- Maintain a normal lumbar curvature throughout.
- Keep the chest up and the head in line.
- Variations include performing with a LifeLine power wheel (c).

Equipment
Stability ball (variation: Lifeline power wheel)

Aims
This is a supplementary exercise to work the anterior core, as well as improving shoulder stability.

Exercise 10.33 Ground conditioning punching on a Powerbag™

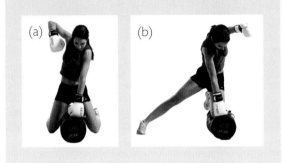

(a) (b)

Equipment
Powerbag™

Aims
This is a supplementary exercise to develop ground conditioning to mimic ground and pound in MMA.

Set-up
• Adopt a kneeling position on the floor on top of a Powerbag™.
• Place one hand on the floor next to the top of the Powerbag™.
• Brace the core.

Execution
• Perform punches onto the Powerbag™ with the same hand.
• Alternate sides every 30 seconds.
• Repeat for the prescribed duration of time.

Technical considerations
• Keep the chest up and the head in line.
• Variations including alternating punches to the Powerbag™ (a) and alternating punches with one knee on the Powerbag™ (b).

Exercise 10.34 Undulating training with ropes

Equipment
Ropes

Aims
This is a supplementary exercise to develop upper body anaerobic conditioning and to work the forearms, arms and shoulders.

Set-up
• Set up the conditioning ropes so that they are attached to an anchor point.
• Brace the core.

Execution
• Perform different types of undulating waves, including double waves, alternating waves, angled waves and lateral waves.
• Vary the type of waves every 30 seconds.
• Repeat for the prescribed duration of time.

Technical considerations

- Keep the chest up and the spine neutral.
- Try to make the pattern of the waves look rhythmical and equal, symmetrical on both left and right, wave after wave.
- Integrate the upper and lower body into the movements.
- Keep your wrist relaxed but 'connected' to the rest of your arms for optimal technique.
- As the wave moves away, pull back on the rope to accelerate the wave all the way to the other end.
- Variations include – hooks, uppercuts, circles in or out, judo rotation throws, waves with reverse lunges, waves with lateral lunges or get-up anyhow waves.

SELF-MYOFASCIAL RELEASE (SMFR) EXERCISES

Exercise 10.35 SMFR, tibialis anterior, prone position

Equipment
Foam roller

Aims
To promote relaxation of the anterior tibialis muscle by applying tension using the foam roller, which will help to increase flexibility and mobility for functional movements.

Set-up
- Position yourself prone on your elbows, anterior aspect of lower leg on roller, opposite leg bent for support.
- If tolerable, cross legs to increase pressure.
- Position the roller on the anterior tibialis (shin muscle).

- Press body down on roller to exert pressure, and lift opposite leg up to increase further.

Execution

- Activate the core/glutes by bracing and squeezing.
- Roll up and down the shin muscle, particularly towards the knee, keeping the knee locked.
- Rotate the hips to apply pressure transversely.
- When a tender spot is found, stop rolling and hold on this point until the pain decreases by about 50–75 per cent.
- Gently invert and evert the foot, and return while holding position.
- When released, continue to 'search' the anterior tibialis for more tender spots and repeat.

Exercise 10.36 SMFR, gastrocnemius, supine position

Equipment

Foam roller

Aims

To promote relaxation of the calf muscle by applying tension using the foam roller, which will help to increase flexibility and mobility for functional movements.

Set-up

- Sit on the floor with legs straight and calves on top of the roller.
- If calves are very tender, then put both legs on the roller at the same time, side by side.
- If tolerable, cross legs to increase pressure on lower leg.
- Place hands next to hips and press body up that hips are elevated above the ground and more pressure is exerted on calf.

Execution

- Roll up and down the calf, keeping the knee locked.
- Rotate the hips to apply pressure onto the medial and lateral areas of the calf.
- When a tender spot is found, stop rolling and hold on this point until the pain decreases by about 50–75 per cent.
- Gently dorsiflex and return while holding position.
- When released, continue to 'search' the calf for more tender spots and repeat.

Exercise 10.37 SMFR peroneals, lateral position

Equipment
Foam roller

Aims
To promote relaxation of the lateral lower leg muscle by applying tension using the foam roller, which will help to increase flexibility and mobility for functional movements.

Set-up
Please follow the steps for the gastrocnemius variation in Exercise 10.36

Execution
- Perform as for the gastrocnemius variation but roll on the lateral lower leg, particularly towards the knee, keeping the knee locked.
- Gently invert and evert the foot, and return while holding position.

Exercise 10.38 SMFR iliotibial band (ITB)

Equipment
Foam roller

Aims
To promote relaxation of the ITB by applying tension using the foam roller, which will help to increase flexibility and mobility for functional movements.

Set-up
- Position yourself laterally on your elbows, lateral aspect of hip on roller, opposite leg bent for support.
- If tolerable, cross legs to increase pressure.
- Position the roller on the ITB.
- Press body down on roller to exert pressure, and lift opposite leg up to increase pressure.

Execution
- Activate the core/glutes by bracing and squeezing.
- Roll up and down the muscle, particularly towards the knee and hip bones.
- Rotate the hips to apply pressure transversely.
- When a tender spot is found, stop rolling and hold on this point until the pain decreases by about 50–75 per cent.
- Gently lift and drop the upper body, and return while holding position.
- When released, continue to 'search' the ITB for more tender spots and repeat.

Exercise 10.39 SMFR latissimus dorsi

Equipment
Foam roller

Aims
To promote relaxation of the latissimus dorsi muscle by applying tension using the foam roller, which will help to increase flexibility and mobility for functional movements.

Set-up
- Position yourself laterally on your elbow, roller positioned just lower than armpit, leg bent for support.
- If tolerable, lift arm to increase pressure.
- Position the roller on the latissimus dorsi near the insertion.
- Press body down on roller to exert pressure, and lift arm to increase pressure.

Execution
- Activate the core/glutes by bracing and squeezing.
- Roll up and down the muscle, particularly towards the insertion, keeping the arm extended.
- Rotate the shoulders to apply pressure transversely.
- When a tender spot is found, stop rolling and hold on this point until the pain decreases by about 50–75 per cent.
- Gently reach with the arm while holding position.
- When released, continue to 'search' for more tender spots and repeat.

Exercise 10.40 SMFR adductors, prone position

Equipment
Foam roller

Aims
To promote relaxation of the adductor muscles by applying tension using the foam roller, which will help to increase flexibility and mobility.

Set-up
- Position yourself prone on your elbows, leg out to the side and medial aspect of thigh on roller, opposite leg on floor.
- Position the roller on the inner thigh.
- Press body down on roller to exert pressure.

Execution
- Activate the core/glutes by bracing/squeezing.
- Roll up and down the adductor muscles.
- Rotate the hips to apply pressure transversely.
- When a tender spot is found, stop rolling and hold on this point until the pain decreases by about 50–75 per cent.
- Gently flex and extend the knee, and return while holding position.
- When released, continue to 'search' for more tender spots and repeat.

Exercise 10.41 SMFR thoracic extension, prone position

Equipment
Foam roller

Aims
To promote mobility in the thoracic extensors of the spine for functional movements.

Set-up
- Position yourself supine over the roller, legs bent for support.
- Position the roller on the thoracic spine.
- Press body down on roller to exert pressure. Activate the core/glutes by bracing to protect lumbar area.
- Support head with hands if more comfortable.

Execution
- Roll up and down the roller, keeping the core tight.
- When a tender spot is found, stop rolling and hold on this point until the pain decreases by about 50–75 per cent.
- Gently rotate the head, and return while holding position.
- When released, continue to 'search' the thoracic spine for more tender spots and repeat.

APPLIED PROGRAMMES

11

The guidelines, advice and information from all of the previous chapters now needs to be summarised, clarified and applied into a variety of different training sessions and programmes, so that a trainer will be able to correctly apply this knowledge. For some parts of designing a training programme, every client can be treated in a similar fashion, since they are all humans and therefore the human movement patterns, limiting factors and assessments will all be the same. However, the goal of the individual, the starting fitness or strength levels, the results of assessments and individual limiting factors will vary from person to person, and would thus require individualisation of the programme. This chapter will review the training principles, give guidelines and explanations on the optimal training parameters, and then a number of examples of training programmes showing how to apply the information related to each movement pattern.

As explained in chapter 1, exercise science is founded on the principles of adaptation, overload, specificity, reversibility, acclimatisation, generalisation and individuality. All training programmes should adhere to these principles in order to successfully reach the goals of the individual. These principles should be adhered to when selecting the appropriate training variables for a given individual. It is then the correct selection and manipulation of the training variables that will ensure that optimal adaptations (improvements) are achieved.

TRAINING VARIABLES
REPS AND INTENSITY

The selection of an appropriate repetition range is probably the most important training variable in resistance training programming. The repetition range will influence other training variables such as the tempo, sets, rests and of course the intensity.

Intensity and repetition range are intrinsically linked and inversely proportional; as the repetition range decreases, the intensity increases. Repetition maximum (RM) infers that the maximum weight is lifted for the number given, i.e. a 6–8RM means that the chosen weight should cause the client to go to concentric failure between the sixth and eighth repetition. No matter what the desired training effect, the client must go to failure in order to elicit that effect. Each particular repetition range has a specific training outcome:

Table 11.1	Specific training outcomes of particular repetition ranges	
Repetition range	**Intensity**	**Dominant training effect**
1–6 RM	85–100 % of 1RM	Relative strength
6–8 RM	79–84 % of 1RM	Functional strength
8–12 RM	70–78 % of 1RM	Hypertrophy
12+ RM	69% of 1RM or less	Strength endurance

Beginners have a low threshold for improvements in strength, and thus will respond to a low intensity with higher repetitions. Using high intensity repetition ranges and advanced training systems with beginners will cause chronic overreaching and will eventually lead to overtraining.

Although strength endurance (12+ repetitions) is beneficial for preparation phases of training, it is important to realise that there is a lot of evidence to show that maximal strength is only achieved at or above 70 per cent of 1RM (McDonagh & Davies, 1984). Some authors have shown that this minimal level may be 60 per cent (Currier and Mann,1983), but this is more likely to only be with those relatively new to resistance training.

Training doesn't need to be the hardest session imaginable every session. When we say that more is better, we mean more than the body is used to, not the most the body can handle or the most that can be squeezed into an hour's session. Again for overload to cause adaptations, it only needs be above what the body is used to, not excessively above what it is used to. For example, elite weightlifters use average loads of 75% ± 2% (Zatsiorsky, 1995), while lifts above 90% per cent generally represented only about 5–13 per cent of the total annual volume (Poliquin, 2004).

Use lower rep ranges:

- With muscle groups with higher percentages of fast twitch fibres (such as the biceps brachii or the hamstrings).
- With athletes with greater amounts of fast twitch fibres (such as those gifted for explosive and speed sports).
- For exercises with a high neurological or coordination demand, such as the Olympic lifts, modified lifts and pulls. With complex, multiple-joint exercises, such as the Olympic lifts, excessive repetitions may bring about undesirable motor learning and technical changes (Poliquin, 2004). With the Olympic lifts the majority of all sets are performed with 1-3 reps; in the snatch only 1.8% of sets are done with 3-4 reps (Zatsiorsky, 1995).
- For exercises with potential stabiliser fatigue, such as front and overhead squats. For assistant exercises to the Olympic lifts like these, the number of reps would be between 1 and 10, with an average of 3-6. For some assistant exercises like the power clean or front squat, excessive repetitions would be counter-productive since some of the stabilising muscles, like the rhomboids, would fatigue quickly and cause changes in the technique. To prevent this, most strength coaches keep the repetitions on the low side, around 4-6, with these exercises.

- If the load is high (85-100% or 1RM) or supra-maximal (up to 130-140% of 1RM), then low repetition ranges must be used.
- As clients or athletes adapt to the repetition ranges, the minimal threshold to elicit a training effect will gradually increase, i.e. the minimal threshold may be 12 reps (70% of 1RM) for a beginner, whereas 4 years later they will need to do 8 reps or less in order to have any influence on maximal strength.
- With progressive resistance tools, such as chains and heavy bands.

Important considerations with reps:

- Do not use low rep ranges and high intensities too frequently or overtraining may result.
- Use mid rep ranges to cause a greater hormonal response and increases in growth hormone (Häkkinen and Pakarinen, 1993).
- Use higher rep ranges with muscle groups with higher percentages of slow twitch fibres, and with clients new to resistance training (as part of their preparation phases).
- Vary rep ranges more with fast twitch athletes and more for the upper body than the lower body.

SETS AND VOLUME

The manipulation of the number of sets when programming is a key parameter in the pursuit of strength. The use of multiple sets will lead to higher and quicker gains in strength, and for each training effect there is an optimal and upper limit to the number of sets required.

Use more sets:

- To elicit gains in size. Hypertrophy gains will be triggered by the greater volume causing increases in testosterone and growth hormone (Kraemer et al, 1990).
- For functional and relative strength. Functional and relative strength gains with high sets will be gained by better recruitment of the fast twitch fibres.
- For athletes with greater percentages of fast twitch fibres, since a greater number of sets will elicit more increases in strength.
- If a programme has only a few specific exercises. At that point more sets should be undertaken on these exercises to focus strength in particular planes or for particular movement patterns.
- If the reps are kept very low because of the issues with technical changes or altered motor learning. At that point the number of sets to elicit

Table 11.2	Guidelines on prescription of sets					
	Reps	Intensity	Time under tension (s)	Rest (s)	Sets/ exercise	Sets/ session
Relative strength	1-6	85-100	1-20	180-300	5-12	6-20
Functional strength	6-8	79-84	20-40	120-180	4-8	8-27
Hypertrophy	8-12	70-78	40-70	90-120	4-8	22-35
Strength endurance	12+	69 or less	50-120	10-90	2-4	16-28

favorable changes will need to be high. A high number of multiple sets help to develop the skill of activating muscle fibres for maximal efforts with such explosive exercises as the snatch.

Use less sets:

- With exercises with larger repetition ranges.
- With exercises with longer time under tension, such as if chains are added to a barbell, increasing the concentric phase.
- In sessions with more exercises.
- With exercises that are more neurologically or metabolically demanding (such as a stiff leg dead lift on a step or power cleans), then the number of sets should be reduced slightly to take this into account.

REST AND RECOVERY

The key to selecting the appropriate rest period is which training goal is being targeted – the higher the intensity and the lower the repetition range, the longer the rest periods.

Adequate rest periods will ensure that the energy system being targeted recovers fully between sets. Relative strength training targets the anaerobic alactate (ATP-CP) system, which takes up to 4–5 minutes to completely replenish the stores of ATP (adenosine triphosphate) and CP (creatine phosphate). It also primarily targets the neurological system, which takes much longer to recover than the muscles being used. Many do not appreciate the importance of these rest periods, and as such only allow a few minutes between sets. This will cause inadequate rest periods and the desired training effect on the neurological system will *not* be achieved.

Important considerations with rest:

- Selection of the rest period will vary depending on the exercise. Exercises which have a longer range of motion, that recruit more muscle mass or are neurologically more demanding will require longer rest periods for adequate recovery.
- Selection of the rest period will vary depending on the client or athlete. The larger the athlete the longer the rest period will need to be (this may be because of the different fibre make-up).
- As an adaptation over a period of time, for any particular time under tension, an athlete may well require less time to recover between sets.
- The rest interval can be manipulated to affect

Table 11.3	Guidelines on prescription of rest			
	Reps	Intensity	Time under tension (s)	Rest period (s)
Relative strength	1-6	85-100%	1-20	180-300
Functional strength	6-8	79-84%	20-40	120-180
Hypertrophy	8-12	70-78%	40-70	90-120
Strength endurance	12+	69% or less	50-120	10-90

the hormonal response. Keeping the rest intervals shorter will increase production of testosterone (Fry et al, 1994) and growth hormone (Kraemer et al, 1990).

- Pairing antagonistic muscle groups, such as push-pull muscles in the upper body, or upper-lower body pairs can allow for shorter rest periods and a larger volume of work for the session.
- Intra-set rest periods of 10–20 seconds should not necessarily be chastised and may in fact favour the recruitment of the higher threshold motor units.
- Take a recovery week off from training approximately every 12 weeks, and perform active recovery activities such as tennis, golf, cycling, yoga, swimming, etc.

TEMPO

Tempo can be defined as the speed of movement for an exercise and variation in the tempo may be critical for prolonged strength development (Bührle and Schmidtbleicher, 1981), particularly for elite athletes in power sports. There are a few different methods for showing the tempo; the following is the most comprehensive:

Example:
Front squat   3 sets   6–8 reps   **4.1.1.0**   120s

This four digit code is used to describe the tempo for the different phases of a resistance exercise: eccentric, isometric, concentric, isometric. Using the example of the front squat, a client would undertake the following tempo:

- **4** seconds for the eccentric phase (the controlling phase from the standing position to the bottom position);

- **1** second for the isometric phase (the pause in the bottom position);
- **1** second for the concentric phase (the exerting phase from the bottom position to the standing position);
- **0** seconds for the isometric phase (the pause in the standing position).

Using this example each repetition would take a total of 6 seconds to complete, which becomes very important when calculating the time under tension for a set. If a trainer wishes to have their client undertake a phase as fast as possible (normally the concentric phase) then an 'X' can be used. So the tempo for the front squat with a fast concentric phase would be written as 4.1.X.0.

This system can cause some trainers or clients to get confused with most pulling exercises, since they tend to begin with the concentric phase first. The numeral system does not change for each exercise, since this would cause more confusion. No matter whether the exercise is executed with a concentric or eccentric phase first, it is always written as **Eccentric. Isometric. Concentric. Isometric**.

The speed of the movement determines a number of things, including the amount of tension developed, the use of mechanical energy (such as the stretch-shortening cycle), and the load (King, 2000). This obviously has implications for the outcome of the training effect; utilising the mechanical properties of the stretch shortening cycle will elicit more neurological adaptations (for relative strength and power), while increasing the muscular tension can elicit more morphological changes (for hypertrophy).

TIME UNDER TENSION

The term 'time under tension' has been used by Ian King for decades and describes how long a muscle or group of muscles is under contractile stress. Time under tension, or TUT, is calculated by multiplying the number of repetitions by the tempo or total time for each repetition. For example, if 6 reps of the front squat are performed at a tempo of 4.1.1.0, then the total TUT for that set would be 6 x 6 seconds, or 36 seconds. The following table describes the training effect elicited from different times under tension:

Table 11.4

The training effect elicited from different times under tension (adapted from King, 2000)

Time under tension (TUT) in seconds	Dominant training effect
1–20	Speed strength/maximal strength
20-40	Functional strength
40–70	Hypertrophy
50–120	Strength endurance

It is critical to know the total TUT for a set, or the desired training effect may not be achieved. For example, a young bodybuilder who races through his 10 reps on the squat, at an estimated tempo of 1.0.1.0, will only take about 20 seconds to complete the set. They believe that they are at an ideal rep range for hypertrophy, but because of the tempo used it will elicit more relative strength gains.

Considerations with tempo and time under tension

- The desired training effect should dictate the total TUT. This should be the first and most important thing when selecting the repetitions and tempo. These training variables are obviously highly interconnected when considering TUT.

- Selection of the eccentric tempo will vary depending on the desired training effect. For preparation and hypertrophy training, the usual range is between 3–6 seconds for the eccentric phase. For functional and relative strength, 1–3 seconds is used. The eccentric duration will also be affected by the range of the exercise, for example, it is easier and safer to undertake a 1 second eccentric lowering on a wrist flexor exercise than a front squat with a larger range of motion. Some exercises will demand a fast eccentric phase, such as the Olympic lifts or a push press.

- Selection of the mid-isometric tempo will vary depending on the desired training effect. If more muscular tension is desired for hypertrophying effects, then the isometric pause should be increased to reduce the effect of the stretch shortening cycle. Research shows that this should be up to 4 seconds to eliminate the elastic energy from the eccentric phase (Wilson et al, 1991). For strength training this period should be between 0–2 seconds and should be 0 seconds for power training.

- Selection of the concentric tempo will vary depending on the desired training effect. The majority of training should be done with concentric tempos of 1 second or less. Some will say that the time taken to complete a heavy squat does not correlate closely enough with a hip extension in sprinting or in a vertical jump. This is true, however, it is more the brain's intent that determines the training effect, not the actual velocity of the bar (Poliquin, 2004). Thus as long as you *try* to move the bar as fast as possible, this will recruit the desired fast twitch fibres.

- Selection of the isometric tempo will vary depending on the desired training effect. There is a strong argument for inclusion of intra-set pauses in a biomechanically advantageous position for the recruitment of fast twitch fibres.
- If the goal is more hypertrophy than relative strength, then the pause can be placed in the disadvantageous position, such as the when the bar is at the chest during the bench press.
- Variations of tempo can be achieved with chains or bands, which will increase the concentric time under tension.
- For fast (signified by an 'X') tempos, it is critical that a basic threshold of strength is achieved prior to commencement of explosive strength regimes.

EXERCISE SELECTION AND ORDER

Certain equipment and certain exercises will be predisposed to the development of certain facets of strength or hypertrophy, while others will be more beneficial for the stimulation of muscle spindles or the enhancement of ankle, knee and hip stability. Medicine balls, for example, only go up to about 10kg maximum weight, which means that they will be very poor for the enhancement of maximal strength because the load is too light. However, if you want to stimulate the muscle spindles of the anterior core, then a dynamic lunge and overhead reach with a medicine ball is more suitable than the same drill with a barbell.

There will always be a difference in what load can be used with a single barbell or a pair of dumbbells. Usually the average person would lift approximately 10 per cent more weight when using a barbell. That is assuming that the person is well balanced and trains often with dumbbells. There can be as much of a 40 per cent deficit with those who only perform the stable barbell variations and never develop the stability and proprioception with dumbbells.

In relation to exercise order, usually any explosive, complex or multi-joint exercises (such as the Olympic lifts) should be undertaken at the beginning of the session, after a warm-up and prior to fatiguing assistant strength exercises, such as squats. If no explosive exercises are being performed, then the heavier, larger strength exercises, like the deadlift or bench press, would come first in the programme.

As mentioned previously, pairing antagonistic muscle groups, such as push-pull muscles in the upper body, or upper-lower body pairs can allow for shorter rest periods and a larger volume of work for the session. This also may increase the potential load used, as some research has shown that motor unit activation can be increased when preceded by a contraction of the antagonist. For example, performing heavy elbow flexion (bicep curls), followed after a rest by a set of elbow extension (weighted dips), may increase the force developed by the triceps, and therefore the potential load used for that set.

When exercises are written as part of a programme, the following letter-number system is used:

Example 1

Order	Exercise	Reps	Rest	Sets
A1	Exercise 1	10 reps	30s	3 sets
A2	Exercise 2	10 reps	30s	3 sets

So, in this example, exercise 1 is super-setted with exercise 2. Exercise 1 is performed for 10 reps, then 30 seconds' rest, then exercise 2 is performed for 10 reps, then 30 seconds' rest, and then back to exercise 1. Each exercise is performed for three sets in total.

Example 2

Order	Exercise	Reps	Rest	Sets
A1	Exercise 1	10 reps	30s	3 sets
B1	Exercise 2	10 reps	30s	3 sets

In this example, exercise 1 is performed for 10 reps, then 30 seconds' rest, and then it is performed again. This continues until all three sets have been completed, before moving on to exercise 2.

PERIODISATION

For every individual that trains with weights, a periodised programme should be developed and followed in order to focus the training towards a particular goal, with time constraints, and to allow for scheduled periods of active recovery. Phases of training would include:

1. Generation preparation
2. Specific preparation
3. (Pre-competitive)*
4. (Competitive)*
5. Transition

*Pre-competitive and competitive phases are listed in brackets because these would not be applicable for the average client who does not compete in sports. For athletes, this would also vary greatly depending on whether they are looking to peak for a particular competition (World Championships or Olympics) or for a season (such as in football and rugby).

Athlete or not, the individual should start with a phase of general preparation, which in terms of our functional triangle would provide the foundation section to each movement pattern. This would include:

- Improving connective tissue strength of required muscles
- Improving required core stability and core strength
- Improving agonist-antagonist strength balance
- Improving agonist-synergist strength balance
- Improving muscular system tolerance to load
- Developing adequate mobility, by releasing immobile joints or myofascial restrictions
- Developing required proprioception to perform all facets of movement pattern

Once this baseline of movement pattern skill, strength and fitness has been developed, maximal strength, size, power and endurance can be sought, depending on the specific requirements of the individual's occupation, sport, daily life or goals. Developing strength will increase the height of the triangle, while the ability to demonstrate this strength at speed, or for long periods, will help to increase the functional range for that movement pattern (or the width of the triangle).

When training to improve functional applied strength, an athlete may reach target strength levels more quickly if hypertrophy methods are used first, followed by strength training methods. Using a variety of different hypertrophy training methods to increase the cross-section of muscle fibres and anaerobic substrate storage (the fuels for anaerobic training) would be used in accumulation phases, where the volume is manipulated as the priority. This phase would then be followed by an intensification phase, where the intensity is the stimulus for adaptation, to enhance motor-unit recruitment and firing rate. In this way morphological adaptations (size) are sought first, before these gains are then applied into the stimulation of fast twitch fibres (high threshold stimulation) with heavy, short duration, low rep sets of maximal effort. It is therefore the manipulation of the training variables to focus more on volume or intensity that will help to avoid plateaus, where adaptations or gains are minimal or non-existent.

During the accumulation or intensification phases of specific preparation training, the following goals should be sought:

Accumulation
- Continuation of structural strength balance
- Increase cross-sectional area of the muscle
- Increase density of muscle fibres per unit cross-sectional area
- Acclimatise body to higher loads and volume from preparation phases
- Maintenance of joint mobility
- Adjustment of nutritional intake, lifestyle and dietary supplements to maximise training

Intensification
- Continuation of structural strength balance
- Maintain cross-sectional area of the muscle
- Increase number of muscle fibres contracting simultaneously
- Increase rate of contraction of muscle fibres
- Efficiency of synchronisation of firing of the muscle fibres
- Maintenance of joint mobility
- Adjustment of nutritional intake, lifestyle and dietary supplements to maximise training gains and promote recovery between sessions

FUNCTIONAL TRAINING PROGRAMMING

Over-utilisation of fixed plane machines and the range of motion required for these exercises decreases the need for these stabilising, synergistic muscles to be activated, thus causing an agonist-synergist muscle imbalance to develop. Training with barbells, dumbbells, kettlebells, Powerbags™ and other freeweights, instead of over-reliance on fixed path machines, will allow for the development of the small synergistic muscles, such as the rotator cuff or core, that also need to be strengthened. Fixed path machines, such as the leg extension or leg curl, are best used as a complement to squat or lift exercises to train the quadriceps or hamstrings in an isolation drill to increase the overload on a specific muscle.

The following programmes will hopefully provide ideas on how best to apply the information in previous chapters on each movement pattern, into comprehensive functional training programmes for a variety of individuals. These programmes are by no means a be-all-and-end-all, but merely help to show how the principles discussed can be practically applied.

SQUAT PATTERN OVERVIEW

The foundation of the squat pattern is to be able to perform bodyweight versions of the squat, overhead squat, split stance, lunge and pistol squat with good form and through a full range of motion.

Any of the listed limiting factors (see page 19) should be identified and corrected prior to the commencement of heavy strength training or more proprioceptively challenging unstable or high velocity exercises. For most individuals this would include mobilising the foot, ankle and hips, developing stability with Vastus Medialis Obliquus (VMO) strengthening, and glute activation. The overhead squat is commonly used as the most comprehensive mobility test for this pattern, and should be supplemented with assessments for tight hip external rotators, limited big toe dorsiflexion, ankle dorsiflexion and hip flexors. The sciatic nerve test, explained in chapter 5, can also be applied. Adhesions or restrictions in the myofascial of the plantarfascia, calves, hamstrings, adductors, iliotibial band (ITB) or tensor fascia latae (TFL) can limit range of motion as well.

The two best exercises to build functional applied strength in this movement pattern are the barbell back squat and front squat. These should form the foundation of the strength exercises, and can be varied slightly for continued improvements by manipulating the stance (normal, narrow, wide, heels raised, etc.), with progressive resistance (chains or thick bands), or by manipulating the rep range, tempo, recovery period or volume. When these cease to provide the means for squat improvement, then unconventional methods such as heavy farmer's walks or super yoke walks, velocity training with power snatches or plyometrics may help to overcome the plateau.

In addition to the heavy, stable exercises for functional applied strength, the functional range of the squat pattern should also look to be improved upon. This can be accomplished using exercises like the split stance squat (flat, front foot raised or Bulgarian), the lunge (sagittal, lateral, crossover), single leg squat (such as weighted pistol squats) and step-ups (sagittal, lateral, crossover). Once these less stable exercises have been mastered, speed can then be applied for continued benefits with plyometrics. Parallel stance squats can be progressed into squat jumps; split squats and lunges into split stance plyometric jumps; step-ups into box drives; and pistol squats into hops.

It is very important that sufficient lower body strength and stability is developed before progressing to advanced forms of training, such as plyometrics or Olympic weightlifting. Plyometrics such as jumps, bounds, hops, box drives and depth jumps require stability at the ankle, knee and hip and varying levels of strength depend on the exercise. For example, to perform a high depth jump an individual should be able to squat 1.5 times their bodyweight. This would demonstrate that they possess sufficient eccentric strength to control a landing from that height and still use the energy for the subsequent jump as elastic energy.

Supplement these knee-dominant movements with exercises to work the erector spinae and hamstrings. Weakness in the back and hamstrings are common limiting factors, and additional strengthening work can help to improve squat function. Improving the hamstring:quad strength ratio has a massive impact on knee stability, and how much load the body will allow to be lifted in this pattern. Exercises such as the bodyweight razor curl, stability ball or suspension system leg curl and the leg curl machines (seated, standing or prone) will help to apply additional overload to the hamstrings if required. Good mornings, deadlifts and reverse hyperextensions can be used to improve the strength of the posterior core muscles. In addition to this, supplementary isolated knee extension exercises, such as the seated leg extension, can be performed. Usually it may be preferable to overload the VMO by rotating the leg outwards, as the majority of individuals will have poor VMO activation and subsequent knee stability.

Isolated calf training can also be performed to assist with the squat pattern, including seated and standing variations to work the soleus and gastrocnemius respectively. Stretch the antagonist muscles before and between sets for optimal agonist recruitment. In this case the hamstrings should be statically stretched between each set of squats, step-ups or any other squat pattern drill or supplementary quadriceps drill.

Exercises such as parallel stance squats on top of a stability ball, or other unstable surfaces, should be avoided since it will have very little carryover to functional capabilities and may in fact teach altered biomechanics of the squat pattern.

Based upon the Siff calculations of weightlifting norms (Sevilla, 2004), the following comparisons can be applied to the squat pattern strength ratios and to other patterns:

- For optimal balance, the barbell front squat should be approximately 86 per cent of the barbell back squat (comparing 1RM to 1RM up to 5RM to 5RM).

- For optimal balance, the barbell front squat should be approximately 137 per cent of the barbell power clean score.
- For optimal balance, the barbell back squat should be approximately 198 per cent of the barbell power snatch score.

Example squat programmes
What follows are a selection of squat programmes to improve various functions.

Key:

LHS	=	left hand side
RHS	=	right hand side
BB	=	barbell
DB	=	dumbbells
OH	=	overhead
SS	=	suspension system (MiloKit, Jungle Gym XT)
PB	=	Powerbag™
(M)	=	Machine

Squat programme to improve knee and hip extension function

WEEKS 1–6

Order	Exercise	Reps	Tempo	Rest	Sets
A1	BB back squat heels raised*	8–12RM	4.2.X.0	90s	5
B1	Cable split squat LHS**	10–12RM	3.1.X.0	45s	4
B2	Cable split squat RHS	10–12RM	3.1.X.0	45s	4
C1	Seated leg extension***	8–12RM	3.1.1.1	90s	4

WEEKS 7–12

Order	Exercise	Reps	Tempo	Rest	Sets
A1	BB front squat	8–12RM	4.2.X.0	90s	6
B1	Peterson step up LHS	10–12RM	3.1.1.1	45s	4
B2	Peterson step up RHS	10–12RM	3.1.1.1	45s	4
C1	DB reverse crossover lunge	20RM	1.0.1.0	60s	4

WEEK 13

Active recovery week

* Performed heels raised to activate VMO with full depth, and assuming limited ankle dorsiflexion.
** Performed with front foot raised on step for VMO activation.
*** Performed with feet turned out.

Squat pattern 6-12-25 or 6-12-30 protocol

This involves performing 6 reps of a heavier exercise, 12 reps of a moderate weight exercise and 25 or 30 reps of a light exercise. All 3 exercises are performed consecutively with 10s to move between exercises.

WEEKS 1–6

Order	Exercise	Sets and reps	Tempo	Rest
A1	BB sumo squat	1 x 6RM	4.1.X.0	10s
A2	DB lunges	1 x 12RM	1.0.X.0	10s
A3	Leg extension	1 x 25RM	3.1.1.1	180s

Repeat x 4

Order	Exercise	Sets and reps	Tempo	Rest
B1	PB depth jump landing	1 x 6RM	X.-.-.-	10s
B2	Alternating box drives	1 x 12RM	1.0.X.0	10s
B3	SS lunge & OH reach	1 x 30RM	X.0.X.0	180s
Repeat x 4				

Example Olympic weightlifting squat session

Order	Exercise	Sets and rep	Tempo	Rest
A1	BB squat snatch, OH squat	5 x 2RM	X.1.X.1	180s
B1	BB squat clean, front squat	5 x 3RM	X.1.X.1	180s
C1	BB Bulgarian split squat	4 x 6–8RM	3.1.X.0	120s

Hypertrophy squat session – German volume training

This system was popularised by Charles Poliquin and normally involves performing 10 sets of 10 reps of a primary exercise like a barbell squat, deadlift or bench press.

Order	Exercise	Sets and reps	Tempo	Rest
A1	Back squat BB	10 x 10RM	3.1.X.0	60s
A2	Calf raise (M)	10 x 12–15RM	2.2.X.1	60s
B1	Lateral step BB LHS	4 x 6–8RM	2.1.X.1	10s
B2	Lateral step BB RHS	4 x 6–8RM	2.1.X.1	10s
B2	Leg extension (M)	4 x 8–10RM	2.1.1.1	90s

Functional strength squat session – mechanical advantage drop set

Order	Exercise	Sets and reps	Tempo	Rest
A1	Heels elevated front squat	1 x 2–3RM	4.1.X.0	10s
A2	Heels elevated back squat	1 x 2–3RM	4.1.X.0	10s
A3	Feet flat back squat	1 x 2–3RM	4.1.X.0	180s
Repeat x 3–5				
B1	DB Bulgarian split squat LHS	4 x 10–12RM	3.1.X.1	60s
B2	DB Bulgarian split squat RHS	4 x 10–12RM	3.1.X.1	60s

LIFT PATTERN OVERVIEW

Assess correct proprioception and technique with bodyweight deadlifts, or hip hinges. This will highlight any client that cannot distinguish between hip flexion and spinal flexion. Focus on tilting the pelvis forward as the torso leans forward to ensure an optimal spinal position is maintained. Check for sciatic nerve restrictions, which will inhibit normal range of motion and posterior chain function. Adhesions or restrictions in the myofascial of the plantarfascia, calves, hamstrings or erector spinae can limit range of motion as well. Assess for optimal strength endurance in the spinal erectors using the back extension endurance test; a poor score in this test will likely show up as poor application or performance in this movement pattern.

Use the split grip bent leg deadlift as the key exercise to improve lifting strength. This grip limits rotation of the bar and will allow the maximum load to be lifted. Ensure you change sides (which hand is pronated and which is supinated) between sets. Working more sets on your weaker preference can correct bilateral strength differences and help you lift more weight in the long run.

Use the fat grip deadlift, the snatch grip deadlift and any single hand barbell deadlift variations to improve grip strength, a common limiting factor for this movement pattern. Try to avoid using straps when lifting as these may help to lift more weight in the session, but over sustained periods may lead to an agonist-fixator strength imbalance developing. As a strength target to aim for, the deadlift 1RM should be approximately 144 per cent of the bench press in achieving a lower-upper body strength balance.

The step and reach exercise can be performed with bodyweight only, with dumbbells, a medicine ball, Powerbag™, sandbag or cables. It is an excellent way of eccentrically loading the hamstrings and glutes in a lifting pattern to stimulate the muscle spindles for increased activation. The load should always be kept light, to maintain the quick tempo, and this exercise is suitable for adding some multi-planar motion, such as reaching to the medial or lateral sides.

Use the vintage dumbbell swing, barbell power cleans and barbell power snatches as drills to apply this strength at speed to develop speed-strength. Heavier loads can be used with the two hand power cleans and power snatches, and are preferred by many strength and conditioning coaches. The vintage dumbbell swing is a unilateral exercise, so is great for improving bilateral differences and for grip overload, but the load on the posterior chain will be less.

Use the kettlebell swings (one or two hand) to apply the posterior chain strength into strength-endurance or power-endurance. Gradually increase the duration of the sets, and always precede with a phase of strength development. Powerbag™ or sandbag lifting drills, such as the lift to shoulder or the swings to shoulder, will provide a method of overloading the lift pattern muscles and grip muscles, with an object that is more difficult to hold and lift than a barbell, kettlebell or dumbbell. These tools also allow some rotation to be added to this pattern, with diagonal deadlifts, diagonal high pulls, diagonal cleans or diagonal snatches. Keep the load lighter for these variations, than the more stable sagittal plane variations.

Supplement this hip extension movement with exercises to work the erector spinae, hamstrings, calves and glutes. Exercises such as the body-weight razor curl, stability ball or suspension system leg curl, leg curl machines (seated, standing or prone), calf raises and superman will help to apply additional overload to these areas if required. Be aware of medial-lateral strength differences in the hamstrings and use variations of some of these drills to overload the weaker side until balanced. Dorsiflexing the ankle on leg curl exercises will increase the overload on the knee flexors (hamstrings), by reducing the involvement of the gastrocnemius, which can also flex the knee as well as plantarflexing the ankle. If this is too hard, then build up to it by performing the concentric phase with the ankle plantarflexed,

and the eccentric phase with the ankle dorsiflexed. The body is stronger eccentrically, and can lower the load, even if it struggles to lift the same load without cramping.

Stretch the antagonist before and between sets for optimal agonist recruitment. In this case the quadriceps and hip flexors should be statically stretched (such as with the split kneeling stability ball hip flexor stretch) between each set of deadlifts, leg curls or any other hip extension or supplementary hamstring drill.

Additional work can be performed on the scapula muscles (rhomboids, trapezius) for strength and stability during lifting, and also on the grip muscles. Fat grip lifting to improve strength, wrist flexion and extension work to improve isolated strength and fat grip carrying exercises, such as the farmer's walk, will also help to improve grip function for lifting.

Include eccentric training on the hamstrings, such as Russian curls for optimal strength development. They will respond best to strength training parameters, more than strength-endurance, and methods of training that would suit hamstring strength gains would include:

- Eccentric training with 120–130 per cent of 1RM
- Progressive resistance training with chains and bands
- Pre- and post-exhaustion sets
- Drop sets
- Double and triple same agonist supersets

Example lift programmes
What follows are a selection of lift programmes to improve various functions.

Key:

LHS	= left hand side
RHS	= right hand side
BB	= barbell
DB	= dumbbells
OH	= overhead
SS	= suspension system (MiloKit, Jungle Gym XT)
PB	= Powerbag™
(M)	= Machine
SLDL	= Stiff Leg Dead Lift

Lift programme to improve hamstring function

WEEKS 1–6

Order	Exercise	Sets and reps	Tempo	Rest
A1	Kneeling hip extension	6 x 6–8RM	3.2.1.1	90s
B1	BB Romanian deadlift	4 x 10–12RM	3.0.2.0	90s
C1	Seated leg curl	4 x 8–10RM	4.0.1.0	90s

WEEKS 7–12

Order	Exercise	Sets and reps	Tempo	Rest
A1	Snatch grip BB SLDL	4 x 10RM	4.1.X.0	10s
A2	Prone leg curl	4 x 8RM	5.0.1.0	120s
B1	Good morning BB	4 x 10RM	3.1.1.0	10s
B2	Supine SS leg curl	4 x 6–8RM	5.0.1.0	120s

WEEK 13

Active recovery week

Lift pattern – 6-12-30 protocol

Order	Exercise	Sets and reps	Tempo	Rest
A1	Barbell deadlift	1 x 6RM	4.1.X.0	10s
A2	Glute-ham raise	1 x 12RM	3.0.X.0	10s
A3	KB swing	1 x 30RM	1.0.X.0	180s
Repeat x 4				
B1	DB vintage swing	1 x 6RM	1.2.X.1	10s
B2	PB lift to shoulder	1 x 12RM	1.0.X.0	10s
B3	MB step and reach	1 x 30RM	X.0.X.0	180s
Repeat x 4				

Olympic weightlifting lift session

Order	Exercise	Sets and reps	Tempo	Rest
A1	BB hang power cleans	6 x 5RM	X.0.X.1	180s
B1	BB snatch grip high pull	4 x 6–8RM	3.1.X.0	120s
C1	BB partial bent over DL	4 x 4–6RM	3.2.X.0	120s

Relative strength lift session – cluster training

This system involves completing more repetitions at a high intensity, than would normally be completed. Using a 3RM intensity and completing 6 sets would normally give a total of 18 reps @ 90 per cent. Cluster training will mean undertaking 25 reps at 90 per cent, leading to a greater time under tension for the fast twitch fibres. This is accomplished by completing 5 sets of 5 intermittent repetitions.

Order	Exercise	Sets and reps	Tempo	Rest
A1	Dead Lift BB	5 x 5RM @ 3RM	4.15.1.1	300s (5 mins)
B1	Standing Leg curl LHS	4 x 6–8RM	3.1.X.0	30s
B2	Standing Leg curl RHS	4 x 6–8RM	3.1.X.0	30s
C1	Overhead Shrugs BB	3 x 4–6RM	1.1.1.1	120s

Other considerations

Based upon the Siff calculations of weightlifting norms (Sevilla, 2004), the following comparisons can be applied to the lift pattern strength ratios and to other patterns: For optimal balance the barbell power clean should be approximately 70–79 per cent of the barbell power snatch score. The power clean represents more the strength-speed end of the power spectrum for the Olympic lifts, while the power snatch represents more the speed-strength end. The balance of these exercises should help a trainer to realise whether the individual needs strength work or speed work.

PRESS PATTERN OVERVIEW

Assess shoulder mobility and scapulo-humeral function before embarking on a press pattern training programme. Limited mobility in shoulder rotation will be indicative of adhesions within the rotator cuff, or medial-lateral external strength imbalances that will affect the ability to efficiently press vertically and horizontally. Ensure adequate strength balance of the pressing muscles by testing the bench press, dips and overhead press exercises. Weakness in one of these planes (horizontal, vertical downwards, vertical upwards) or the associated muscles will limit overall pressing ability. For example, a weak overhead press may be a limiting factor for a plateaued bench press. Weakness in the antagonist muscles, such as those responsible for external rotation, may also limit pressing performance. Limited thoracic mobility or a weak core may cause pain or discomfort when pressing overhead and each of these factors should be assessed.

The barbell bench press (biacromial grip), weighted dips and standing overhead press (barbell/dumbbell) are the key exercises to improve functional applied strength in the various pressing planes. These should be varied over phases to ensure that over-dominance in a certain plane, or plateauing does not occur. Varying the grip width, using dumbbells instead of a barbell and adding chains/thick bands will help to provide a variation of stimulus.

In addition, bodyweight drills, such as suspension system presses, press-up variations, cable presses and medicine ball/sandball throws will help to integrate the core muscles with the pressing muscles at lower intensities. Although not as effective at overloading the agonist muscles, these exercises help to integrate the rest of the body and to apply the press motion at speed (medicine ball/sandball throws). Use cable pressing exercises to develop strength endurance and core integration, but the maximal load usually available with this exercise (without additional stability) may be only 40 per cent of the subject's bodyweight (Santana, Vera-Garcia & McGill, 2007).

Overhead pressing with two hands (barbell) and one hand (side press, bent press, vintage press) have been a key test of pressing ability for well over a century. Standing overhead pressing requires hip, core and shoulder stability and can be performed with a variety of conventional (barbell, dumbbell, kettlebell) or unconventional (Powerbag™, sandbag) equipment. The lateral core and hips should be strengthened with exercises like the side plank and windmill prior to lifting heavy loads in one hand above the head. In order to adequately load the agonists, the surface should be stable (i.e. performed on the floor) and not on a stability ball or BOSU. Functionally this vertical upwards pattern would have been performed to a higher volume than the vertical downwards pattern (dips), and this should be replicated in a modern programme.

In addition, plyometric exercises such as the medicine ball chest pass, single arm chest pass, or plyometric press-ups can help to convert the slow-speed strength into power. This can also be accomplished with heavy overhead drills such as the barbell push press and jerk.

Isolation exercises to work on the agonists can be performed including chest flies, and triceps extension (standing or supine) using cables, dumbbells and bars. These exercises do allow for a greater overload on the agonists, and should be performed in a stable position to allow for a greater neural drive. Normally these will be performed bilaterally to assist with balance. Because of the degree of pressing exercises undertaken within most people's programmes, additional anterior deltoid exercises are probably not required, unless specifically for rehabilitation or specific strength. Many individuals will include additional sets of front raises, which will only increase the anterior to posterior agonist-antagonist strength imbalance. Triceps strength can be diminished if the biceps or brachialis has shortened, and become hypertonic because of the agonist-antagonist relationship between the elbow flexor and extensors.

Supplementary work should also be undertaken on the retractors and external rotators to ensure an optimal agonist-antagonist strength balance training and to prevent internal rotation of the arms and potential shoulder pain. When training the external rotators, the infraspinatus is trained with the arm abducted, while the teres minor is preferentially recruited with the arm down. In relation to how to programme best to work these muscles, Kinakin (2004) recommends that 'All rotator cuff exercises should be done at the end of the workout or on an off day. This prevents fatigue of the small stabilising rotator cuff muscles, which are needed when using the larger muscles, such as the pectorals or deltoids, for pressing movements.'

Poliquin (2006), on the other hand, recommends completing a set of shoulder external rotator work in between every set of chest work in order to achieve the optimal volume within a session, and to prioritise this development of strength (rather than leaving these exercises to the end of the session when you are fatigued). He believes that using compound sets, an individual will be able to bring the size and strength of the shoulder external rotators in balance with the agonists without compromising the development of chest mass or strength.

Release work on the pectorals, medial shoulder rotators, lateral shoulder rotators and thoracic spine using a foam roller, tennis ball or by a therapist will help to ensure optimal range of motion for pressing. The elbow extensors can be overloaded with a variety of barbell, dumbbell and cable exercises – explained later in this chapter.

A press programme could be broken down in a few different ways:

- Pure press session – including horizontal pressing, vertical pressing upwards and downwards.
- Horizontal pressing within one session and vertical pressing within another. These are usually paired with the corresponding pull pattern.
- Chest and triceps for one session (horizontal and vertical downwards press) and shoulders for another session (vertical upwards press).

Bodybuilders would usually prefer to follow the last method, since this fits into their current mentality of training muscle groups. Examples of different sessions within these categories are shown on the next page.

Key:

LHS   = left hand side

RHS   = right hand side

BB   = barbell

DB   = dumbbells

AMRAP = As many reps as possible

Example pure press session

Order	Exercise	Sets and reps	Tempo	Rest
A1	Standing DB jerk LHS	5 x 4–6RM	X.0.X.1	60s
A2	Standing DB jerk RHS	5 x 4–6RM	X.0.X.1	60s
B1	DB inclined chest press*	4 x 8–12RM	3.1.1.0	45s
B2	Seated DB ext rotation	4 x 8–12RM	4.1.1.0	45s
C1	Weighted dips	4 x 6–10RM	5.1.X.0	90s

* Performed close grip with rotation

Example horizontal press-pull session

Order	Exercise	Set and reps	Tempo	Rest
A1	Barbell bench press*	4 x 6–8RM	4.1.X.1	60s
A2	Supine pull-ups	4 x AMRAP	3.1.X.1	60s
B1	Standing cable press	4 x 10–12RM	3.0.X.0	45s
B2	Single arm DB row	4 x 8–12RM	3.1.X.0	45s
C1	Supine EZ triceps extension	3 x 8–10RM	3.1.X.1	30s
C2	SS biceps curl	3 x 8–10RM	3.1.X.0	30s

* Performed with a biacromial grip

PULL PATTERN OVERVIEW

Assess shoulder mobility and scapulo-humeral function before undertaking a pull pattern training programme. Limited mobility in shoulder rotation will be indicative of adhesions within the rotator cuff that will affect the ability to efficiently pull vertically and horizontally. Poor mobility will likely affect posture during pulling exercises and can potentially stress the structures of the gleno-humeral joint. For example, when performing a lat pull down, a lack of external rotation will cause the individual to hyperextend through the lower back to accommodate the range of motion. Back musculature imbalances can be assessed using a variety of exercises, such as an upright row, seated/standing row, or lat pull down. Upper to lower trapezius muscle imbalances will be commonly seen as shoulder girdle elevation during the pull. With a horizontal pull there should not be any elevation occurring throughout the range. With a vertical pull upwards there will be upper trapezius activation, but if this is premature then this would demonstrate a dysfunction. With a downwards pull, such as with a lat pull down or pull up, the shoulders should start in an elevated position prior to the commencement of the concentric phase. If the shoulders shrug during the mid or end of the concentric phase, then this would demonstrate a muscle imbalance.

The pull-up can be used to assess an individual's basic level of strength and pulling function. This may seem unrealistic, but every individual near their optimal body mass should be able to pull their own weight up. Most individuals, following a correct pulling preparation training programme, can gain the required strength to perform a pull within 6–12 weeks. Boyle (2004) believes that males should be able to achieve a minimum of 10–15 reps of bodyweight supinated grip chin-ups for athletic performance, while females should perform a minimum of 3–5 reps. Poliquin (2006) believes that an optimal pull:press ratio can be calculated using the supinated grip chin-up and the biacromial grip width barbell bench press. He states that the chin-up should be 87 per cent of the load for the bench press (weight calculated as bodyweight plus external load). As long as the repetition max is the same, these exercises can be compared whether it is 1RM:1RM or as down to 6RM:6RM. The pull-up should be trained with a variety of grips, in order to sufficiently work the range of motor units of the back and elbow flexor muscles. It should initially be performed with bodyweight only, and then additional weight can be added to provide the overload with the use of belts or a vest.

To overload the upward pulling muscles the Olympic lifts and modified lifts should be used. These include the barbell snatch, clean, power snatch, power clean, high pulls, low pulls and power shrugs. These exercises allow for significant load to be used, as well as linking the pulling muscles, with the lift muscles and the core. Dumbbell and kettlebell variations of these exercises can also be used, but the load will be significantly lower than the more stable barbell variation.

Use cable pulling exercises (horizontal and upwards), suspension system exercises to develop strength endurance and core integration, as these exercises (like their pressing counterparts) will be limited by stabilisation ability of the body. As such the actually load on the agonists may not be as great as more stable exercise variations, but the connection and activation of accessory and stabilising muscles will likely be greater.

Weakness in the upper trapezius muscles will show itself as the head being held forward of the thoracic cage (Kinakin, 2004), while a weak middle and lower trapezius and rhomboids will present as an elevated and protracted scapula and a kyphotic position in the torso. A weak latissiumus dorsi will allow the shoulder to elevate and move anteriorly in a standing posture (Kinakin, 2004). The upper trapezius can be trained with upwards pulling or diagonal upwards pulling exercises, such as the upright row or high pulls. They can also be isolated with shrugging exercises. Shrugs are commonly performed with a barbell and the arms holding the bar with a pronated grip. This has the impact of causing internal rotation at the shoulder, and will cause torsion and shear forces on the acromioclavicular and sternoclavicular joints. Dropping the chin during shrugs places more stress on the cervical vertebrae when the neck is flexed. The shrug is best performed with weights held by the side of the body to ensure optimal posture, and minimal stress on the joints. This can be performed with dumbbells, cables, barbells or any other load that can be held in one hand. The load should be sufficiently heavy as to initiate an overload of these muscles, and the load used for shrugs is commonly quite high. Poliquin (2010) suggests that the best option is to use a barbell held in one hand, so that there is no dragging of the weight against the body when lifted, to increase the range of motion, and for greater activation of the infraspinatus and teres minor. This can also be achieved using a single cable and moving slightly away from the column. The single hand barbell shrug will also be excellent for improving grip strength and endurance, depending on the load and time under tension selected for the set.

Just as with the lift pattern, poor grip strength is probably one of the most common limiting factors for the pull pattern. Many individuals will find that it is their grip, which fails when they are performing pull-ups. They are either unable to hold their weight (grip strength) or to hold onto the bar for the duration of the set (grip endurance). This is further worsened as the bar diameter increases, such as fat grip pull-ups. Performing grip-emphasised pulling exercises, such as fat grip dumbbell rows, fat grip pull-ups and supine pull-ups, and supplementary forearm and grip drills will help to correct this deficit.

Supplement this movement pattern with exercises to work the retractors, elevators and depressors of the scapula. Exercises such as the stability ball superman, shrugs, and reverse flies will help to apply additional overload to these areas if required. The elbow flexors can be overloaded with a variety of barbell, dumbbell and cable exercises – explained later in this chapter.

An example pull programme could be broken down in a few different ways:

- Pure pull session – including horizontal pulling, vertical pulling upwards and downwards.
- Horizontal pulling within one session and vertical pulling within another. These are usually paired with the corresponding press pattern.
- Back and biceps for one session (horizontal and vertical downwards pull) and upper back and shoulders for another session (vertical upwards pull, usually as part of an Olympic lifting session).

Examples of different sessions within these categories are shown on the next page.

Key:

LHS	= left hand side
RHS	= right hand side
BB	= barbell
DB	= dumbbells
AMRAP	= As many reps as possible

Example pure pull session

Order	Exercise	Sets and reps	Tempo	Rest
A1	BB snatch high pull	5 x 4–6RM	X.0.X.1	90s
B1	Pull-ups pronated grip	4 x AMRAP	3.1.1.0	60s
B2	Seated DB ext rotation	4 x 8–12RM	4.1.1.0	60s
C1	Standing cable rope row	4 x 12–15RM	3.1.X.0	60s

Example horizontal press-pull session

Order	Exercise	Sets and reps	Tempo	Rest
A1	Dumbbell chest press	4 x 8–12RM	4.1.X.1	60s
A2	Supine pull-ups	4 x AMRAP	3.1.X.1	60s
B1	Standing DB vintage press	3 x 10–12RM	3.0.X.0	45s
B2	Standing cable pull	3 x 8–12RM	3.1.X.0	45s
C1	Dips	3 x AMRAP	3.1.X.1	45s
C2	KB dead clean	3 x 12–15RM	1.1.X.1	45s

Advanced pull session – drop/extended sets

Once an individual can perform at least 12 supinated grip pull ups, or can perform 6–8 pull-ups with at least 10 per cent of their bodyweight, then the following types of pull-up overload session can be applied:

Sessions 1–6: Biomechanical extended set

Order	Exercise	Reps	Rest	
A1	Wide grip pronated	AMRAP	15s	Repeat for a total of 3–5 extended sets
A2	Narrow grip pronated	AMRAP	15s	
A3	Medium grip supinated	AMRAP	180s	

Sessions 7–12: Grip extended set

Order	Exercise	Reps	Rest
A1	Fat grip wide grip pronated	AMRAP	15s
A2	Normal grip wide grip pronated	AMRAP	15s
A3	Strapped wide grip pronated	AMRAP	180s

Pull sessions can be performed with supplementary exercises for the elbow flexors (sets completed post-pull, so as not to pre-fatigue) or with elbow extensors (triceps). The reasoning behind performing elbow extensor work would be to allow these muscles to be trained when fresh, so that a greater overload can be applied to these exercises. For example:

Example session A

Order	Exercise	Sets and reps	Tempo	Rest
A1	Pull-ups	6 x 8–12RM	3.1.X.1	120s
B1	Standing cable rope pull	4 x 8–12RM	3.1.1.1	120s
C1	Seated DB hammer curl	4 x 6–8RM	4.1 X.0	120s

Example session B

Order	Exercise	Sets and reps	Tempo	Rest
A1	Pull-ups	6 x 8–12RM	3.1.X.1	60s
A2	BB seated half press	6 x 6–8RM	4.1 X.0	60s
B1	Standing cable rope pull	4 x 8–12RM	3.1.1.1	60s
B2	Supine EZ triceps extension	5 x 6-8RM	4.1 X.0	60s

ROTATION AND SMASH OVERVIEW

The rotation and smash patterns should not be trained as completely separate sessions, as these muscles do not require as much volume of training as the lift, squat, press or pull muscles. As mentioned in the introduction chapter, 'not all movement patterns are created equal', and this would be an example of that. It is important that these muscles and movements are trained, but to apply the same volume would lead to overtraining.

For the rotation and smash patterns ensure adequate hip mobility and thoracic mobility through stretching, self-myofascial release (SMFR) and treatments. Areas to focus on will be the hip rotators, hip flexors and the lateral line muscles (tensor fascia latae and iliotibial band). Thoracic mobility can be improved with foam roller and tennis ball exercises, and will be linked to restrictions with the rotator cuff as well.

The upwards rotation movement will be trained as part of the lift pattern, by adding a rotation to it, such as a Powerbag™ or sandbag lift with rotation. Kettlebell diagonal snatches and reverse woodchops (cable or freeweight) will also help to work this movement pattern with the training programme.

The horizontal rotation is the pure rotation movement, and it should always be included within the programme, both as part of preparatory training to ensure adequate core stability and to maintain it. Many weightlifters will show great strength in the sagittal plane, but because the snatch, clean and jerk, only really develop strength in this plane, injuries can occur when the individual has to rotate. Including rotation exercises may not increase the performance in these lifts, but it will stop the athlete becoming injured, which in itself will limit performance. Cable rotations are the purest method of training the horizontal rotation, since the load will pull along the correct vector, and will not be negatively influenced by gravity as freeweight horizontal exercises will be.

The downwards rotation movement is a combination of the rotation and smash pattern and can be trained by diagonally curling the body, such as a cable judo throw, a band woodchop or a medicine ball woodchop throw.

To train the smash pattern a variety of drills can be used to train different properties. Exercises that load the spinal flexors at a fast velocity, such as suspension system lunge with overhead reach, will stimulate the muscle spindles helping to increase activation of the muscle. Prone plank exercise variations will improve the stability of the smash pattern muscles, which will be required for overhead pressing activities, while hammer slams on a tyre, or sandbag slams onto the floor will help to develop ballistic strength. The smash pattern muscles can be trained with slower heavier drills, such as loaded crunches, but these should only form a small part of the smash pattern exercises included within an annual programme.

These exercises are commonly performed at the end of a lift, squat, press or pull session, as the loaded used are much lighter and pre-fatiguing the core muscles would have a negative impact on the performance of these exercises. In preparatory sessions, there can be a rotational or smash emphasis in order to develop core strength and stability, prior to the commencement of heavier, more specific phases of training. An example of such a session would be:

Key:

LHS	=	left hand side
RHS	=	right hand side
BB	=	barbell
DB	=	dumbbells
AMRAP	=	as many reps as possible
SS	=	suspension system
OH	=	overhead
PB	=	Powerbag™

Rotation-smash emphasis whole body session

Order	Exercise	Sets and reps	Tempo	Rest
A1	Dumbbell press LHS	3 x 8–12RM	4.1.X.1	30s
A2	SS lunge and OH reach	3 x 12–15RM	X.0.X.1	30s
A3	Dumbbell press RHS	3 x 8–12RM	4.1.X.1	30s
B1	Supine pull-ups	4 x 8–12RM	3.1.X.1	30s
B1	PB reverse woodchop	4 x 10–12RM	3.0.X.0	30s
C1	Standing cable press LHS	3 x 10–12RM	3.1.X.0	10s
C1	Sandbag slams	3 x 10–12RM	X.0.X.0	10s
C3	Standing cable press RHS	3 x 10–12RM	3.1.X.0	60s

This session provides a solid core emphasis by working the posterior core on the supine pull-ups, the lateral core with single arm overhead presses, the rotational core with the reverse woodchop and cable press, and the core flexors with the sandbag slams.

GAIT AND LOCOMOTION AND MOVING-CARRYING LOAD OVERVIEW

It is important that any structural or biomechanical issues are assessed using gait analysis and lift analysis or any other appropriate tests. These will help to identify areas that will be overloaded when running or swimming for long periods, or when moving under load. If these dysfunctions are not corrected, then stress on the joint structures or soft tissue will result when the intensity or volume of training is increased.

To work the full spectrum of the gait and locomotion movement pattern, walking, jogging, running, swimming and crawling drills should be encouraged. When running, speed is critical, specific drills to improve acceleration, deceleration, agility and maximal speed can be trained using tools such as cones, hurdles, bands and ladders.

The moving and carrying load movement pattern includes carrying loads on the shoulders, the chest, above the head, in the hands, dragging and pushing heavier loads, and moving load from the floor to a standing position. All of these should be trained in different phases of training, to ensure well-rounded development and no gaps occur in the spectrum of functional range.

To work the pattern of moving load from the floor, exercises like the Turkish get-up, get-up anyhow and sit-up get-up are most appropriate, and can be trained with fit bars, barbells, kettlebells, dumbbells, Powerbags™ or sandbags. Exercises using the tyre or sled for dragging, backwards dragging, sideways dragging or pushing will not only work the muscular system, but will provide a great overload for the cardiovascular system as well.

When deciding the number of reps, distance or time, it will depend on the goal of the individual:

- Relative strength/anaerobic alactate power 1–10s TUT
- Relative strength/anaerobic alactate capacity 11–20s TUT
- Functional strength/anaerobic lactate power 20–40s TUT
- Functional strength/anaerobic lactate capacity 41–70s TUT

These can also be combined with carrying drills such as the farmer's walk, which will improve grip strength and endurance, ankle stability and core stability as well as the main muscles worked, and the stress on the cardiovascular system. Sessions usually last between 40–60 minutes (including the warm up and cool down), with some examples given below:

Moving-carrying load – strongman session

Order	Exercise	Reps/Time/Distance	Rest	Sets
A1	BB* farmer's walk	60m	120s	8
B1	Sled push	30s	120s	8

* Barbell

Moving-carrying load – strongman circuit session				
Order	**Exercise**	**Time**	**Rest**	**Sets**
A1	Sled push	20s	10s	5
A2	Rock push press*	20s	10s	5
A3	Tire wrestle**	20s	10s	5
A4	Hammer slams	20s	10s	5
A5	Sled drag	20s	10s	5
A6	BB*** overhead walk with chains	20s	240s	5

* Some heavy rock
** Performed against a partner
*** Barbell

This session could be incorporated within a weekly programme as follows:

Weekly programme for moving-carrying load session	
Day	**Session**
Mon	Whole body strength in gym
Tue	Strongman circuit
Wed	Rest day
Thur	Whole body strength in gym
Fri	Strongman circuit
Sat	Off
Sun	Off

ARM TRAINING

Increases in the size of a person's arms will be related to concurrent increases in lean body mass. Many individuals that strive to achieve larger, stronger arms struggle because a limiting factor could be the overall lean body mass. The reason is the body will not allow you to develop 20in arms, while having a skinny body, just like it would not allow you to develop bodybuilder legs with a waif-like upper torso. Poliquin (2010) estimates about a gain of 15lbs of lean body mass per inch increase in the size of the arms.

Training legs with the squat, lift and moving-carrying load movement patterns will assist in helping to gain size on the arms, while obviously also improving your functional capabilities. Poliquin (2010) states that he believes the three best exercises for the elbow extensors are:

1. Dips
2. Close grip bench press
3. Lying triceps extension

And the best three exercises for the elbow flexors:

1. Scott curls (aka preacher curls)
2. Inclined dumbbell curls
3. Standing reverse curls

Biceps and forearm

Different bicep exercises, grips, positions and equipment should be used to adequately cover and overload all of the ranges of the flexion movement, and recruit the different motor pools of the biceps:

- Barbells should be used with elbow flexion as they allow the greatest loads to be used.
- Dumbbells can be used to allow semi-supinated grip and to allow supination during the elbow flexion. This should occur at or before 90 degrees of flexion.
- The preacher or scott curl overloads the beginning range, the standing curl the middle range and the concentration curl the end range.
- Standing barbell and dumbbell curls will train the brachialis and short head of the biceps.
- Seated inclined dumbbell curls will train the long head of the biceps.
- Reverse curls with EZ bar or dumbbell hammer curls will increase the stress on the brachialis muscle.
- Pronated or semi-pronated grip increases stress on brachioradialis and brachialis.
- The brachioradialis is responsible for flexion at the elbow in a semi-supinated grip position, such as in hammer curls, and is more active at a higher velocity than a slow tempo (Kinakin, 2004), and thus it is better to programme a fast concentric phase (signified by an 'X' in the four-digit tempo method) than a slow one.

- Supinated grip pull-ups work the biceps well as they are stronger above the head.
- A weakness in the elbow flexors may be due to tight triceps (thus statically stretch between sets of biceps).

A weak forearm is usually indicated with such symptoms as tennis or golfer's elbow (lateral or medial epicondylitis respectively), and is usually due to the development of adhesions within the forearm muscles. These can be corrected with soft tissue release methods, such as rolfing or active release techniques (ART).

To train the forearm muscles, work on the following exercises/movements:

- Dumbbell hammer curls (will work the brachialis and brachioradialis)
- Reverse EZ curls (will work the brachioradialis)
- Dumbbell wrist extension curls (to work the forearm extensors and ensure optimal forearm agonist-antagonist strength balance)
- Barbell/dumbbell/cable wrist flexion curls (to work the forearm flexors).

Triceps

Different triceps exercises, grips, positions and equipment should be used to adequately cover and overload all of the ranges of the extension movement, and recruit the different motor pools of the triceps:

- Barbells should be used with elbow extension as they allow the greatest loads to be used.
- The triceps is one muscle with three heads – the long head, medial head and lateral head.

- The lateral and long head exert minimal force with elbow extension unless the load is heavy and the intensity high.
- Weakness in the triceps may cause difficulty in locking out when performing the bench press or dips.
- The close grip bench press and supine triceps extension are good for recruiting the long head with heavy loads (8RM or less).
- Heavy cable push-downs and dumbbell kick-backs will recruit the lateral head.
- Dips are an excellent method of recruiting the triceps, since the load that can be generated by the triceps is greater when the arm is below the shoulders than above.

This system involves tri-setting, or compounding three exercises that work the same muscle groups, with minimal rest between. The first and third exercises are the same exercise, which should be an isolation exercise, with the second exercise being a compound exercise. This will produce a lot of lactate and significant overload for the selected muscles.

Example hypertrophy session arm – double tri-sets

Order	Exercise	Sets and reps	Tempo	Rest
A1	Reverse curl EZ	4 x 8 reps	4.1.X.0	10s
A2	Seated hammer curl DBs	4 x 8 reps	5.1.1.0	10s
A3	Reverse curl EZ	4 x 6 reps	4.1.X.0	120s
B1	Supine tri ext EZ	4 x 8 reps	3.1.1.0	10s
B2	Seated half press (Smith M)	4 x 8 reps	3.1.1.0	10s
B3	Supine tri ext EZ	4 x 6 reps	3.1.1.0	120s

REFERENCES

Alter, M.J. (2004). *Science of Flexibility*. Human Kinetics.

Anderson, K.G. and Behm, D.G. (2004). 'Maintenance of EMG activity and loss of force output with instability', *Journal of Strength & Conditioning Research*. 18 (3): 637–640.

Behm, D.G., Anderson, K. and Curnew, R.S. (2002). 'Muscle force and activation under stable and unstable conditions', *Journal of Strength and Conditioning Research*. 16(3): 416–422.

Bompa, T.O. (1999). *Periodization for Sports*. Human Kinetics.

Boyle, M. (2004). *Functional Training for Sports*. Human Kinetics.

Bührle, M. and Schmidtbleicher, D. (1981). 'Kompo-. nenten der Maximal- und Schnellkraft', *Sportwissenschaft*. 11:11–27. 6.

Burkhardt, E. and Garhammer, J. (1988). 'Biomechanical comparison of hang cleans and vertical jumps', *Journal of Applied Sports Science Research*. 2: 57.

Bynum, B., Barrack, R. and Alexander, A. (1995). 'Open versus closed chain kinetic exercises after anterior cruciate ligament reconstruction', *American Journal of Sports Medicine*. 23: 401–406.

Canavan, P.K., Garrett, G.E. and Armstrong, L.E. (1996). 'Kinematic and kinetic relationships between an olympic style lift and the vertical jump', *Journal of Strength and Conditioning*. 10: 127–130.

Calock, J.M., Smith, S.L, Hartman, M.J., Morris, R.T., Ciroslan, D.A., Pierce, K.C., Newton, R.U., Harman, E.A., Sands, W.A. and Stone, M.H. (2004). 'The relationship between vertical jump power estimates and weightlifting ability: A field-test approach', *Journal of Strength and Conditioning*. 18(3): 534–539.

Chandler, T.J., Wilson, G.D. and Stone, H.M. (1989). 'The squat exercise: attitudes and practices of high school football coaches', *NSCA Journal*. 11(1): 30–34.

Chek, P. (2001). *Golf Biomechanics Manual*. C.H.E.K. Institute.

Currier, D.P. and Mann, R. (1983). 'Muscular strength development by electrical stimulation in healthy individuals', *Physical Therapy*. 63: 915–921.

Dunn, B., Klein, K., Kroll, B., McLaughan, T., O'Shea, P. and Wathen, D. (1984). 'Coaches round table: The squat and its application to athletic performance', *Journal of Strength and Conditioning*. 6: 10–22.

Escamilla, R.F., Francisco, A.C., Fleisig, G.S., Barrentine, S.W., Welch, C.M., Kayes, A.V., Speer, K.P. and Andrews, J.R. (2000). 'A three-dimensional biomechanical analysis of sumo and conventional style deadlifts', *Medicine and Science in Sports and Exercise*. 32 (7): 1265–1275.

Escamilla, R. F., Lowry, T.M., Osbahr, D.C. and Speer, K.P. (2001). 'Biomechanical analysis of the deadlift during the 1999 Special Olympics World Games', *Medicine and Science in Sports and Exercise*. 33: 1345–1353.

Escamilla, R.F., Fleisig, G.S., Zheng, N., Barrentine, S.W., Wilk, K.E. and Andrews, J.R. (1998). 'Biomechanics of the knee during closed kinetic chain and open kinetic chain exercises', *Medicine and Science in Sports and Exercise*. 30: 556–569.

Fleck, S.J. and Kraemer, W.J. (1987). *Designing Resistance Training Programmes*. Human Kinetics.

Fry, A.C., Smith, J.C. and Schilling, B.K. (2003). 'Effect of knee position on hip and knee torques during the barbell squat', *J. Strength Cond. Res.* 17(4): 629–33.

Fry, A.C., Kraemer, W.J., Stone, M.H., Warren, B.J., Fleck, S.J., Kearney, J.T. and Gordon, S.E. (1994). 'Endocrine responses to over-reaching before and after 1 year of weightlifting training', *Canadian Journal of Applied Physiology*. 19(4): 400 –410.

Fu, F., Woo, S.-Y. and Irrgang, J. (1992). 'Current concepts for rehabilitation following anterior cruciate ligament reconstruction', *Journal of Orthopaedic Sports Physical Therapy*, 15: 270 –278.

Garhammer, J. and Gregor, R.J. (1992). 'Propulsion forces as a function of intensity for weightlifting and vertical jumping', *Journal of Applied Sport Science Research*. 6: 129–134.

Häkkinen, K. and Pakarinen, A. (1993). 'Acute hormonal responses to two different fatiguing heavy-resistance training protocols in male athletes', *Journal of Applied Physiology*. 74: 882–887.

Hori, N., Newton, R.U. and Andrews, A.W. (2008). 'Does performance of hang power clean differentiate performance of jumping, sprinting and change of direction?', *Journal of Strength and Conditioning Research*. 22: 412–418.

Hori, N., Newton, R.U. and Nosaka, K. (2005). 'Weightlifting exercises enhance athletic performance that requires high-load speed strength', *Journal of Strength and Conditioning*. 27: 50–55.

Kalenak, A.K. and Morehouse, C.A. (1975). 'Knee stability and knee ligament injuries', *JAMA*. 234(11): 1143–1145.

Karpovich, P.V., Singh, M. and Tipton, C.M. (1970). 'The effect of deep knee squats upon knee stability', *Teor Praxe tel Vvch*. 18: 112–122. Cited in Chandler, T.J. and Stone, M.H. (1991). The Squat Exercise in Athletic Conditioning: a Review of the Literature. *Journal of Strength and Conditioning*. 13 (5): 52–58.

Kinakin, K. (2004). *Optimal Muscle Training*. Human Kinetics.

King, I. (2000). *Speed of Movement*. See: www.pton-thenet.com/displayarticle.aspx? ArticleID=1022

Klein, K. K. (1962). 'Squats right', *Scholastic Coach*. 32(2): 36–38, 70–71.

Klein, K. K. (1961). 'The deep squat exercise as utilised in weight training for athletes and its effect on the ligaments of the knee', *Journal of the Association for Physical and Mental Rehabilitation*. 15: 6–11.

Koshida, S., Urabe, Y., Miyashita, K., Iwai, K. and Kagimori, A. (2008). 'Muscular outputs during dynamic bench press under stable versus unstable conditions', *Journal of Strength and Conditioning Research*. 22: 1584–1588.

Kraemer, W.J., Marchitelli, L., McCurry, D., Mello, R., Dziados, J.E., Harman, E., Frykman, P., Gordon, S.E. and Fleck, S.J. (1990). 'Hormonal and growth factor response to heavy resistance exercise', *Journal of Applied Physiology*. 69(4): 1442–1450.

Marshall, P.W.M. and Murphy, B.A. (2006). 'Increased deltoid and abdominal muscle activity during Swiss ball bench press', *Journal of Strength and Conditioning Research*. 20: 745–750.

McDonagh, M.J.N. and Davies, C.T.M. (1984). 'Adaptive response of mammalian skeletal muscle to exercise with high loads', *European Journal of Applied Physiology*. 52: 139–155.

McGill, S. (2002). *Low Back Disorders*. Human Kinetics.

McGuigan, M.R.M. and Wilson, B.D, (1996). 'Biomechanical analysis of the deadlift', *Journal of Strength and Conditioning Research*. 10(4): 250–255.

Meyers, E.J. (1971). 'Effect of selected exercise variables on ligament stability and flexibility of the knee', *Research Quarterly*. 42(4): 411–422.

Michaud, T.C. (1997). 'Ideal motions during the gait cycle': in *Foot orthoses and other forms of conservative foot care 2nd edition*, Williams & Wilkins. 27–56.

Paton, M.E. & Brown, J.M. (1994) An electromyographical analysis of functional differentiation in human pectoralis major muscle. *Journal of Electromyography and Kinesiology*. 4, 161-169

Poliquin, C. (2004). *PICP Theory Manual Level 1*. Poliquin Performance Centre.

Poliquin, C. (2006). 'The truth about full squats', Notes from FitPro Convention 2006.

Poliquin, C. (2010). *Bigger, Stronger Arms :The Poliquin Way*. Poliquin Institute.

Salem, G.J. and Powers, C.M. (2001). 'Patellofemoral joint kinetics during squatting in collegiate women athletes', *Clinical Biomechanics*. 16: 424–430.

Santana, J.C., Vera-Garcia, F.J. and McGill, S.M. (2007). 'A kinetic and electromyographic comparison of the standing cable press and bench press', *J. Journal of Strength and Conditioning Research* 21(4): 1271–1277.

Saxon, A. (1905). *The Development of Physical Power*. Healthex Publishing.

Sevilla, A. L. (2004). *Siff Score and Russian Standard Computation for Powerlifting, Weightlifting and Assistance Exercises*. See: http://anton.free.net.ph/siff_score-v4.xls

Shelbourne, K. and Nitz, P. (1990). 'Accelerated rehabilitation after anterior cruciate ligament reconstruction', *American Journal of Sports Medicine*. 18: 292–299.

Siff, M.C. (2004). *Supertraining*. Supertraining International.

Signorile, J.F., Zink, A.J. and Szwed, S.P. (2002). 'A comparative electromyographical investigation of muscle utilization patterns using various hand positions during the lat pull-down', *The Journal of Strength and Conditioning Research*. 16(4): 539–46.

Stone, M.H., Byrd, R., Tew, J. and Wood, M. (1980). 'Relationship between anaerobic power and Olympic weightlifting performance', *Journal of Sports Medicine and Physical Fitness*. 20(1): 99–102.

Vera-Garcia, F.J., Grenier, S.G. and McGill, S.M. (2000). 'Abdominal muscle response during curl-ups on both stable and labile surfaces', *Physical Therapy*. 80(6): 564–69.

Waller, M., Townsend, R. and Gattone, M. (2007). 'Application of the power snatch for athletic conditioning', *Journal of Strength and Conditioning*. 29: 11–20.

Wilson, G.J., Elliott, B.C. and Wood, G.A. (1991). 'The effect on performance of imposing a delay during a stretch-shorten cycle movement', *Medicine and Science in Sports and Exercise*. 23(3): 364–370.

Zatsiorsky, V.M. (1995). *Science and Practice of Strength Training*. Human Kinetics.

INDEX

acclimatisation 12
accumulation 285
adaptation 11, 18
agility ladders 35–6
agonist-antagonist strength balance 19
agonist-synergist strength balance 20
ankles 49–50
arm training 304–6
   programme example 306

barbells 32–3
biceps training 305
   exercises 257–62
Biering–Sørensen back extension test 89–90
bodybuilding 5–7

cables 42
conditioning ropes 41
core 114–16, 145, 204
core plates 42
core stability 7–8
core supplementary exercises 263–71
   ground conditioning punching on a
     Powerbag™ 270
   jackknife 269
   reverse crossover step and lateral overhead
     reach 263
   roll out 268
   side planks 266–7
   undulating training with ropes 270–1
   windmill 264–5
crawling 223

diagonal upwards rotation exercises 181–5
   diagonal lift to shoulder 184
   reverse woodchops 181–3
   thigh to thigh rotations 185
downward pull exercises 173–6
downward rotation exercises 192–4
downwards press exercises 138–9
dumbbells 32

elbows 117, 146
exercise selection 116, 145–6, 283–4

Fat Gripz™ 41–2
feet 49–50
fighting pattern 15
fixed path machines 5–6, 42
foam rollers 34–5
forearm training 305
functional capacity 16–17, 22–3
functional training
   equipment and methods 30–42
   history of 2–10
   modern concepts 14–18
   parameters 13
   principles of 11–14, 18–30
   programming 285–306
   variables 277–85
functional triangle 16–18, 22

gait and locomotion pattern 15, 222–3
   overview 302–3
   programme example 303–4

gait and locomotion pattern exercises 224–32
    bounds 227
    crawls 225, 232
    other exercises 232
    run-throughs 229–30
    shuffles 231
    sprints 228
    walks 224, 226
generalisation 12–13
glutes 90
grip strength 26–7, 90, 146, 204

hammers 40
hamstrings 90
hips 86–7, 179–80, 196
horizontal press exercises 130–7
    bench press 130
    chest presses 133–4, 136–7
    press-ups 131–2
    vintage supine press 135
horizontal pull exercises 164–72
    high pulls 169–70
    rows 165–8, 170–2
    one-arm 169–71
    two-arm 164–8, 172
horizontal rotation exercises 186–91
    cable rotations 187
    high bridge rotations 191
    plank with leg sweep 186
    rotation throw 189
    seated rotations 190
    standing rotations 188
hurdles 35–6
hypertrophy 5–6, 12–13, 45, 279
    programme example 306

individuality 13
injuries 17, 18, 19, 20–1, 22, 112

intensification 285

kettlebells 30–1
knees 51–2

lift pattern 15, 22, 84–90
    limiting factors 86–90
    overview 290–1, 294
    programme examples 292–3
lift pattern exercises 91–110
    barbell lifts 91–9, 108–10
    cleans 107, 108–9
    deadlifts 91–7, 99, 108
    dumbbell lifts 100–1, 109–10
    good morning 98
    kettlebell lifts 102–4, 109–10
    one hand lifts 96–7, 101, 103–4
    sandbag lifts 105–7
    snatches 109
    step and reach 100
    swings 101–4, 109
    two hand lifts 91–5, 98–100, 102–3, 105–7
lift pattern supplementary exercises 235–43
    hamstring curl 240–1
    kneeling hip extension 235
    kneeling razor curl 236
    kneeling Russian curl 237
    leg curl machine 238
    leg curl stability ball 239–40
    quad and hip flexor stretch 242–3
    Superman 241–2
lifting chains 38
linear variable resistance training (LVRT) 37–8
lower back 51, 89–90

medicine balls 33–4
movement patterns 14–15
    assessment of 18, 19

limiting factors 19, 20
and training principles 18–30
moving and carrying load pattern 15, 22, 202–4
limiting factors 203–4
overview 302–3
programme example 303–4
moving and carrying load pattern exercises 205–21
drags 213–17, 220
get-ups 207–11
other exercises 218–21
pushes 217–18
walks 205–6, 212–13
multi-planar training 9

overhead squat test 52–3
overload 11, 18

performance 17, 20–2, 44–5
periodisation 12, 13–14, 284–5
physical culture 3–5
Poliquin's upper body structural balance scores 113
postural correction 9
Powerbag™ 39
powerlifting 5–7
prehabilitation 45–6
press pattern 15, 20, 111–17
functions/importance 112–13
limiting factors 113–17
overview 294–5
programme examples 296
press pattern exercises 118–40
downwards press 138–9
horizontal press 130–7
other exercises 140
vertical press upwards 118–29
press pattern supplementary exercises 246–54
chest flyes 246–8

external shoulder rotations 248–50
triceps exercises 251–4
pull pattern 15, 141–6, 297–300
functions/importance 142–4
limiting factors 144–6
overview 297–8
programme examples 299–300
pull pattern exercises 147–176
downward pull 173–6
horizontal pull 164–72
other exercises 177
vertical upwards pull 147–63
pull pattern supplementary exercises 255–62
biceps 257–62
upper back 255–6

range of motion (ROM) 20–1, 24, 44
rehabilitation 45–6
repetition maximum 277
reps and intensity 277–9
resistance bands 37–8
rest and recovery 280–1
reversibility 12
rotation pattern 15, 178–80
limiting factors 179–80
overview 301
programme example 302
rotation pattern exercises
diagonal upwards rotation 181–5
downward rotation exercises 192–4
horizontal rotation 186–91

sandbags 38–9
sandballs 39
scapula 117, 146
sciatic nerves: tension in 87–9
self-myofascial release (SMFR) 34–5, 196
exercises 271–6

sets and volume 279–80
shoulders 52, 117, 146
sleds 39–40
slump mobilising drill 88–9
smash pattern 15, 22, 195–6
    limiting factors 196
    overview 301
    programme example 302
smash pattern exercises 197–201
    crunches 199–200
    kneeling overhead throw 201
    slams 197–8
specificity 11–12, 21, 27
squat pattern 15, 20, 43–53
    full squat debate 46–9
    functions/importance 44–6
    limiting factors 49–53
    overview 286–7
    programme examples 287–90
    terminology/subcategories 44, 45
squat pattern exercises 54–83
    back squats 54–5, 83
    front squats 57–8, 61–2, 68, 83
    hop over hurdles 76–7
    jump onto step 77–8
    lunges 69–75
    overhead squats 60, 65–7
    Peterson drag 83
    pistol squats 63–5
    split stance squats 58–60
    squat – sumo stance 56
    squat jump 75–6
    step-ups 78–82, 83
squat pattern supplementary exercises 243–5
stability balls 34
straight leg raise test 87–8
strength 27–30
    and biomotor abilities 28

categories of 29
    and squat pattern 45
supplementary exercises 25–6, 233–76
    core 263–71
    lift pattern 235–43
    press pattern 246–54
    pull pattern 255–62
    SMFR 271–6
    squat pattern 243–5
suspension system training 31
swimming 223

tempo 281
time under tension (TUT) 282–3
thorax 180, 196
triceps training 305–6
tyres 40

unconventionl training 10
unstable surface training (UST) 8–9, 35
upper back exercises 255–6

vectors 24
vertical press upwards exercises 118–29
    one-arm 119, 124–9
    two-arm 118, 120–3
vertical upwards pull exercises 147–63
    cleans 155–6, 157, 159–60
    high pulls 149–51, 152–3, 158, 162
    one-arm 150–7, 162–3
    snatches 151–2, 153–4, 160–1, 163
    swings 152–4, 156
    two-arm 147–50, 158–61
    upright rows 147–8
vintage training 3–5

weighted vests 36
wrists 52